"The twenty-first century is the post
unsettling divide shaped by the desire for tradition or the pressing need for
relevance reveals itself through Christian worship expressions. Oftentimes,
this tension manifests itself in the choice of music used for corporate worship.
Without a doubt, music making has a significant role in realizing Christian
worship, a role comparable to ritual actions and the art of rhetoric in earlier
eras. To that end, Constance Cherry in *The Music Architect* has strategically
and helpfully unpacked the purpose, functions, and implications of music
making in the context of worship in our day. Shaped by Cherry's overarching
concern for leadership formation in enabling congregational singing, this
book offers much guidance to those who are preparing to serve or are already
serving in the fields of worship and sacred music. It is a timely gift for all of
us who are in the forefront of nurturing God's people in song."

—**Lim Swee Hong** (林瑞峰), Deer Park Assistant Professor of Sacred
Music and Director, Master of Sacred Music Program, Emmanuel
College of Victoria University in the University of Toronto

"Constance Cherry has given the church and its leaders a gift: a book that the
church needs. She has successfully repositioned discussions of the church's
music to be theologically grounded, liturgically functional, spiritually formative, and congregationally conceived. Along the way she provides practical
insights for choosing songs, engaging congregants, establishing flow, and
creating vision. Cherry's contribution to congregational song provides the
church a foundational source that it has been missing. Her work has resituated
the discussion of congregational music by offering music leaders, worship
leaders, pastors, congregants, and scholars a new place to restart this much-
needed conversation. This book is a must-read for all who are involved in
music and worship ministry. It will shape the thoughts and practices of the
next generation."

—**Randall Bradley**, Ben H. Williams Professor of Church Music,
director of the Church Music Program, and director of the Center
for Christian Music Studies, Baylor School of Music

"I can't think of anyone more qualified to teach and write about the connection between worship and music than Constance Cherry. *The Music Architect*
is a must-read for anyone wanting to think and minister on a deeper level.
Her thoughts on being a pastoral musician as well as her insights on spiritual
formation in worship are truly trailblazing."

—**Rory Noland**, director, Heart of the Artist Ministries

Other Books by Constance M. Cherry

The Worship Architect: A Blueprint for Designing Culturally Relevant and Biblically Faithful Services

The Special Service Worship Architect: Blueprints for Weddings, Funerals, Baptisms, Holy Communion, and Other Occasions

the MUSIC architect

Blueprints for Engaging
Worshipers in Song

Constance M. Cherry

Baker Academic
a division of Baker Publishing Group
Grand Rapids, Michigan

© 2016 by Constance M. Cherry

Published by Baker Academic
a division of Baker Publishing Group
P.O. Box 6287, Grand Rapids, MI 49516-6287
www.bakeracademic.com

Printed in the United States of America

Library of Congress Cataloging-in-Publication Data
Names: Cherry, Constance M., 1953– author.
Title: The music architect : blueprints for engaging worshipers in song / Constance M. Cherry.
Description: Grand Rapids : Baker Academic, 2016. | Includes index.
Identifiers: LCCN 2016004354 | ISBN 9780801099687 (pbk.)
Subjects: LCSH: Music in churches. | Church music.
Classification: LCC ML3001 .C5 2016 | DDC 264/.23—dc23
LC record available at http://lccn.loc.gov/2016004354

16 17 18 19 20 21 22   7 6 5 4 3 2 1

In memory of Ann Baas,
who unknowingly influenced me
toward a lifetime of music ministry in the church.

Thank you.

Contents

Acknowledgments

The writing of any book requires many long hours alone at one's desk, usually in a quiet room. This was the case for me, as evenings and weekends I sat in my home office, concentrating on this manuscript. Yet a strange thing happened in my solitude. Week after week I found myself reflecting often on many individuals from my past who unknowingly played a significant role in starting or keeping me on the path of music ministry in the local church. Their faces have flashed before me more than once as the chapters unfolded. Some spoke encouragement into my life when I was a young child, others when I was a teenager, collegian, or young adult in ministry. And on it goes. I marveled as I recalled each one and was struck again by how instrumental they were at certain points in time. I was not alone at my desk after all. I had my own personal great cloud of witnesses.

It strikes me as appropriate to acknowledge their virtual role in the writing of this book, for even though their influence spans my lifetime, each one has ultimately contributed greatly to this endeavor of the moment. I owe them a great deal of thanks, for I would not be in a position to undertake this project without the contribution each made in their own way. Most of these folks would not consider themselves to have been significant, but they were. I therefore wish to acknowledge a few of them, though this roll call of saints is only representative (there have been many more). They include Ann Baas, children's Sunday school superintendent of the First United Brethren Church of Lansing, Michigan; Bishop Ray Seilhamer, pastor of College Park United Brethren Church in Huntington, Indiana; Dr. E. Dewitt Baker, president of Huntington College; Hugh T. McElrath, hymnology professor; Carlos Harrow and Charlie Walker, two church custodians (church custodians are very wise people); Joanne Neikirk, encourager; Mary Kirk, organist extraordinaire and friend; Dorothy Wells, daring layperson who was obedient to the voice of God; Bonnie Pollock and Alberta Duncan, church secretaries (and as wise as custodians); and Daisy Vollrath, woman of hospitality and prayer. Only God knows the critical roles you have played at junctures in my life. Thank you for helping me to run with perseverance the race marked out for me.

Certain of my need for the prayers of others while undertaking this venture, I am grateful that a group of ten people, representing various ages, places, ethnicities, and vocations, agreed to lift me daily before God as members of a prayer circle. Thank you so very much. Though I did not hear your prayers, I felt them. Thanks also go to my dad, the Rev. Dr. Harold Cherry, who maintains a vital prayer ministry for his family and many others. I am aware that a number of my colleagues at Indiana Wesleyan University have prayed for me throughout this project as well. It has meant so much. If this book makes any contribution to the kingdom's work, it is because of those who have prayed for it.

I express sincere thanks to Indiana Wesleyan University, its academic support for the writing of this book through the Hinds Fellowship Award, and my exceptional colleagues within the School of Theology and Ministry who express interest in and support for my ongoing work. I especially thank Elaine Bernius and Chris Bounds, who generously served as consultants in their respective fields of biblical studies and theology.

This book has emerged (as have the other books) as my attempt to fulfill a curricular need for the classroom and ultimately for the church. The delightful students at IWU, as well as those at The Robert E. Webber Institute for Worship Studies, inspire me. Their probing questions and insights shape my perspectives and challenge my thinking. Their influence is represented in the pages of the book. Thank you.

Special thanks to Kelly Bixler for her superb work in formatting and editing.

I very much appreciate the support and friendship of Bob Hosack at Baker Publishing for yet another opportunity for publication. Thanks to all of the fine people at Baker for seeing this project through from beginning to end. I am honored to work with you.

I conclude with gratitude to God, the source and subject of the Christian's song. Better is one day in your courts than a thousand elsewhere.

Prelude

You and I have something in common. If you are holding this book in your hands or perusing it digitally, chances are we share a passion for at least two things: worshiping the triune God of Scripture and making music in community as a primary means to do so. This is a book about the connection between music and worship. I imagine that you have experienced the wonder of worship through song. Perhaps you, like me, are a participant in the song or a leader of it. If so, at times you've probably found yourself wondering how you can become a better participant or a more effective leader of worship music. You're not alone. Every worship leader I know has real questions—not so much about how they can become a better musician, as important as that is, but how they can lead worship as a musician. If that's you, then this book will help.

Why a Book about Worship Music?

The church faces a daunting dilemma today. There are many musicians serving in worship services who are very talented but far fewer who have had any real education in worship. They have incredible voices, they can play drums and pianos, organs, and guitars beautifully, and they direct excellent choirs and vocal teams of all kinds—yet they have had virtually no formal training in what amounts to the most important ongoing event of a Christian community: its worship. Even most pastors have not had the privilege of taking courses dedicated to worship in their ministerial preparation. This has left us with a lot of talented, well-intentioned but underprepared individuals when it comes to leading God's people in the most important work to which we are called. This book stands in the gap between the underequipped worship leaders and those sincere Christians gathered before them, who together worship God on a weekly basis.

Yet while this is a book about musical leadership in the church, it's not just for musicians. There are many people who have responsibility for music in worship, including pastors, sound technicians, accompanists, and graphic artists—a whole array of people routinely have some type of leadership role in the music of worship. One of the greatest needs of the church today is for its leaders to have a clear understanding of music's purpose and a shared vision for its proper role, not only on its own merits but also in relation to the whole service. While this book is about music in the local church, it doesn't attempt to train musicians to become better at performing music. Instead, it seeks to guide all persons vested in the music ministry of the local church (musicians or not) to think more deeply and prayerfully about music in worship so that it can best fulfill its God-given purposes.

The Architect Metaphor

With this in mind, all sorts of people qualify as "music architects"—any persons who share responsibility for providing music in worship. The role of an architect is used lightly as a metaphor in various places in the book. Building architects don't design only functional spaces; they design *beautiful* functional spaces—places where order and beauty meet. They are not just construction engineers but artists too. Even though they are obligated to follow certain necessary steps to create a trustworthy edifice, their work is not predictable or cookie-cutter. Each building is conceived differently according to those who will dwell there. While building architects are faithful to construction principles, they are keenly aware of how the structure will serve the relationships of those who will use the building. They design physical parameters that support the building's purposes, but they are skilled enough to do so while placing their own imprint on the design. When the building is complete, the occupants are set free to enjoy the purposes for which the space was created. The architect then delights in the results that often far exceed what he or she imagined in the design phase.

Music architects also bring order and beauty together, arranging for the necessary parameters for music to best function in worship that will enhance the relationship that occurs there between God and people. They understand music's place in the worship service, its relationship to other components, and its capabilities for encouraging holy encounters. Order and beauty are both put into play; they are not mutually exclusive. They are partners in a common purpose, in this case bringing glory to God through the music of worship in a particular time and place in ways that are far from predictable—unique to each community. Music architects make the arrangements for the people's participation in song and then set them free to enjoy the meaning and beauty that comes as a result. It is often much more than the music architects dreamed.

What the Reader Can Expect

This book is distinctly different in several ways from other books about worship music. First, worship and music have come to be used synonymously these days. Sadly, in many places music is referred to *as* worship, as if to assume they are one and the same. Some books add to this confusion of terms. This book seeks to help leaders understand worship and music as related but separate entities. Second, probably because of such confusion, "worship leader" has come to mean only those involved in making music. This book defines the worship leader much more broadly to include anyone who has responsibility for music in worship, including, but not limited to, musicians. Third, I have intentionally chosen to refer to worship music rather than church music. The term "worship music," in present standard use, has come to refer almost exclusively to the songs that the gathered church sings. Since that is the primary focus of this book—the congregation worshiping through its songs—it simply makes sense to use this term. The field of church music traditionally entails a wide range of needed expertise with an emphasis on the classic musical development of the leader. It typically encompasses such things as graded choir systems, the development of instrumental and vocal ensembles, musical programming, congregational song choices and leading, service planning, and the administration of music departments within the church. I appreciate the great tradition of church music. I simply wish to be clear that if you are a church musician who is looking for help along all of those lines, you will be disappointed to find most of these topics unaddressed; fortunately, those needs are well met in other places. Here, however, you will find insight and practical assistance in performing your primary duty: leading the church's song.

The Music Architect is at once both narrower and broader in focus than that of church music. It is narrower in that it concentrates almost entirely on just one thing—the song of the church (and how to lead it in one's context); it is broader in that it takes this one thing and examines it widely from multiple perspectives, each of which is critical for leading music effectively. This is why I use both words strategically throughout the book: "song" to refer to that which is sung by worshipers and "music" to refer to the larger domain of which song is a part. In short, this book attempts to help leaders (1) think about worship music holistically and (2) disciple worshipers as the primary participants of the church's song. It is a comprehensive guide for various leaders in the church to help worshipers fully engage in their calling to sing unto the Lord in corporate worship. The main thrust of *The Music Architect* is congregational song and the leaders who employ it thoughtfully, faithfully, and prayerfully for the sake of the church's worship.

I write this book out of my experience as a worship leader who has served the church vocationally in this capacity for more than four decades as both musician and pastor. I have had the good fortune to serve churches in small, medium, and megachurch sizes, representing various styles, with people who can't read music and with superb professional studio musicians. I have served in Anglo churches and multicultural churches, in rural areas and huge metropolitan areas. Early on, I completed music degrees to prepare me for this area of ministry, and I enjoyed developing my skills and helping others make music in the house of God. However, before long I was hungry to understand much more of the relationship between music and worship. I knew that one was not the other. Still, how did they relate? Thankfully, I had the opportunity to complete graduate programs in theology and liturgical studies, which answered some of my questions. I'm still working on the integration of theology, liturgy, music, and ministry. I anticipate it being a lifelong pursuit. I make no claims at having all the answers, or even very many, but I relish the collaborative spirit of all who are pursuing God's ways and will in these matters, as together we seek to have the mind of Christ.

Precisely because my own leadership will always be a work in progress, I have attempted to write this book more conversationally, as someone who is speaking *with* others not *at* others. I therefore have occasionally included voices of a few current worship leaders whom I have met along the way. I have also used first- and second-person pronouns so as to create a sense that we are not teacher/pupils or expert/novices but colleagues, regardless of our level of expertise or experience. Read this book as if you are sitting with the author and other readers on couches in a local coffee shop discussing these matters of great interest and significance, not only to us but also to the people we serve. With this prelude, I hope you can begin to smell the coffee perking.

How This Book Can Help

This book is the third volume in The Worship Architect series. The first, *The Worship Architect: A Blueprint for Designing Culturally Relevant and*

Biblically Faithful Services (Baker Academic, 2010), is a book about planning the whole service of worship from beginning to end, from the concept stage to leading it in real time. Two chapters are dedicated to providing the worship architect with a very basic introduction to incorporating congregational song into worship as one component among many others. The second volume, *The Special Service Worship Architect: Blueprints for Weddings, Funerals, Baptisms, Holy Communion, and Other Occasions* (Baker Academic, 2013), applies the principles of worship preparation to the sacraments/ordinances, life passages, and other special occasions of worship. Music is not addressed other than song suggestions made for each service. Both volumes are presently being used in academic institutions to train future ministerial leaders and in local church settings to sharpen pastoral and lay leadership. These books are available not only in English but also in other languages. This final volume undertakes a third, more specific aspect of worship: its music. It is my prayer that this book will also find its way into the hands of teachers, both in the academy and in local churches, to help them disciple others in the ministry of music in worship.

The three books share a few things in common. First, the reader will find a consistent philosophy of worship that runs throughout them. Second, all three volumes unite theology and practice. The church needs leaders who are deeply rooted in biblical, theological, historical, cultural, and pastoral principles that inform their practice in local ministry. Third, the approach to the issues presented in each volume is trans-denominational in nature. While I minister from within the Wesleyan tradition personally, the reader will see that the discussion takes place at a level where all Christian leaders can find much resonance. Leaders must always seek ways to interpret and apply common principles as fitting for their context. Fourth, I seek to take a pastoral approach to worship issues. Leadership in the church is very challenging. Change is difficult and delicate. The strategies presented in each book suggest leadership approaches that demonstrate care and love for the people with whom one serves. Fifth, the organization of each book follows the same plan. Each chapter begins with "Explore," a set of questions to help the reader begin to think about the topic at hand. "Expand" provides significant content to inform and shape the leader's thinking. Each chapter then concludes with "Engage"—practical suggestions for application in one's context. Within each chapter key vocabulary words are shown in bold type and then defined at the end of the chapter. Also included at the end of each chapter is a list of additional resources.

The book begins and ends with a look at the person of the worship leader because *who we are* will always have greater ministerial impact than *what we do*. Chapter 1 unwraps the idea of the "pastoral musician," a term that is used in conjunction with "music architect" throughout the book in ways that I hope will be clear. Chapter 12 describes the leader in pursuit of excellence, especially in terms of spiritual leadership. These two chapters frame the discussion that takes place in between—ten chapters that address distinct topics to help music architects carry out their duties with a high level of competence. These chapters address, in order, the following:

- Music in relation to the big picture of worship
- Music's particular role and functions in worship
- Placing songs effectively in the order of worship
- Evaluating worship music
- Maximizing shorter song forms
- Maximizing longer song forms
- Distinguishing between worship style and worship voice
- Techniques for leading congregational song
- Raising the level of engagement among worshipers
- The formational nature of worship

An interlude (a brief introduction to using a wide variety of congregational song) and a postlude (conclusion) round out the book.

So, if you wish to discover how to take your own musical participation or leadership to the next level in your local worshiping assembly, wherever that may be, you have come to the right place. Pull up a chair and bring your coffee mug. There's room at the table for you.

Constance M. Cherry
Pentecost Sunday 2015

1

Becoming a Pastoral Musician

Expand

We are often defined by our titles. For better or for worse, titles establish our identities. Notice how often when called on to introduce ourselves in a public gathering, we do so by saying what we do: "I'm a stay-at-home dad"; "I am a principal at the local high school." Whether titles are formal ("senior defense attorney for the city of Los Angeles") or informal ("mama"), they serve as a clue to who we are and what we do. What we do, of course, is not the same thing as who we are. First and foremost, we are children of God made in the *imago Dei*, apart from what our job might be. At the same time, who we are and what we do are often related, for our interests, natural talents, spiritual giftedness, cultural contexts, and so on not only help to form who we are but also often determine the trajectories of our lives, leading us naturally to our primary vocations. The connection between who we are and what we do is all but unavoidable in Western cultures.

Many folks engaged in musical leadership in the church, whether paid or not, have a title that describes their role: worship leader, pastor, worship pastor, director of music, minister of music, worship arts pastor—these are just a few of the common ones. Options have proliferated in recent years, as a visit to any ministry job-search website will attest. But is there a title that combines both *what* you do and *who* you are?

In this chapter we will examine just such a title in depth: **pastoral musician**. While any number of titles can be appropriate for persons invested in worship music leadership, this one holds profound potential for capturing much more than one's duties to be performed; it also represents how leaders approach their duties in a particular way as a result of who they are. The purpose of this book is to assist persons charged with musical leadership in the local church with carrying out their duties in ways that are glorifying to God and edifying to worshipers. The title "pastoral musician" reflects a multidimensional type of leadership that combines both being *and* doing—a leader who is being conformed to the image of Christ and, as a result, is able to do God-focused ministry with others. This term will be used broadly to include any and all persons with responsibilities for any aspect of the music in corporate worship. (This approach will become clearer as we go along.) Remember that pastoral musicians are also worship architects. As explained in the prelude to the book, worship architects are those persons with responsibility for designing and leading a full service of worship in its many aspects, from concept stage to the service itself to its evaluation. One dimension of such responsibility is the musical leadership for the service of worship; in that sense we are music architects in particular.

Defining the Pastoral Musician

The term "pastoral musician" has had a distinguished history in some sectors of Christianity while unknown in others, but it is a term with much merit. A definition will help to describe what is meant:

A pastoral musician is a spiritual leader with developed skill and God-given responsibility for selecting, employing, and/or leading music in worship in ways that serve the actions of the liturgy, engage worshipers as full participants, and reflect upon biblical, theological, and contextual implications, all for the ultimate purpose of glorifying God.[1]

There are several key phrases and ideas found in this definition. First, pastoral musicians are spiritual leaders; they lead out of their relationship with Jesus Christ, and their leadership is offered for the spiritual development of the church. Next, pastoral musicians have developed skill. They possess more than natural talent; they have intentionally invested in training to maximize their skill set(s) as a means to serve Christ and his church in a manner that is worthy of their calling. They seek to honor God through the ongoing nurture of the gifts God has given them. Pastoral musicians also have God-given responsibility for some aspects of the music employed in worship. Whether remunerated or volunteer, they have been placed in designated leadership for this ministry by the will of God and the church. Pastoral musicians understand that music serves the greater purposes of biblical worship, and they help participants to become fully engaged in the fulfilling of those purposes. They also give thoughtful consideration to theological reference points that undergird their ministry so as to ground it faithfully in biblical and historical Christianity. At the same time they are aware of contextual and cultural realities as they seek to offer the music of the community most fitting in a given locale. Last, pastoral musicians are deeply committed to enabling all worshipers to sing of God's glory.

Describing the Pastoral Musician

Definitions can be very helpful; however, sometimes a *description* of the type of person and ministry can be equally advantageous. Below is a series of succinct descriptive statements that begin to tease out the definition of the pastoral musician. The statements describe three dimensions: the *person* of the pastoral musician, the *vision* of the pastoral musician, and the *role* of the pastoral musician. Following each group of statements, which are comprehensive but not exhaustive, I will elaborate on some of the principal themes, while leaving others to be addressed at length in the succeeding chapters.

1. Constance M. Cherry, *The Worship Architect: A Blueprint for Designing Culturally Relevant and Biblically Faithful Services* (Grand Rapids: Baker Academic, 2010), 180 (adapted). Based on ideas from J. Robert Clinton.

The Person of the Pastoral Musician

Pastoral musicians begin by recognizing who they are as God's beloved and redeemed creation on a journey of growth and service.

Characteristics of the person include the following:

- Fully embraces and lives the Christian faith
- Demonstrates a developing spiritual maturity
- Demonstrates awareness of personal spiritual gifts
- Senses a vocational call to worship ministry[2]
- Embraces, encourages, and loves the persons in the community God has given him or her to oversee
- Is committed to lifelong learning
- Is accountable to God and to others for his or her ongoing development as a pastoral musician

The *person* who you are in ministry will affect your ministry more than any skill or quality you possess. In the end, who you are will leave a more lasting impression than what you do. Our personhood is rooted in the *imago Dei*. We are humans made in the likeness of God (Gen. 1:26). Beyond this, we also become children of God through faith in Christ Jesus (Gal. 3:26). Our identity as persons is found first and foremost in our relationship with God by virtue of our creation (made in the image of God) and in our re-creation (becoming children of God). While the source of our identity is rooted in our relationship with God, our personhood develops and matures over time; it is a lifetime process. The person of the pastoral musician (whom we have become, are becoming, and will become) possesses several important characteristics: is a disciple of Jesus Christ, has a deepening spiritual maturity, is a member of the church, and has a sense of vocation.

Disciple of Jesus Christ. The starting place for a true pastoral musician is that she or he is a fully devoted follower of Jesus Christ. As a leader, one's relationship with Christ is the foundation for ministry. Non-Christians can fulfill tasks in a religious setting, but they cannot do *ministry* apart from a relationship with the One in whose name they minister.[3] Pastoral musicians

2. This does not necessarily suggest an official ecclesial credential, though a leader may hold one. A pastoral musician is better defined by the way he or she goes about worship and music ministry than whether he or she is credentialed.

3. That is not to say that God will not use the work of non-Christians for the benefit of the church; this happens frequently by God's grace. It is to say that ministry is how one lives out his or her vocational call from God, which presumes that he or she is a devoted Christ-follower.

will identify themselves as Christians; they will demonstrate love and devotion to the triune God and love and compassion for others. They will be committed to the orthodox tenets of Christianity and embrace the Scriptures as authoritative for life and ministry. They will name Jesus as Lord and live according to his teachings. Being in Christ is a prerequisite for true ministry.

Deepening spiritual maturity. Pastoral musicians not only declare their faith as Christians; they also commit themselves to a lifelong pursuit of spiritual maturity. Our growth in Christ cannot be separated from our growth in leadership, for how we develop as leaders is deeply linked to how God is forming us into the likeness of his Son. Our view of leadership shifts over time in relation to our experience of God at work in our lives. It is common for young leaders to embrace secular models of leadership for ministry, sometimes overlaid with Christian terminology in order to authenticate its use in the church, only to discover that the biblical portrayal of leadership looks quite different. (Chapter 12 will elaborate on servant leadership as a favored model for Christian leaders.)

Spiritual maturity occurs through the gracious initiatives of God, followed by our intentional cooperation with God in those initiatives. There is no better means for our growth in Christlikeness than our participation in the classic spiritual disciplines of the church.[4] Spiritual disciplines provide the normative ways and means for our spiritual formation. Transformation is God's work—it is the gift of grace at work for a lifetime. At the same time, God accomplishes spiritual transformation when we offer ourselves willingly as full participants in the process. The point is that pastoral musicians are conscientious about their growth in Christ. It is never growth for growth's sake; rather, it is an honest, dynamic pursuit of holiness so that our will comes into conformity with God's will. It is that type of "long obedience in the same direction"[5] that is worthy of the pastoral musician. It is that kind of conformity that will produce effective pastoral musicians to lead the church of Jesus Christ.

Member of the church. The pastoral musician's relationship to the church is also central to who we are. The church is not an organization; it is a living organism. As such, it is a dynamic, eternal, worldwide community of Christ-followers who name Jesus as Lord. As baptized believers, we are members of Christ's holy church; we are in union with Christ and all true believers—past, present, and future—who make up the church. Pastoral musicians serve the community of faith in fulfilling their duties. The local church is our context

4. A great starting place for exploring the spiritual disciplines is Richard J. Foster's *Celebration of Discipline: The Path to Spiritual Growth*, rev. ed. (New York: Harper & Row, 1988).
5. I recommend Eugene H. Peterson's *A Long Obedience in the Same Direction: Discipleship in an Instant Society*, 2nd ed. (Downers Grove, IL: InterVarsity, 2000).

for doing the ministry that we are called to do. There would be no point in serving as a pastoral musician apart from the local church or its parachurch ministries. Pastoral musicians understand the nature of the church and fully embrace its God-given role in the kingdom of God. They view themselves as citizens in a cosmic, universal community who think globally and serve locally. Enabling the music of worship in a local church setting becomes much more than it seems when pastoral musicians serve out of their love for Christ and his church.

Sense of vocation. It is, in fact, the church that helps pastoral musicians make the shift from seeing their duties as employment versus vocation. Some pastoral musicians are paid while others are not, but this is immaterial to the idea of vocation. To embrace a vocation is to recognize a sense of call in relation to one's duties. The English word **"vocation"** comes from the Latin word *vocatio*, meaning "calling."[6] It is possible to fulfill a list of duties without a call to ministerial-type service in the church. Plenty of people contract their services with local churches to fulfill a need both for themselves and the church. By contrast, while pastoral musicians will perform certain duties specified by the local church, they will do so out of a strong conviction that God has compelled them, through the Holy Spirit's direction, to offer their service in music ministry for the benefit of the church. Perhaps it can be stated this way: *a pastoral musician is not a musician who happens to serve in a church but a vocational minister who happens to be a musician.*

When speaking of vocation, we are not talking about holding an ecclesial credential, though that may be the case. A credential (e.g., ordination, certification, license, etc.) may be a beneficial and appropriate step to take, but it is not required to be a pastoral musician in most cases. What is required is that we hear the call of God and we answer that call. The vocational call of God usually follows the path of discernment, preparation, and consecration. First is the *discernment* of the call itself. We discover (often slowly) and become convinced that God is moving us toward particular service in the kingdom. The call is heard in concert with input from others in the community of faith. A true call from God does not rest entirely on our individual and singular conviction; other devoted followers who know us well, and recognize along with us that God is speaking, play their needful role in affirming our sense of vocational calling. Next there is *preparation* to fulfill the duties of the call. This will include some type of training, either formal (e.g., courses of study in a program), or informal (e.g., internships/mentoring), or both. At some

---

6. Richard A. Muller, *Dictionary of Latin and Greek Theological Terms* (Grand Rapids: Baker Books, 1985), 329.

point after discerning the call there will likely be a point of *consecration* for the work to be undertaken. (Depending on the situation, this may overlap in time with one's preparation.) The church often ratifies the call in some way, either through the laying on of hands, or a document authorizing one's preparation for ministry, or simply by hiring an individual deemed ready to fulfill the stated duties of a particular ministry. Last, vocational servants are committed to lifelong learning and are accountable to God and to others for their ongoing development as a leader in the church.

To summarize, a pastoral musician's primary asset for ministry is the person he or she is. This is what Paul had in mind when he wrote to the Corinthians indicating that the lives of the believers in Corinth were the result of Paul and Timothy's personal ministry among them (see 2 Cor. 3:1–3). Paul claims that letters of recommendation were not needed in order to commend their work among the believers there. Instead, their very lives were their credentials; their ministry stood for itself on the basis of who they were. The result? The believers themselves were seen as an open letter from Christ himself, testifying to the personal ministry of Paul and Timothy among them. At its fundamental level, the gift we bring to ministry is the person we are becoming in Christ.

The Vision of the Pastoral Musician

Pastoral musicians must develop a vision for music in worship that goes both deep and wide. At this point I am not speaking of casting a vision in the managerial sense, though that must happen over time as the leader's metavision comes into focus. I am simply calling pastoral musicians first to an ever-enlarging understanding of what music in worship is all about foundationally and comprehensively.

Characteristics of the visionary pastoral musician include the following:

- Is captivated with pursuing God's view of worship
- Has a solid understanding of biblical worship and its meaning
- Views the core content of worship to be the story of God—what the triune God is doing from creation to re-creation
- Celebrates the Christian year so as to proclaim the story of God in Christ
- Has an awareness of the historical significance of more than two millennia of Christian worship
- Embraces the dialogical nature of worship as revelation/response
- Is able to theologically reflect on worship in light of present culture
- Rejects **anthropomorphic worship** in favor of **christocentric worship**

- Understands that worship is primarily to be relevant to God (while connecting to the people)
- Recognizes that biblical worship is multidirectional in nature (both vertical [Godward] and horizontal [toward one another])
- Understands biblical worship to be primarily corporate in nature
- Rejects passive worship done *for* the community and strives for participative worship done *by* the community
- Understands that worship always forms worshipers, explicitly and implicitly
- Views worship as a larger entity than exclusively music
- Understands the interrelationship (interplay) between music and all the other acts of worship in the whole service
- Views music as a servant of the written text of worship (biblical and liturgical)
- Views the pastoral musician's duties holistically, with sensitivity to the larger purposes of worship, the Christian year, orthodox praxis, and so on
- Views the entire service as prayer, while enabling the Christian community to sing the more specific actions of the liturgy (proclamation, petition, praise, exhortation, call to action, etc.)
- Embraces a wide variety of congregational song drawing from psalms, hymns, and spiritual songs
- Is convinced that the gospel invites a variety of emotions, from gladness to sorrow, from comfort to conviction
- Understands that excellence is a journey, not an end

Pastoral musicians with a broad vision for music in worship will see their duties not as tasks to be accomplished but as ways and means that not only help people to worship locally but also contribute in some way to the global church at worship. Christ has a worshiping church. At any given moment, Christian corporate worship is happening somewhere on our beautiful earth. What's more, worship is eternal; our earthly worship occurs simultaneously with the unceasing worship of heaven—always. This way of thinking returns us to the idea of what it means to think globally and worship locally. Essentially, pastoral musicians must work to enlarge their understanding of what is at play when the church gathers to worship, and they must do so informed by certain scriptural imperatives and historical practices. Yet recognition of these necessities is not enough; we must commit ourselves to leading in such a way that these imperatives and practices become evident in actual services of worship and that the worshipers under our care begin to experience the largeness of worship as well.

To this end, here are a few "musts" to help us begin to expand our vision for corporate worship.

Biblical principles. Pastoral musicians must gain a solid understanding of biblical worship and its meaning. Pursuing God's view of worship motivates us. There is no such thing as a singular, detailed order of worship provided for us in the Bible, nor is there one way to go about worship. Nevertheless, there are critical, significant, general principles of worship that explicitly guide our work when we carefully examine what is actually said about corporate worship in the Scriptures. These universally true principles must undergird worship in every time and place.[7]

Historical consciousness. Pastoral musicians must minister with an awareness of the historical significance of more than two millennia of Christian worship. Local church services of worship do not take place as "stand-alones," uninfluenced by historical reference points. They do not occur in isolation; they have not simply dropped out of the stratosphere. Whether it's admitted or not, every service of worship is situated in some historical context. Depending on one's tradition, the historical line may be traced backward to varying degrees of success; nevertheless, there is a longer line of worshipers who have contributed to each expression of corporate worship. Wise leaders will investigate the grand sweep of thousands of years of worship to find and evaluate worship practices in which the church has always found meaning. The point is not to attempt to re-create historical worship practices—as if we even could (or should)—but to identify worship practices that seem to be central to worshiping God in every age and rendering them in a manner that is relevant for today's worshipers. To think and act historically not only means looking to the past but looking to the future as well. History is not stagnant; it is dynamic. Therefore, every generation will make its own contribution to the historical stream of worship practices that is ever evolving. As pastoral musicians, we should encourage new but meaningful worship practices and also find ways to interpret ancient practices for the present and future. We do so not to prove that we are historical for tradition's sake; we do so to emphasize the larger view that we do not worship in a vacuum—we worship with the sense of a joyous continuum of worship that has gone uninterrupted for many centuries.

7. For an examination of some of these foundational principles, see Cherry, *Worship Architect*, chaps. 1 and 2.

Spiritually forming. Pastoral musicians must understand that worship always forms worshipers, both explicitly and implicitly. We are forever shaped by what we do (or fail to do) in corporate worship. If we fully understood the power that worship holds to influence us in our love for God and others, we would take it far more seriously than we often do. Over time, pastoral musicians should expect that the services of worship they have planned and led will result in individuals who have been formed in direct relationship to what has transpired in public worship. Our vision of worship is greatly enlarged when we understand that the very choices we make in planning and leading the music of worship will influence others in more ways than we ever dreamed. Recognizing the formational power of worship and its music is critical for the pastoral musician.

Theological reflection. The pastoral musician's vision for worship must also include theological reflection on worship in light of the surrounding culture. Every worshiping community's context is influenced by the greater culture that surrounds it. Wise leaders are both students of culture and students of worship. They are able to prayerfully discern when and where the intersection between culture and worship is appropriate and when and where the leader must disallow secular influences in order to preserve Christian worship as truly Christian. Pastoral musicians will neither dismiss the culture in order to hang on to some mistaken view of "pure worship" nor absorb the culture in an indiscriminate manner. They will be careful not to mistake the call for relevancy to include practices that are questionable in light of biblical teaching. Instead, they will prayerfully engage in parsing the culture in which they find themselves so that the worship that they plan and lead will be faithful to God's vision for worship and voiced in a manner that relates to persons who find themselves worshiping in a certain place and time.

The previous paragraphs have attempted to flesh out some of the ways in which pastoral musicians must begin to enlarge their vision for worship in general and for music in particular. In the process, remember that the vision is dynamic—it will grow over the course of a lifetime, for it is directly related to our spiritual, musical, and ministerial development as well. Our limited and somewhat parochial views must be challenged. We will be able to lead our people only where we ourselves have gone first.

The Role of the Pastoral Musician

Pastoral musicians have one essential role: to enable musical worship of God in Christian community. This takes place by assuming many particular roles that support the primary one.

Characteristic roles of the pastoral musician include the following:

- Has designated responsibilities in worship and music ministry[8]
- Selects and employs music not for its own sake but to serve a greater purpose—that of enabling corporate conversation with the triune God
- Enables the Christian community to both proclaim the truth and respond to the truth through music
- Enables the community to sing both praise and lament
- Prayerfully arrives at a canon of song appropriate to his or her community by applying standards of theological, musical, and lyrical integrity
- Seeks to help his or her God-given community discover its "worship voice" (a meaningful way of communicating with God that is expressive of the community's particular culture)
- Strengthens and balances the musical style that is normative for his or her community
- Helps worshipers view their worship as connected to the worship of Christian sisters and brothers all over the world
- Helps worshipers view their worship as eternal worship—worship that has been and will always be ongoing—on earth as it is in heaven
- Connects public worship with pursuing justice for others here and now
- Connects public worship with private worship

Pastoral musicians will fulfill particular roles in their ministries. Notice that the roles of pastoral musicians flow from the persons they are becoming and the visions they are developing. What we do in music ministry is derived from who we are and what we believe about music in worship. Vision is translated into implementation. Specific tasks are critical to fulfilling one's vocational call, *but they must be viewed as a way to express the call rather than be viewed as the call itself.* Again, what we do isn't essentially who we are; nevertheless, the particular responsibilities pastoral musicians have, like those listed above, are very important to identify and fulfill. The church is depending on this kind of clarity and breadth of leadership. At the same time, perhaps these roles can be grouped into two primary ones as described below.

Worshiper among worshipers. One primary role of all musicians is simply this: they must understand themselves to be a worshiper among worshipers. Musicians must be worshipers themselves. This may seem obvious; however,

8. This may be full-time or part-time, paid or volunteer.

this is not always the case. Occasionally musicians view themselves as professionals who are leading others in music making in the context of a service. This can easily happen, even among leaders with the best of intentions—those who are sincerely devoted to God and desire nothing more than God-honoring worship. We often naturally default into a leadership role and quickly forget that we ourselves are, in fact, worshiping in real time as members of the gathered community. Frankly, we may arrive at home after leading the service(s) only to find ourselves exhausted from the demands of musical leadership. We may ask ourselves, "When do *I* get to worship?"

That's a good question. There are two perspectives that can help us here. First, it will always be true that once we are pastoral musicians we are occupied with on-the-spot leadership during the service, ranging from directing the congregational singing to participating as an instrumentalist to monitoring the technology to observing the engagement of the people, and so on. With so many jobs to do, we may not feel like a worshiper in that moment. Good news! Our work *is* our worship! One of the biblical words often translated as the word "worship" is *leitourgia*, a Greek term from which we get our English word "liturgy."[9] In English Bibles *leitourgia* is translated as "service" or "ministry." It is also faithfully translated as "worship." It refers to the holy duties of those who minister before God, especially those functioning as priests (see Luke 1:23 [Zechariah]; Heb. 9:21 [Moses]; and Heb. 8:1–2 [Christ]). It is fair to say that our worship is our service to God, or we can also say, our service is our worship of God. Either way, to worship is to minister. I have found that when I undertake my responsibilities for musical leadership while at the same time offering them to God and the community as an act of worship, it changes everything. It allows me to joyfully accept my God-given duties and transform them into opportunities for offering a sacrifice of praise. I no longer have to ask, "When do I get to worship?" The answer is, "I just did."

Second, I have carefully worded the phrase "worshiper among worshipers," as opposed to "lead worshiper." The term "lead worshiper" has become popular in recent years, and while there is arguably nothing wrong with its use, it may not most accurately depict our role. Being a worshiper among worshipers suggests that we are part of the community endeavoring to engage in the very event to which we call the community. It simply affirms that we, as pastoral musicians, seek to worship among our sisters and brothers even as we lead them. "Lead worshiper," on the contrary, suggests that the worship leader is the model worshiper to whom others look to imitate. While leaders

---

9. The Hebrew word used in the Old Testament is *abad*, translated also to mean "worship" (in the performance of priestly/ministerial duties).

do present a necessary disposition for worship that will hopefully encourage others, technically speaking, *people* are not really the lead worshipers. That is the role of Jesus Christ. Christ is our true lead worshiper. It is the role given him by God the Father. The author of Hebrews uses the Greek term *leitourgos* to refer to Christ as the leader of our worship; he is "a minister in the sanctuary" (Heb. 8:2). Chapter 2 will expand on this idea further.

One of the primary roles, then, of pastoral musicians is to foster their own participation as a worshiper among worshipers. This role is related to their own spiritual development and their development as a leader.

Bishop of souls. The second primary role of pastoral musicians is to be shepherd of the worshiping community. By now it should be evident that a pastoral musician has a calling to superintend an event in such a way that God's people are shepherded toward a real encounter with God and one another. To be a pastoral musician is really about overseeing the flock of God in worship. For this, once again, we look to Jesus as our example. In fact, he is called just that—the "Overseer of your souls" (1 Pet. 2:25 NIV). This stunning phrase is translated as "bishop of your souls" in the King James Version: "For [you] were as sheep going astray; but are now returned unto the Shepherd and Bishop of your souls." The word "bishop" is the Greek word *episcopos*, meaning overseer. It is comforting to know that we have an Overseer of our souls—Jesus—who stands guard over us as a Shepherd, someone who will provide the watchful care we need as we live the life of worship. That's the role of the pastoral musician—to oversee, to cast a watchful eye on all the actions and participants of worship while discerning the movement of the Holy Spirit in real time. *A pastoral musician is a bishop of worshiping souls.* While leading worship, pastoral musicians will cast their spiritual gaze heavenward—watching for the movement of God's Spirit; at the same time they will have an eye toward those under their care, praying for them as worship is under way, guiding them toward doxology. Pastoral musicians watch and listen; they guide and exhort as they lovingly lead fellow worshipers to the throne of God. God has entrusted us to oversee God's people in worship. Pastoral musicians are bishops of souls. This role is the most important of all.

Conclusion

In some cases, who we are and what we do can seem almost inseparable due to the overwhelming passion with which we invest our lives vocationally. This is the sense one gets when reading Paul's story in the New Testament. Notice how Paul introduces himself in each of his letters. Nine out of thirteen epistles begin with Paul describing himself with the title "apostle."[10] This title was not one he claimed for himself; rather, it was given to him by the will of God (see 1 Cor. 1:1; 2 Cor. 1:1; Eph. 1:1; Col. 1:1; etc.). The preponderance with which he uses the term "apostle" is telling. The term relates directly to what Paul does as a life calling: he is sent to be an ambassador of the gospel. This is a formal title, entailing Paul's ministry of apostolic teaching, preaching, church planting, evangelizing, mentoring, and more. When needed, Paul appealed to his title for authority in the first-century church. His title seems to center on what Paul does. Yet it is all but impossible to read the Acts of the Apostles and Paul's letters and separate who he is from what he does. His passion for his God-given vocational ministry was all-consuming. For Paul, "living is Christ"; he states, "If I am to live in the flesh, that means fruitful labor for me" (Phil. 1:21–22). Formerly he found his identity in his race and in his impressive pedigree (Acts 22:3; Phil. 3:4–6); after his conversion and as his ministry progressed, Paul found his identity through who he was in Jesus Christ and in becoming like him in his sufferings and death (Phil. 3:10). In short, Paul's person and work seem almost one and the same due to his singular focus and full abandon to the will of God.

We have now come full circle. This chapter began by distinguishing between what we do and who we are in ministry. Sometimes our titles reflect our job responsibilities more than the manner in which we go about ministry. As an exception, Paul's perspective seems to suggest a holy synthesis between Paul as a person and his vocation as apostle. Likewise, the designation of "pastoral musician" suggests not only one's ministry responsibilities (musician) but also how these responsibilities are undertaken to God's glory (pastoral). In the end, our goal is like that of Paul: living is Christ!

Key Terms

anthropomorphic worship. Human-centered worship; the opposite of theocentric worship.

christocentric worship. Christ-centered worship.

pastoral musician. A spiritual leader with developed skill and God-given responsibility for selecting, employing, and/or leading music in worship in ways that serve the actions of the liturgy, engage worshipers as full

10. See Rom. 1:1; 1 Cor. 1:1; 2 Cor. 1:1; Gal. 1:1; Eph. 1:1; Col. 1:1; 1 Tim. 1:1; 2 Tim. 1:1; Titus 1:1.

participants, and reflect upon biblical, theological, and contextual implications, all for the ultimate purpose of glorifying God.

vocation. From the Latin word *vocatio*, meaning "calling."

To Learn More

Books

Funk, Virgil C., ed. *The Pastoral Musician.* Vol. 5 of *Pastoral Music in Practice.* Washington, DC: Pastoral Press, 1990.

Westermeyer, Paul. *The Heart of the Matter: Church Music as Praise, Prayer, Proclamation, Story, and Gift.* Chicago: GIA, 2001.

Websites

National Association of Pastoral Musicians. http://www.npm.org.

Engage

Bring your music ministry into focus by answering these questions:

1. How has your ministry in music leadership been described thus far? Whether paid or volunteer, what is your present title? If you do not have a title, what do you suppose it would be if your local church leaders were asked to give you one based on your present responsibilities?
2. Imagine that you were given the opportunity to change your title (without changing your ministry responsibilities) to more accurately describe your vision for who you are and what you do. What title would you choose?
3. From your perspective, how would this title describe your vocation more accurately?

2

Pouring the Footing

God-Focused Song

Explore

Before reading this chapter, discuss the following ideas with someone involved in the music ministry of your church or organization:

1. Brainstorm a list of every purpose that music serves in culture today. Be specific.
2. How would you go about determining the purpose of any type of music?
3. Complete this thought in one sentence: The purpose of music in Christian worship is to _____.

Expand

Every type of music has a purpose. Some music is composed for dance, while some for mourning; some is written for coronations of royalty or for soothing the savage beast. Music is created for religious purposes and for sheer entertainment, to sell a product, or to promote school spirit. Even when a musician composes "just to compose," it is serving a purpose—satisfying the innate personal desire to create—whether or not anyone else ever hears the music. Persons acquainted with the history of Western music have probably encountered the term "absolute music"—a type of musical genre that is portrayed as having no particular meaning outside itself; it "is free from extra-musical implications."[1] In contrast to songs (where words present an explicit message) or program music (instrumental music intended to suggest a scene or story line),[2] absolute music could be argued to be music for music's sake. Philosopher and theologian Nicholas P. Wolterstorff counters this argument by claiming that "all music, with the rarest of exceptions, is composed or used for the service of something or other."[3] While it may not have a particular message (a Haydn string quartet, for instance), it certainly has a function: "Almost all music is composed or used . . . for some social function."[4] Wolterstorff concludes that essentially all music is functional, from the concert hall to divine liturgy; the only question is which function is it serving.[5]

In worship, music does not exist for music's sake. It is not written to be admired. Musician and theologian Don Saliers explains by comparing the music of worship with the sacred use of icons. He writes,

> Music can be regarded as offering acoustical icons. Just as the theological significance of the icon can be set aside to appreciate the image as an artifact of human making, so music can be simply admired for its structure, its elements, and for how it gives us pleasure. But the theological import of music requires a kind of active receptivity that is more akin to prayer, to contemplation, and to attending [to] the world with a sense of wonder and awe.[6]

The use of religious icons involves more than our seeing the icon with physical eyes but instead involves our learning to let the figure(s) in the icon gaze upon us while we open the "eyes of our hearts" to be read by God.[7] In the same way, the music of worship does not exist for us to stand at a distance and admire the musical accomplishments of gifted composers and lyricists; this admiration can distract us from full participation in the divine relationship under way in corporate worship. The music of worship has a purer, God-given purpose instead.

The music of Christian worship exists for the adoration of the triune God. The music will take many forms, of course, and will naturally include many

1. *Harvard Dictionary of Music*, 2nd ed., rev. and enlarged, ed. Willi Apel (Cambridge, MA: Belknap Press, 1972), s.v. "absolute music."
2. Ibid.
3. Nicholas P. Wolterstorff, "Thinking about Church Music," in *Music in Christian Worship*, ed. Charlotte Kroeker (Collegeville, MN: Liturgical Press, 2005), 5.
4. Ibid.
5. Ibid., 7.
6. Don E. Saliers, *Music and Theology* (Nashville: Abingdon, 2007), 69.
7. Ibid.

themes and aspects of what it means to give God glory. It will also include inspiring one another to glorify God while worshiping together. To ensure that music glorifies God, music architects begin the building of a service by pouring the footing that will anchor the foundation.[8] The footing consists of core truths concerning Christian worship on which musical foundations will subsequently be laid—a footing that is established beforehand and that provides a base for laying a solid foundation when considering music's role in worship.

What type of footing must be established in order to ensure the God-focused nature of music in a worship service? On what basis will we lay our foundations for all aspects of our musical leadership? What connection is there between the fundamental footing of Christian worship and the decisions we make related to worship music? The answer to these questions will derive from our understanding of the appropriate biblical footing for corporate worship that is poured first. A clear concept of what worship is all about and a thorough understanding of the general principles of worship must precede any discussion of particular aspects of the service, such as music, prayers, sermon, and so on.

This chapter will attempt to install a solid footing for musical leadership by affirming that the music of worship is God-focused. The *music* of worship must be God-focused because *worship* is, first of all, God-focused. In other words, if we believe that worship focuses on God, then pastoral musicians are committed to God-focused musical leadership as well, so that the larger, central purposes of worship are fulfilled. This chapter seeks to help pastoral musicians identify and accept the footing of worship at its most basic level on which they will then lay foundations for musical leadership. (Chapter 3 will help pastoral musicians lay the foundations related to music in corporate worship.) Specifically, this is accomplished when worship proclaims and celebrates the story of God, when the person and work of Jesus Christ is portrayed as central to that story, and when a Trinitarian ethos provides the context for the songs the Christian community sings in worship. We'll address these one by one, but first we'll look at what Christian worship is.

What Is Christian Worship?

What is worship? Worship occurs in many places and takes many forms. Most of the time we use the word "worship" to refer to outward actions

8. A foundation begins with an underground, poured concrete track in which it is anchored so as to stabilize the entire structure. As the building is erected, it is grounded in that which will secure its longevity so as to fulfill its ultimate purpose.

and internal devotion that people offer to give honor and adoration to a deity.[9] The worship of gods has played a central role in cultures of all time. But what is *Christian* worship? Christian worship is the outward actions and internal devotion that believers offer to the one true God in Jesus Christ through the Holy Spirit. It involves many expressions that are individual and corporate, outward and inward, "24/7" and on the Lord's Day. These things being noted, the primary setting for Christian worship is the context of the church. Notice that its context is not in *a* church. "Church" is not a building, though it is perfectly fitting to refer to a building as a church. *The* church is the living community of Christ-followers—past, present, and future—who name Jesus as Lord. The church is established by God with Christ as its head (Eph. 4:15). Together, all true Christians compose Christ's holy church, and the worship of God in Christ is its central activity. The gift of worship given by God to the church often takes place in buildings (churches) that serve as gathering places for local believers. But we don't just go to church; we *are* the church!

There is no singular, complete, perfect definition of what Christian worship is, but Robert Schaper offers one that is very helpful to music architects as they pour the footing on which their musical leadership rests: "Worship is the expression of a relationship in which God the Father reveals himself and his love in Christ, and by his Holy Spirit administers grace, to which we respond in faith, gratitude, and obedience."[10] There are several strong features of Schaper's definition for corporate Christian worship. It portrays worship as highly relational, an important aspect given that the story of God is all about the relationship between God's creation in general and God's people in particular. The definition also suggests a rhythm of revelation and response—God reveals his character and being; therefore, it is God's own self-revelation to which we respond. Worship does not begin with us; we do not approach God as the first act of worship, nor do we respond to ourselves, which sometimes is attempted in worship. Instead, God approaches us and calls us to worship; our response of worship is predicated on God acting first. Additionally, the definition is Trinitarian in scope (more is said about this below). Last, the definition gives us biblical means for our response: faith, gratitude, and obedience. Obedience is especially key in helping us to link corporate worship with service to the needy and pursuing justice for the oppressed.

9. We also use the word apart from religious meanings. For instance, one might say, "I worship the ground she walks on." However, as evidenced by most dictionaries and common usage, the primary use of the term is related to religious adoration of a deity.

10. Robert Schaper, *In His Presence: Appreciating Your Worship Tradition* (Nashville: Thomas Nelson, 1984), 15–16.

Worship can't be captured entirely in a definition, though that is a great starting place. These basic ideas must be fleshed out as we turn to the Scriptures and the teaching of orthodox Christianity to help us arrive at a mature understanding of the worship event. It is critical that worship leaders, in concert with their local church leaders, arrive at nonnegotiable principles that will undergird their worship. There is no master list that is universally followed; nonetheless, an appropriate start must be made, for the principles we embrace concerning worship will drive the decisions we make. There are some things that are true about Christian worship that transcend time, place, culture, geographical location, style, and denomination. Worship leaders are very wise to identify these central "musts" of worship that serve as orienting markers to keep us true to God's expectations for worship. Below is one example of just such a list. It is composed of "transcultural norms" that serve as principles for fashioning services of Christian worship.[11] The norms are quoted directly from the source (italics are original); the parenthetical comments are my attempts to briefly summarize and interpret the principles.

1. Christian worship should be *biblical.*

   (The Bible is our primary *source* for direction concerning our worship practices as well as our primary *text* for worship, both in prominent readings of Scripture and as the basis for many of our worship elements such as prayers, songs, etc.)

2. Christian worship should be *dialogic and relational.*

   (Worship carries out the public dimension of our corporate relationship with God, which is relational and hence conversational.)

3. Christian worship should be *covenantal.*

   (Corporate worship is an opportunity to renew our covenant with God as God's people [vertical] and with one another [horizontal].)

4. Christian worship should be *Trinitarian.*

   (The words and actions of worship honor the biblical view of God in three persons: Father, Son, and Holy Spirit.)

5. Christian worship should be *communal.*

   (Believers offer worship together, representing the unity and mission of those called into fellowship in a given place.)

11. Carrie Titcombe Steenwyk and John D. Witvliet, eds., *The Worship Sourcebook,* 2nd ed. (Grand Rapids: Calvin Institute of Christian Worship/Faith Alive Christian Resources/Baker Books, 2013), 16–17.

6. Christian worship should be hospitable, caring, and welcoming.

   (Worship convicts, prepares, and empowers believers to offer loving acceptance of and ministry to broken people.)

7. Christian worship should be *"in but not of" the world.*

   (While worship takes place within a given culture and/or subculture, it is not fashioned by the culture in ways that run counter to the gospel.)

8. Christian worship should be a generous and excellent outpouring of ourselves before God.

   (The worship offered to the triune God is worthy of our best efforts.)

9. Christian worship should be *both expressive and formative.*

   (Worship is profound enough to welcome the honest expressions of our lives while at the same time shape us through the event, in unexpected ways, to the glory of God.)

We started by addressing the question, what is Christian worship? This is the essential first step. Pastoral musicians cannot begin their vocational ministry without first understanding the event that is being served by the music they lead. As we will see in chapter 3, music serves the liturgy, not the other way around. **Liturgy** is a very important word in worship studies. Regrettably, some sectors of Christianity hold a bias concerning the word, which stems from misunderstanding. The English word "liturgy" is from the Greek word *leitourgia*, translated into various English words including "service," "ministry," or "worship." It is found in several places in the New Testament (see Luke 1:23; Rom. 12:1; Heb. 8:6; 9:21). Thinking broadly, "liturgy" refers to the complete collection of worship acts that the people do in the course of any given worship service.

Every worshiping community has liturgy—even those who think they do not. Whether spontaneous or planned, whether written or not, all services of Christian worship employ actions, words, gestures, and symbols that, when performed with the right intentions, constitute the corporate worship of God. Liturgy isn't just the order of service; it is everything we do to offer our body, soul, mind, and strength to minister to God as a gathered community—*it is the people's work.* The music of worship plays a very special role in all of this as it is uniquely favored to enable the liturgy of any church, any style, any place, at any time.

There is so much more to say about the corporate worship event that is simply beyond the bounds of this chapter. Suggestions for learning more about worship are found at the end of this chapter to help the worship architect get started. At this point, the important thing is this: understanding worship is the key to understanding the leadership of music in worship. It would be a grave error (that too many make) for the worship musician to provide musical leadership without a well-grounded understanding of what is taking place when God's people gather to worship. Pastoral musicians who also serve as worship architects must understand (intellectually, biblically, experientially, and spiritually) what corporate worship is all about. Only then will they truly be able to live out their vocation.

Worship Proclaims and Celebrates the Story of God

First and foremost, pastoral musicians must embrace the reality that Christian worship is the proclamation and celebration of the **story of God** in community. The story of God—the acts of the eternal, triune God from creation to re-creation—constitutes the content of worship and, to some degree, the order of worship. (This will be explained in greater detail in chap. 4.) This single reality dramatically affects what is said and done in worship.

We live in an interesting time in history. There was a period in the West when a particular view of reality—based on the biblical narrative as expressed in the Christian Scriptures—was more or less accepted as a way to orient and explain life and culture. Not all persons knew of or adopted the biblical narrative, of course, and those who did embraced it to varying degrees of certainty or commitment. Nevertheless, the story of God in Christ factored prominently in the cultural worldview, often even with those who made no claim to be Christians themselves. God's story was simply presumed to be true, for Christians and many non-Christians alike.

However, for years this wide acceptance of the biblical narrative as true has been diminishing by the day. Robert Webber notes, "At one time the Western world was narrated by the Christian God and the biblical story of his work. . . . Today, this story of God's cosmic salvation has been lost in the West. In Europe the light has nearly flickered out, and in North America the light is growing dim."[12] We now live in a time that is witnessing ever-increasing secularization. One recent example of this is a remark made in a movie theater overheard by someone waiting to watch Mel Gibson's *The Passion of the Christ*: "I hear this film is based on a true story." The demise of a "universally" accepted metanarrative does not mean that *no* story is valid. Rather, with the influence of postmodern thought it is suggested that *multiple* stories are valid. Any number of metanarratives is viable around which one may orient one's life in order to describe reality.

12. Robert E. Webber, *Who Gets to Narrate the World? Contending for the Christian Story in an Age of Rivals* (Downers Grove, IL: InterVarsity, 2008), 11.

The Scriptures suggest otherwise. There is one story line that is true—a metanarrative of redemption—that travels from Genesis to Revelation. It is the story of God's activity of his love for the world and everything in it that he created. Christian worship expresses the claim that there is, indeed, one narrative that truly depicts reality. There is a story—a story that is true whether acknowledged or not—a narrative that is unapologetically proclaimed and celebrated when the church gathers for worship. Worship has changed over the past several decades in some places to the point where anthropomorphic worship predominates. Webber critiques that "much of our worship has shifted from a focus on God and God's story to a focus on me and my story."[13] One of the consequences of self-focused worship is narcissism[14]—a preoccupation with the satisfaction of self. Biblical worship, on the contrary, boldly centers on God's story as the central narrative of reality (God-focused worship). Anthropomorphic worship is misguided worship. Indeed, "a dominant error of some Christians is to say, 'I must bring God into *my* story.' The ancient understanding is that God joins the story of humanity to *take us into his story*. There is a world of difference. One is narcissistic; the other is God-oriented. It will change your entire spiritual life when you realize that your life is joined to God's story."[15] Our stories matter a great deal, of course. But we must be clear: it is the intersection of our story with God's story that is of significance in Christian worship. God doesn't alter his story to ours; we alter our story to God's. "In summary, here is what biblical worship does: It remembers God's work in the past, anticipates God's rule over all creation, and actualizes both past and future in the present to transform persons, communities, and the world."[16]

If Christian worship is the proclamation and celebration of the story of God in community, then music contributes to the telling of that story. Singing the songs of faith proclaims and celebrates the story. As church musician Paul Westermeyer asserts: "the church's song is about the story."[17] The themes of our songs will be both deep and wide, for it takes many a song to tell the sweeping narrative of what the eternal, triune God is doing from creation to re-creation. Pastoral musicians help people to sing God's story. Objective psalms, hymns, and spiritual songs best retell the story. Pastoral musicians

---

13. Robert E. Webber, *The Divine Embrace: Recovering the Passionate Spiritual Life* (Grand Rapids: Baker Books, 2006), 231.

14. Ibid.

15. Robert E. Webber, *Ancient-Future Worship: Proclaiming and Enacting God's Narrative* (Grand Rapids: Baker Books, 2008), 23.

16. Ibid., 43.

17. Paul Westermeyer, *The Heart of the Matter: Church Music as Praise, Prayer, Proclamation, Story, and Gift* (Chicago: GIA, 2001), 39.

also help believers sing their story in relation to God's story. More personal songs of testimony, witness, and experience help to position our story within God's story for proper perspective. Pastoral musicians will see to it that the whole story of God is sung over time. Stories are to be told and retold so that people remember the characters and the plot, the conflict and the resolution. The music of worship carries the story line of the Christian narrative—episode by episode, chapter by chapter. Pastoral musicians are sensitized to how well the musical repertoire of their congregational song is suited to tell the whole story of God over time, and they lovingly add to or subtract from the local body of song so as to ensure that the whole of God's story, as well as our place in that story, is clear.

Worship Is Centered on the Person and Work of Jesus Christ

We have said that worship proclaims and celebrates the story of God in community. The very heart of that story is God's Son, Jesus Christ. He is the cornerstone of worship. In fact, this one reality is what makes Christian worship truly *Christian* worship. Various New Testament passages refer to Christ as the cornerstone of our faith, providing the trustworthy basis for a spiritual dwelling place for God (see Matt. 21:42; Eph. 2:19–22; 1 Pet. 2:4–7). The cornerstone of any building represents an honored place, for the building is constructed according to its true, level, and stable placement. If it is situated properly, the entire edifice is secure. Jesus Christ has been given the honored place in worship by the will of the Father. The honor that is due to Christ is not one that was demanded by him; rather, it was given to him. God the Father "highly exalted him and gave him the name that is above every name" (Phil. 2:9). The stone that was once rejected, God made to be the chief cornerstone. "This is the LORD's doing; it is marvelous in our eyes" (Ps. 118:23).

The significant, even cosmic role that Jesus plays in worship is at least twofold: Christ receives our worship, and Christ leads our worship. It is a great mystery that one Being can fulfill two seemingly opposing functions at once, but that is exactly what Jesus is qualified to do as the God-man, incarnate God. As God, Jesus is worthy of worship; as human, he is one of us in worship. In this way, the person and the work of Jesus Christ is central to our worship.

Christ Receives Our Worship

First, as God, Christ is worthy to receive worship. Such a statement does not, of course, suggest that God the Father and God the Holy Spirit are not also worthy of worship. All persons of the triune God are worshiped both through individual reference and as one God in three persons (see "Trinitarian Worship" below). This practice is seen in Scripture;[18] it is also affirmed by the church fathers as summarized in the Nicene Creed of AD 381: "We believe in the Holy Spirit. . . . With the Father and the Son he is worshiped and glorified."[19] Notice the emphatic assertion that all persons of the Godhead are equally worshiped. The creed "was reflecting a continuous tradition that extended from at least the time of the apostles onward in the threefold name found in the church's hymnody."[20]

At the same time, God's will is that the Son is the recipient of worship in a unique way—a way that glorifies God in return. The worship of Jesus Christ is the eternal plan of God. Before the beginning of time, God willed that the Son would receive the worship of eternity, for "when he brings the firstborn into the world, he says, 'Let all God's angels worship him'" (Heb. 1:6). It is also the worship of Christ that will be the grand climax of the story when God puts all things under his feet (1 Cor. 15:25) and the angels once again sing with full voice, "Worthy is the Lamb that was slaughtered to receive power and wealth and wisdom and might and honor and glory and blessing!" (Rev. 5:12). Immediately after his resurrection, Mary Magdalene and the other Mary worshiped at Jesus's feet when he met them early in the morning on that day (Matt. 28:9). At his ascension the disciples worshiped him (Matt. 28:17). The risen Lord did not refuse these acts of devotion. Evidence of New Testament prophets and teachers "worshiping the Lord" (Acts 13:2) suggests Christ as the referent of that worship.[21] Jesus, who was and is and is to come, receives worship to the glory of God the Father (Phil. 2:11) throughout eternity. Historian Larry Hurtado further demonstrates that Jesus was corecipient of devotion (with God) by the earliest Christians—a most radical development, given Judaism's hallmark of monotheism. Hurtado notes that prayer is now offered through and to Jesus, Jesus's name is invoked as a source of grace, ritual acts are directed toward Jesus, Jesus is confessed to be Lord, Jesus is the name invoked in

18. The number of references in the Bible supporting the worship of God the Father is abundant. Numerous occasions in the New Testament attribute the worship of Christ as normative following the resurrection (Matt. 28:9; Luke 24:52; Phil. 2:10–11; Heb. 1:6; Rev. 1:6; 5:11–14, etc.). The worship of the Holy Spirit is seen in the various Trinitarian invocations found in the context of worship in the New Testament. Examples of these include baptism (Matt. 28:19) and benedictions (2 Cor. 13:14).

19. Joel C. Elowsky, ed., "We Believe in the Holy Spirit," in *Ancient Christian Doctrine* (Downers Grove, IL: InterVarsity, 2009), 4:246.

20. Ibid.

21. Larry W. Hurtado, *At the Origins of Christian Worship: The Context and Character of Earliest Christian Devotion* (Grand Rapids: Eerdmans, 1999), 76.

baptism, Jesus authorizes the Lord's Supper, Jesus is sung to devotionally in worship, and more.[22]

When Christians gather for corporate **Lord's Day worship**, they do so to honor the triune God; this is accomplished through the adoration of Jesus Christ. Bryan Chapell writes, "The heart of Christian worship is love for Christ. We cannot love him without extolling his greatness, confessing our weakness, seeking his goodness, thanking him for his grace, and living for his glory. So, out of love for him, we worship him in these ways."[23] Caution is in order. In worship we certainly do not want to fall into the "Jesus only" heresy found in some segments of the modern church,[24] praying and singing to and otherwise referencing a benign Jesus who is romanticized as he is worshiped. That is an approach foreign to biblical and historic Christianity. However, with caution duly noted, Christ remains the central figure of worship by God's design. We need not worry; the persons of the Trinity are not in a spiritual tug-of-war for attention when Christ becomes the center of our worship. Instead, the Godhead is well pleased, for when the Son is worshiped, God is glorified.

If Christ is to be the center of Christian worship, then we, like the earliest Christians, must be intentional in naming the name that is above all names as we worship. We must reverently recognize the remarkable recipient of our worship. We must sing to and of him, invoke his name in prayer, remember his life and death in our participation of the sacraments, place him at the heart of God's story that we celebrate as we proclaim each episode of that narrative over time, and never forget to herald him as *Christus Victor*—the Anointed One who has not only done battle with but triumphed over Satan forever—"to whom be the glory forever and ever. Amen" (Heb. 13:21).

Christ Leads Our Worship

Because most Christians readily acknowledge that Jesus Christ is worthy of worship, we rarely think imaginatively about this idea. The scriptural passages mentioned above, and the long-standing practices of the church, secure Christ's role as one who receives our praise. However, the second role that Christ plays in worship—Christ is our premiere worship leader—while also

22. Ibid., 74–92. Hurtado elaborates on these and many examples of early Christian Christ-devotion.

23. Bryan Chapell, *Christ-Centered Worship: Letting the Gospel Shape Our Practice* (Grand Rapids: Baker Academic, 2009), 112–13.

24. Susan J. White, "What Ever Happened to the Father? The Jesus Heresy in Modern Worship," 2004, http://www.kintera.org/atf/cf/%7B3482e846-598f-460a-b9a7-386734470eda%7D/WHITE.PDF.

true, may stretch our human imaginations to a greater degree. Remarkably, the author of Hebrews refers to Jesus using that very term *leitourgos* (Heb. 8:2), to be interpreted as the leader of our worship. As James B. Torrance makes crystal clear: "The real agent in worship, in a New Testament understanding, is Jesus Christ who leads us in our praises and prayers."[25] Through his incarnation, Christ is uniquely positioned by God to mediate our worship to the Father. Christ plays this priestly role—a desperately needed one—so that our woefully inadequate worship is made perfectly presentable to God. Christ is our high priest, mediating our prayers (1 Tim. 2:5) and mediating our praises (Heb. 2:12). Torrance elaborates,

> Jesus comes to be the priest of creation to do for us, men and women, what we failed to do, to offer to the Father the worship and the praise we failed to offer, to glorify God by a life of perfect love and obedience, to be the one true servant of the Lord. . . . He comes to stand in for us in the presence of the Father, when in our failure and bewilderment we do not know how to pray as we ought to, or forget to pray altogether. . . . This is the "wonderful exchange" (*mirifica commutatio—admirabile commercium*) by which Christ takes what is ours (our broken lives and unworthy prayers), sanctifies them, offers them without spot or wrinkle to the Father, and gives them back to us, that we might "feed" upon him in thanksgiving. He takes our prayers and makes them his prayers, and he makes his prayers our prayers, and we know our prayers are heard "for Jesus' sake."[26]

Just as Jesus sanctifies our prayers, he sanctifies our song, as New Testament scholar Reggie Kidd maintains: "Jesus cleanses consciences and he cleanses songs one would have thought foul beyond redemption."[27] We all stand in continued need of the mediating work of Jesus Christ in worship. God graciously makes ongoing provision for the church at worship through the continuing priestly ministry of Jesus Christ, our *leitourgos*. Truly it is because of Jesus's role as great high priest that we may come before God with boldness (Heb. 4:14–16); we are able to worship with confidence that Jesus has transformed humanly offered worship into divinely offered worship to the glory of God.

Yet even as Christ facilitates our worship, he is also with us as a worshiper. As Hebrews also makes clear, "Jesus is not ashamed to call them brothers and sisters, saying, 'I will proclaim your name to my brothers and sisters, in

25. James B. Torrance, *Worship, Community and the Triune God of Grace* (Downers Grove, IL: InterVarsity, 1996), 23.

26. Ibid., 14–15.

27. Reggie Kidd, *With One Voice: Discovering Christ's Song in Our Worship* (Grand Rapids: Baker Books, 2005), 127.

the midst of the congregation I will praise you'" (Heb. 2:11b–12). Quoting Psalm 22:22, Jesus places himself among the humans he came to redeem; the fellowship of the family of God is his community with which he identifies as he leads them in worship of the Father.

From our vantage point as pastoral musicians, perhaps the most remarkable image of Christ as our lead worshiper is that of the singing Jesus. Christ is the eternal singer. He sang as the world was created (Job 38:4, 6–7),[28] he sang during his earthly life (Mark 14:26; Matt. 26:30), and he continues to sing following his ascension (Heb. 2:12: "I will praise [*hymnesō*] you [God]"). Michael O'Connor notes that Jesus sang as a way of life during his earthly ministry: "Jesus grew up in a lyrical culture and worshiped in a setting that used musical/lyrical forms regularly and with ease. It would have come naturally to him to sing at prayer; indeed, it would have been *unnatural* not to do so."[29] As a well-initiated Jew in ancient Palestine, Jesus would have no doubt sung at play, social events, in the home, at synagogue, at temple, at prayer, while reading Holy Scripture, and so on. The public reading of Scripture in the synagogues, in which Jesus participated (Luke 4:16), was intoned, as were the prayers.[30] O'Connor affirms: "Likewise at times of prayer with his disciples, perhaps even when teaching them the Our Father, it can be assumed that Jesus would have used some kind of cantillation."[31] Singing was a way of life. It was also a way of death, for as O'Connor also points out, the psalms on the lips of Jesus while on the cross would have reflected that "a reminiscence of musical prayer accompanies the final moments of Jesus' life."[32]

Of particular interest for our purposes as we pour the footing of worship, is that Jesus sings *with* us in corporate worship. The risen Lord is present through the Holy Spirit every time the church gathers. Returning to Hebrews

28. For a fascinating account of the Jesus who sings eternally, see Michael O'Connor's "The Singing Jesus," in *Resonant Witness: Conversations between Music and Theology*, ed. Jeremy S. Begbie and Steven R. Guthrie (Grand Rapids: Eerdmans, 2011), 443–45. O'Connor cites the work of Johann Mattheson (1681–1764) to suggest the cosmic comprehensiveness of the God who sings. Mattheson uses a passage in Job to argue that when the foundation of the earth was laid, "the morning stars sang together and all the children of God shouted for joy" (Job 38:7). By implication he credits Jesus with participating in the song (1) by virtue of Jesus referring to himself as the bright morning star (Rev. 22:16) and (2) that he is the firstborn of all creation (Col. 1:15) and would therefore have been among the children of God (Hebrew, "the sons of God"). While O'Connor recognizes that Mattheson's argument by implication has its limitations, O'Connor embellishes the viability of the singing Jesus throughout the chapter substantially.
29. Ibid., 439.
30. Edward Foley, *Foundations of Christian Music: The Music of Pre-Constantinian Christianity* (Collegeville, MN: Liturgical Press, 1996), 54–55.
31. O'Connor, "Singing Jesus," 437.
32. Ibid., 439.

2:12, we find that Jesus is "in the midst of the congregation" praising the Father. He is both proclaiming the Father's name to his fellow worshipers and praising the Father among them. O'Connor states it so well:

> Christ sings among his people when they are gathered to worship on earth. This is part of his promise to remain among them even to the ends of the age (Matt. 28:20). The singing of Jesus in the church shows who he is (Son of the Father) and who his disciples are (no less than his brothers and sisters). Christ is the leader and initiator of Christian worship, the High Priest of the sacrifice of praise offered to the Father by those who serve him (see Heb. 8:1–2). The eternal Son's loving obedience toward the Father, translated into human form in the incarnation (which is his priesthood) is now shared with all of his brothers and sisters.[33]

This perspective of Jesus being our worship leader is long-held among noted church leaders throughout the centuries. Among them are John Calvin, who affirmed, "Christ leads our songs . . . and is the chief composer of our hymns,"[34] and John Wesley who, referencing Hebrews 2:12, views Jesus's role as worship leader as not only something he performed in the midst of his apostles at the Passover meal the evening before his death but as something he still does, and will continue to do in the church throughout all generations by his word and his Spirit.[35]

What is happening here? The ascended Jesus "now sings the Father's praises as Firstborn among the firstborn. The song of the church below . . . is antiphon to this voice from heaven."[36] In short, the songs of worship produce the sounds of antiphonal singing—the resounding interplay of Jesus's song with our song as the incarnate Lord, both ascended and yet present among his sisters and brothers, sings to the Father. What difference does this make?

> Somehow our singing is more his than ours. It is unspeakable joy for me to take my place as a worshiper among my brothers and sisters, knowing that Jesus, the Chief Liturgist, has already taken his place. My Sundays would be miserable if I thought otherwise. In his real presence, our posture is simultaneously more trembling and more relaxed. He is in *control* rather than we, so we can relax. *He*—who, like C. S. Lewis's Lion-Christ Aslan, is not safe, but is good—*he* is in

33. Ibid., 442–43.
34. Ibid., 442. O'Connor cites John Calvin, *Commentaries on the Epistle to the Hebrews*, trans. and ed. John Owen (1853; Grand Rapids: Eerdmans, 1949), 66–67.
35. John Wesley, *Explanatory Notes upon the New Testament* (London: Epworth Press, 1948), 815–16.
36. Kidd, *With One Voice*, 115.

control, so we tremble. We become at one and the same time more circumspect and less manipulative, more disciplined and yet more free.[37]

So which is it? Is Jesus Christ the recipient of our worship or the leader of our worship? The answer is "yes." Jesus is both/and. This is a job only Jesus, Incarnate God, can fulfill. As God he receives our worship; as human he enables our worship. Hurtado substantiates the understanding of this dual role in the earliest days of the church: "Jesus is very often the content and occasion for worship and liturgical song or chant, and is also characteristically the one through whom the worship and praise is efficacious."[38] Kidd summarizes the matter eloquently:

> Here in a nutshell is the entire glorious mystery of the New Testament. By virtue of his resurrection, Jesus is alive in such a way that he can be both "with us" and "for us." Simultaneously he is "in the midst of the assembly" and in the heavenly Jerusalem ever interceding for us. A permanent Singer has been installed. From one perspective, he sings with us in the church; from another he intercedes for us in heaven. When the church gathers in worship, earth and heaven converge. When we sing we are not singing by ourselves. There is a higher song going on above ours and a deeper song going on beneath ours.[39]

Thanks be to God!

Trinitarian Worship

Ultimately, Christian worship is Trinitarian worship. I have made the claim that worship celebrates the story of God and that Christ is the center of that story. While these assertions are true, the sum of the matter is this: the one true God of the Christian faith is God in three persons—Father, Son, and Holy Spirit. God-focused, Christ-centered worship in no way detracts from the Trinitarian nature of worship, for the presence and action of one God is indivisible in character. Sometimes concerns are raised when one person of the Godhead is emphasized.[40] This is understandable, for as worship scholar John Witvliet writes, "In human terms, when we focus on one person, we inevitably take our focus away from another."[41] But Witvliet goes on to say

---

37. Ibid., 117.
38. Hurtado, *At the Origins of Christian Worship*, 90.
39. Kidd, *With One Voice*, 115.
40. For example, see White, "What Ever Happened to the Father?"
41. John D. Witvliet, "The Joy of Christ-centered, Trinitarian Worship," *Worship Leader*, April 14, 2015, http://worshipleader.com/the-joy-of-christ-centered-trinitarian-worship.

that "this zero-sum logic makes no sense when it comes to God."[42] Why? Because the oneness of persons reflects their oneness of purpose. When one person of the Godhead is fulfilling some eternal purpose (Creator, Redeemer, Comforter, etc.), all are fulfilling their purposes as coparticipants. Also, the oneness of persons deflects the glory they receive so that all persons are equally honored; when one person of the Godhead is recognized, all are recognized. In summary, "When we attend to Jesus, we inevitably 'see' God the Father, and come to discover the work of the Holy Spirit that has already been going on in and around us. 'Christ-centered' and 'Trinitarian' each refer, ideally, to the very same thing."[43]

Trinitarian worship is rooted in relationship. Corporate worship, by its very nature, is a relational encounter between God and people. The basis for the relational nature of worship is found in the eternal Trinitarian relationship between God the Father, God the Son, and God the Holy Spirit. This interrelationship of mutual love and self-giving is described by the church fathers as *perichoresis*—derived from a combination of Greek words that can be interpreted "to dance around in a chorus."[44] As William Dyrness affirms, "This image represents the most fundamental assertion one can make about the character of the Christian God: the nature of God is a dynamic movement of love and beauty."[45] And this eternal, mutual, and loving fellowship of the persons of the Godhead—the very fellowship that the triune God enjoys—forms the ultimate fellowship into which all believers are invited. The fellowship that is the reality of the one God in three persons is the real basis for the oneness that is also our reality in worship; we are one with Christ and one in fellowship with all true disciples of Jesus Christ when we gather for the express purpose of corporate "appointed-time" worship. Remarkably, the mutually indwelling, utterly relational bond of one God in three persons becomes the all-embracing congregation into which we are invited when we worship! By God's gracious initiative, we are invited to the dance. *Perichoresis*, the eternal, joyful union of Father, Son, and Holy Spirit, is real and ongoing. And it is into this ongoing reality that we enter—a dance of worship that is already under way to which we are invited. It's like arriving at the dance a little late. The dance has begun, the music is playing, people are moving, and there is laughter and lighthearted energy. While we may have arrived thirty minutes late to the dance, someone meets us at the door, invites us in, and we

42. Ibid.
43. Ibid.
44. William A. Dyrness, *A Primer on Christian Worship: Where We've Been, Where We Are, Where We Can Go* (Grand Rapids: Eerdmans, 2009), 82.
45. Ibid., 82–83.

participate by dancing. But our participation in the dance didn't change the fact that a dance was already under way; we were simply drawn in as participants.

Trinitarian worship is "worship under way." It is the fellowship of the triune God in motion, and we have the blessed privilege of being welcomed into that reality. We worship God when we step into the participatory relationship of the triune God that is the welcoming community for all worshipers. It is something unseen but nonetheless real. How do we do this? We do this by faith every Lord's Day when we enter a gathering with the intention of fully offering ourselves in sincere worship. In doing so, we have affirmed once again that we are part of the ongoing, joyful union of the triune God that is likewise a larger union—that of every faith-filled follower who genuinely worships God.

All this discussion about the Trinity can appear like it's much ado about doctrine; one might wonder what the fuss is about. Affirming Trinitarian worship is not simply a matter of getting one's theological house in order; it is ultimately for the purpose of proper worship. It has been said that right worship (orthodoxy—literally, "right praise") leads to the formation of right practice (orthopraxy), which, in turn, leads to right affections (orthocardia)—the love of God, neighbor, and the created order. Put another way, with improper worship, we are formed improperly in practice and this, in turn, leads to improper affections—disordered love. Ultimately, our doctrinal constructs that lead to knowledge of God have one purpose: true worship. Theologian Beth Felker Jones captures it well: "The heart of the doctrine [of the Trinity] is about who we worship, and there is nothing more wonderful, life giving, or joyous than to worship the true and living God. . . . The most proper and important fruit of the doctrine is worship."[46]

The music of worship must portray the Trinitarian God of Christianity. How reflective of our view of the Trinity are the songs we use in worship?[47] The words of our songs will either aid or hinder our view of one God in three persons. This matter is also a part of the fleshing out of the story of God, for God's story is one of Father, Son, and Holy Spirit at work in creation and re-creation. Intentionality is called for when establishing the repertoire of song for the church, not only so that we believe the right thing but also worship the true God in the right way.

46. Beth Felker Jones, *Practicing Christian Doctrine: An Introduction to Thinking and Living Theologically* (Grand Rapids: Baker Academic, 2014), 75.
47. For an insightful analysis of the use of Trinitarian language in modern worship music, see Lester Ruth, "How Great Is Our God: The Trinity in Contemporary Christian Worship Music," in *The Message in the Music: Studying Contemporary Praise and Worship*, ed. Robert Woods and Brian Walrath (Nashville: Abingdon, 2007).

Conclusion

We have discovered that Christian worship is God-focused worship. "Worship is a narrative—God's narrative of the world from its beginning to its end. How will the world know its own story unless we do that story in public worship?"[48] God's story is the story of the triune God, with Jesus Christ at the center of the narrative. Pastoral musicians help the church to tell that story by planning and leading music for worship in which a proper orientation to "worship as the story of God" predominates. There will always be potential obstacles to worship that will test its purpose. Our approach to these obstacles will call for biblically, theologically, and historically informed responses. An excellent starting place is to return to the solid footing you have poured for Christian worship such as those expanded on in this chapter.

Now we are ready to discover how worship music figures into the biblical understanding of worship.

Key Terms

liturgy. The complete collection of actions, words, gestures, and symbols that facilitates the prayerful worship and full participation of all worshipers in the context of corporate worship.

Lord's Day worship. The biblical and historic phrase for the day on which the primary service of worship occurs for Christians. It refers to the Day of the Resurrection (the first day of the week) and therefore signifies the presence of the risen Lord in the worshiping community, both then and now.

story of God. The narrative of who God is and what God is doing from creation to re-creation.

To Learn More

Cherry, Constance M. *The Worship Architect: A Blueprint for Designing Culturally Relevant and Biblically Faithful Services.* Grand Rapids: Baker Academic, 2010.

Torrance, James B. *Worship, Community and the Triune God of Grace.* Downers Grove, IL: InterVarsity, 1996.

48. Ibid., 39–40.

Webber, Robert E. *Ancient-Future Worship: Proclaiming and Enacting God's Narrative*. Grand Rapids: Baker Books, 2008.

Engage

Strategize practical ways to pour solid footing for worship in your context by following the suggestions below.

1. Examine the content of your worship services during the past two months. Where do you see evidence of anthropomorphic worship?
2. List three ways that you could make your worship service more christocentric.
3. List three ways that you could make your worship service more Trinitarian in ethos.
4. Review the nine foundational principles of worship given in this chapter. List two additional principles that you would add to this list as appropriate for Christian worship in your context. Then ask: Are these two principles truly universal for all believers?

3

Laying the Foundations

Music's Role in Worship

Explore

Before reading this chapter, discuss the following ideas with someone involved in the music ministry of your church or organization:

1. Try to imagine worship services at your church with absolutely no music whatsoever included. What would that be like for you and why?
2. Brainstorm together and list the specific functions that music plays in your service.
3. Have there ever been occasions when you felt uncomfortable with the music in worship? If so, in what way?

Expand

It's hard to imagine worship without music, isn't it? It is simply difficult to conceive of worship anywhere without the lovely, inspiring, and sometimes poignant sounds of music filling sacred space. Music has always played a vital role in Judeo-Christian practices of worship. From songs of deliverance on the far banks of the Red Sea to the elaborate vocal and instrumental music of the glory-filled temple, from the chanting of psalms in the earliest Jewish

37

synagogues to the Christian daily office, from the ancient sung liturgies of both the Roman and Eastern churches to the exuberant songs of revivalism on the American frontier, from the high-vaulted sanctuaries of ornate cathedrals to open-air worship in remote parts of less-developed nations, music has held its prominent place—so much so that in some places music has *become* worship. It's just hard to conceive of worship without it.

But have we ever paused to reflect deeply on the actual roles or functions that music plays in worship? We know that music is useful, but is it a tool? We sense that music moves us, but is inspiration its primary purpose? We realize that the music itself speaks beyond words, but what is it saying? And who is engaged in the conversation? Is all music appropriate for worship? Are there parameters for music set forth in Scripture? To what degree does the music of worship relate to the music of its surrounding culture? Critical questions such as these are raised all the time among worship leaders who meet up at local coffeehouses with other church staff, or blog on the internet, or attend worship conferences. Worship leaders are earnestly trying to sort it all out as they are confronted with the pressing issues of music in worship today. It will take more than a leisurely cup of coffee or a worship conference to get to the bottom of it all, but one thing is sure: we need a place to start.

In this chapter, I will begin to lay some solid foundations that build on the footing poured in chapter 2. We can't talk about the foundations of *music* in worship without first discovering the essentials of *worship*; music isn't worship per se, although it is a dimension of it. It's important to realize that *the music of worship is always accountable to the greater principles of worship*. We need to get first things first, so keep chapter 2 in your sights as you read this chapter. Likewise, subsequent chapters will address many particular aspects of musical leadership that are based on the foundations explained in this chapter. Leaders must challenge themselves to discern where their present views come from as they seek to establish biblically faithful and reasonable foundations that will support vital musical leadership in any given worship context.

To begin, music has one primary *role* in worship. At the same time, music has many functions in fulfillment of that singular role. Although the words "role" and "function" are often used interchangeably, I will use them to help distinguish between the purpose of music in worship (one role) and the means through which this purpose is fulfilled (many functions). I will identify several functions below (although there are others not mentioned), each of which constitutes a primary building block for understanding music in worship. As each block is firmly set, music architects will find themselves laying a solid foundation for God-pleasing and relevant music.

The Role of Music in Worship

When I speak with worship leaders around the world, I often ask the question: What is the role of music in worship? Very often the responses include such comments as these: music sets the mood for worship; music helps us to express ourselves to God; it helps us to connect with culture; it adds life and vitality to a worship service; music inspires us; it helps us to draw nonbelievers to church; and it is our primary form of praise to God. There is no doubt that music is related to each of these things and more, as we shall see. For now, simply notice how these ideas represent quite a variety of purposes. Notice also how music is represented in a highly utilitarian way—something we use to achieve particular results. We've probably all thought about music in at least some of these terms. Intuitively we know that music serves worship in myriad ways. Yet how do these many ways relate to one another? Or are they independent functions that just happen as we employ music in worship? Let's begin by establishing the central role of music in worship.

The role of music in worship is to facilitate the proclamation and celebration of the story of God. The claim was made in chapter 2 that worship enacts God's story—it remembers, rejoices in, and anticipates what God has done, is doing, and will do to bring to fullness the kingdom of God. Music cannot operate independently from the ultimate purpose of worship, a purpose that it should support in every way. It does not play a role unto itself. In worship, music cannot be employed for music's sake. Neither can we say that music exists simply to give God praise without connecting our praise to the glorious character and saving actions of God. Praise is given for who God is and what God has done. Music, therefore, is placed in service to worship, not the other way around; worship doesn't exist as a platform for musical engagement but to facilitate worship in fulfilling its God-given purpose: proclaiming and celebrating God's eternal narrative.

As we meet to worship we participate in a liturgy that facilitates an encounter between God and people. There's the "L" word again: liturgy. Chapter 2 explained that liturgy is nothing more or less than those elements that a group uses to help worshipers fully engage in their holy duty of corporate worship. Nicholas Wolterstorff clarifies: "[This] is what I mean when I speak of the liturgy: the liturgy is the service. If the word 'liturgy' evokes for you connotations of elaborate rites and rituals, replace it with the word 'service.'"[1] Regardless of your preferred term, music functions to facilitate the service.

---

1. Nicholas P. Wolterstorff, "Thinking about Church Music," in *Music in Christian Worship*, ed. Charlotte Kroeker (Collegeville, MN: Liturgical Press, 2005), 9.

Music can serve corporate worship in at least the following ways, as suggested by Wolterstorff.[2] First, music is intuitive to worship; it serves as a natural unfolding of the corporate event. To make the claim that worship services *need* music overreaches; nevertheless, music is a gift from God for the sake of worship and has, therefore, played an incredibly prominent role in Judeo-Christian practice from its inception. Second, music can enhance any or all of the actions of worship. No doubt some of what is normally spoken in worship would benefit from the added dimension of musical settings. Third, music helps the congregation to become the primary participants of the actions of the liturgy. Congregational song, in particular, is very well suited for engaging the corporate voice of worshipers. Fourth, the musical character of each sung action helps to depict the nature of the action. Simply put, the music accompanies what is said and done in a manner that is fitting to it and thereby emphasizes the worship act itself. Fifth, music assists in carrying the sacred conversation of worship in a style that relates to a particular people group in a particular location—one with which the worshipers can identify. Each worshiping community hears and sings the music to which it has been naturally oriented given its context. That is appropriate. It is not to say that musical styles cannot be expanded on but that leaders must introduce songs of other styles effectively so that the songs do not interfere with but rather assist in the actions of worship for that community.

No doubt, additional ways can be identified in which music serves worship. The main point is this: pastoral musicians understand that worship is the primary event and that music helps to enable it to be the glorious occasion that it is. While most leaders will likely agree with this perspective, we sometimes ignore or forget this principle when we prepare our services. We get lost in the many aspects of music planning or become overly enthused about the music we enjoy. Sometimes we do musical things in worship simply because we *can*, not because we *must*. Pastoral musicians will set music free in worship and also restrain it if need be, according to its servant role in the liturgy in any given circumstance. Caution is in order any time music takes center stage and becomes the focus of worship. This is too close to "music for music's sake." Instead, music should help to facilitate corporate worship.

Once the role of music is perfectly situated as a partner in proclaiming the story of God, we can look more specifically at a great variety of

2. Ibid., 11–16. Wolterstorff presents a number of principles, which I have reframed, restated, and elaborated on.

helpful functions that music plays as it serves its purpose for worship. The remainder of the chapter is largely given to explaining the *functions* of music in support of its God-given *role*: assisting the worshiping community in proclaiming and celebrating the story of God. *In this way, each function is related to the other functions in serving a common purpose.* We no longer view music as an independent tool to achieve something in worship. Instead, we are aware of how the various functions work together to support worship as God's story.

The Functions of Music in Worship

Worship music functions in many ways in support of its primary role. Music is described throughout Scripture as multifunctional. It is amazing to note the remarkable number of ways that music accompanied, accommodated, or even accomplished God's purposes. Music *accompanied* the creation of the world (Job 38:6–7), communal celebration dances of worship (2 Sam. 6:12–15; Exod. 15:19–21), the dedication of the temple (2 Chron. 5:12–13), the ancient ministry of prophesying (1 Chron. 25:1b),[3] and various liturgical services at the temple,[4] to give a few examples. Music also *accommodated* worship by virtue of moving the liturgy along by advancing significant actions. To accommodate is to oblige someone or something. Music obliges worship as it sets the stage for the action of the liturgy to advance. In this way, songs accommodated the Passover liturgy; for example, the singing of a hymn concluded the formal Passover meal and advanced the action of Jesus's final hours (see Matt. 26:17, 30). Music accommodated the Lord's Day worship of the earliest Christian believers (1 Cor. 14:26). In addition, music sometimes *accomplished* God's purposes. The blasts of trumpets were the signal that brought down a city wall as Canaan was settled (Josh. 6:1–5, 20), and the mellow music of a harp reversed the demonic activity of a king (1 Sam. 16:23). In short, music has a number of functions. Let's examine the few mentioned above: music accompanies the actions of worship, music accommodates the dialogue of worship, and music accomplishes the communal ministry of worship. At the end of the chapter we will take a look at some factors that could potentially weaken the musical foundations we have carefully laid.

---

3. A number of Bible translations, including the NRSV, use the word "prophesy." The New Living Translation renders the action as "to proclaim God's messages to the accompaniment of lyres, harps, and cymbals" (1 Chron. 25:1b). Hence, to prophesy is to proclaim God's message.

4. See Andrew E. Hill, *Enter His Courts with Praise! Old Testament Worship for the New Testament Church* (Nashville: StarSong, 1993), 203–5.

Music Accompanies the Actions of Worship

Corporate worship not only consists of words that carry on a dialogue; it also comprises prescribed actions. Perhaps it is best to say that Christian worship is an active conversation! As we celebrate and maintain our relationship with God, we *do* things: we assemble, praise, proclaim, exhort, present offerings, intercede, share the Lord's Table, kneel, bow, testify, surrender, declare our faith, listen, and disperse the assembly in order to serve. Each of these things, and more, are called for in Scripture, either as prescribed or described actions that are normative for believers.[5]

The many actions of worship have been, and continue to be, accompanied by music to varying degrees, depending on one's tradition. Much of what is *said* in worship can be *sung* in worship with great benefit. I do not mean to suggest that worship needs sound to be effective—far from it. True silence is a powerful and very beneficial aspect of active worship. Rather, I am suggesting that songs or instrumental music can sometimes raise the actions to a new level of appreciation or internalization for worshipers. In this section, let's consider representative ways that music, especially congregational songs, functions in key actions of worship: sung proclamation, sung praise, sung prayer, and sung exhortation.

Sung proclamation. Proclamation is the public declaration of claims that are held to be true. It is to announce to others what one believes. Christians engage in proclamation as a means of making known the story of God, of publicly announcing the gospel of Jesus Christ according to the Scriptures. The New Testament Greek word *kerygma* is translated "proclamation" and may refer to the content of the gospel, the message of the sermon, or the act of preaching.[6] In fact, the verb form, *kēryssō*, means "to preach" or "to proclaim."[7] To proclaim the gospel involves telling the truth as it relates to the nature and work of the triune God, most especially as expressed in the ministry of Jesus Christ. To state succinctly, "In current NT scholarship the term [*kerygma*] is used to describe the content of the early Christian message. It contains within its scope the life and work of Jesus."[8]

---

5. Those persons who follow the *regulative principle* attempt to do only that which they interpret as commanded in Scripture, and therefore deemed necessary for worship, omitting that which is not explicitly commanded. (John Calvin and others favored this view.) Those who follow the *normative principle* include that which is not forbidden in Scripture for public worship. (Martin Luther and others favored this view.) The lines between the two are admittedly arguable. Regardless of what any group approves, nevertheless, some worship actions are necessary for biblical worship to take place.

6. D. S. Ferguson, "Kerygma," in *Evangelical Dictionary of Theology*, ed. Walter A. Elwell (Grand Rapids: Baker, 1984), 602.

7. Ibid.

8. Ibid., 602–3.

Corporate songs have functioned as proclamation throughout the many centuries of Judeo-Christian worship. Two notable canticles will suffice for now. One perfect example is the story of God's great deliverance of Israel, as sung by the whole community on the shores of the Red Sea after Israel's mass exodus from Egypt. The song proclaims in sequential detail the miracle God performed (Exod. 15:1–18, 20–21). The song of Mary in the New Testament is also a proclamation song—announcing the good news of God's favor (Luke 1:46–55). It has been sung by Christians ever since. Songs of many different types serve as excellent proclamation songs. Hymnals and databases are full of them. The well-known hymn by Philip P. Bliss demonstrates proclamation:

> "Man of Sorrows!" what a name for the Son of God, who came
> ruined sinners to reclaim! Hallelujah, what a Savior!
>
> Bearing shame and scoffing rude, in my place condemned he stood,
> sealed my pardon with his blood; Hallelujah, what a Savior!
>
> Guilty, vile, and helpless, we, spotless Lamb of God was He;
> full atonement! can it be? Hallelujah, what a Savior!
>
> Lifted up was He to die, "It is finished," was his cry;
> now in heav'n exalted high: Hallelujah, what a Savior!
>
> When He comes, our glorious King, all His ransomed home to bring,
> then anew this song we'll sing, Hallelujah, what a Savior![9]

The truth is, "Much of the church's musical heritage is exegetical or proclamatory. Music proclaims, interprets, breaks open the Word of God."[10] Music has the power to exegete a biblical text not only with the lyrics but with melodies and rhythm too.[11] Great hymns, songs, and psalm settings partner with the liturgy in their God-given role of proclaiming the story of God.

One of the features of proclamation songs is that they major in objective statements; they state facts rather than opinion. To identify proclamation songs, look for songs that accurately paraphrase some dimension(s) of the Christian story or doctrine. Are the lyrics clearly set forth as true on the basis of Scripture and not laden with personal perspective? If so, chances are the song is functioning as proclamation.

9. Philip P. Bliss, "'Man of Sorrows,' What a Name," 1875, public domain. See, e.g., Tom Fettke, ed., *The Celebration Hymnal: Songs and Hymns for Worship* (Nashville: Word Music/ Integrity Music, 1997), hymn #311.

10. Paul Westermeyer, *The Heart of the Matter: Church Music as Praise, Prayer, Proclamation, Story, and Gift* (Chicago: GIA, 2001), 32.

11. Ibid., 35.

Pastoral musicians must intentionally plan for some of the songs of the church to announce the good news of God's love, mercy, and salvation. Jesus came to proclaim this gospel, to say, "The time is fulfilled, and the kingdom of God has come near; repent, and believe in the good news" (Mark 1:15). The church must sing of this same good news. Some of our songs will proclaim that the time is fulfilled and the kingdom of God has come near.

Sung praise. There is nothing like music to enable praise to God! The psalmists knew this well and exhorted worshipers to let their praises resound: "Rejoice in the LORD, O you righteous, and give thanks to his holy name!" (Ps. 97:12); "Enter his gates with thanksgiving and his courts with praise" (Ps. 100:4a); "Praise God in his sanctuary" (Ps. 150:1b); "Let everything that breathes praise the LORD!" (Ps. 150:6a). The corporate praises of God's people have been, are, and will be the central feature of musical worship. God is worthy of all praise, and it is the church's joyous privilege and duty to sing God's worth now and throughout eternity. As Paul Westermeyer notes, "The organization of the Psalter toward everything that breathes singing a song of praise to God is not just a rhetorical device. . . . It's where the cosmos is headed."[12]

Praise, of course, is deeply connected to proclamation, though the two are distinct in purpose. When we proclaim the mighty deeds of God, we cannot resist praising the one who acts so graciously on behalf of all creation. (For example, note the acclamation of praise that appears at the end of each stanza of the proclamation hymn previously quoted: "Hallelujah, what a Savior!") God's praise cannot be separated from God's actions. Still, the focus of each one is different. The focus of proclamation is to make known the story of God while the focus of praise is celebrating that story. Though inseparable, each function's particular purpose predominates. (The use of instrumental music played in praise to God is addressed in chap. 9.)

Songs of praise are identifiable in their sheer offering of glory to God. The lyrics celebrate the attributes, character, being, and actions of God as depicted in Scripture. The musical settings tend toward joyful melodies and robust tempos but not always, of course. Praise is cast in more reflective types of songs as well. Hymns and songs of praise are most often addressed to the triune God directly. However, it is also very common for songs to address the community to sing of God's praiseworthiness. The classic contemporary song "Great Is the Lord" is a fine example of the latter that includes the words, "Great is the Lord; now lift up your voice."[13]

12. Ibid., 15.
13. Michael W. Smith and Deborah D. Smith, "Great Is the Lord," 1982, Meadowgreen Music (administered by EMI Christian Music Publishing).

Many centuries of Judeo-Christian worship provide a very deep treasure chest of sung praise from which the church may, and should, draw. "All Creatures of Our God and King," a thirteenth-century text by St. Francis of Assisi, is timeless. It currently appears in 197 hymnals[14] and is experiencing rebirth through modern worship artists as well.[15]

> All creatures of our God and King,
> lift up your voice and with us sing
> Alleluia, Alleluia!
> O burning sun with golden beam,
> and silver moon with softer gleam,
> O praise him, O praise him,
> Alleluia, Alleluia, Alleluia!
>
> Let all things their Creator bless,
> and worship him in humbleness,
> O praise him, Alleluia!
> Praise, praise the Father, praise the Son,
> and praise the Spirit, Three in One,
> O praise him, O praise him,
> Alleluia, Alleluia, Alleluia![16]

Music architects must select and lead the church's sung praise. They should also encourage original, fresh expressions of praise by qualified musicians and lyricists. Take care to ensure that the lyrics of praise songs are rooted in scriptural allusions and are rich in biblically poetic metaphor.

Sung prayer. Corporate worship services, in their entirety, are in themselves one large prayer that worshipers offer to God. The whole liturgy *is* prayer in the sense that it consists of God and people in conversational relationship. At the same time, particular prayers are offered during the liturgy that guide our conversation with God in certain directions. Specific "little prayers," prayed within the liturgy, help us to carry on the "big prayer" of worship. Prayers are highly functional in that they give us words for the dialogue: they help us acknowledge and welcome God's presence (invocation), seek forgiveness (confession), and call on God for help (petitions and intercessions), to mention just a few.[17] Some or all of these prayers may be sung—they have been

14. St. Francis of Assisi, "All Creatures of Our God and King," 1225, public domain, http://www.hymnary.org/text/all_creatures_of_our_god_and_king.
15. David Crowder, e.g., has arranged a popular setting of this medieval text.
16. St. Francis of Assisi (1182–1226), "All Creatures of Our God and King," public domain.
17. For an overview of types of prayers in worship, see Constance M. Cherry, *The Worship Architect: A Blueprint for Designing Culturally Relevant and Biblically Faithful Services* (Baker Academic, 2010), chap. 9.

throughout the centuries. The remarkable history of the development of the daily office,[18] so important to early medieval piety and to the present day, is a prime example of the community at sung prayer. Another is the contemporary Taizé community,[19] popular among young adults from all over the world. Some Christian traditions have historically emphasized sung prayer in corporate worship: "The prayer of the assembly is primarily sung prayer since singing deepens, expresses, unifies, and vitalizes common prayer. Singing is no esthetic shell for the assembly's prayer together; rather, it is the modality of prayer."[20] Not every prayer in worship, of course, must be sung—though at various times and places this was the case in Christianity—but the music of worship does play a special function in helping the church to pray. To sing a prayer is to add an important dimension of experience to prayer: it engages additional senses, helps to express the emotional dimension of the prayer, enables the community to capture the pathos of the prayer corporately, and establishes the prayer deep into the memory of the participants for years to come. Every style of worship has a repertoire of prayers that are sung regularly. Perhaps we have just not noticed how many of our songs are, in fact, prayers. Many times we think we are simply selecting theme-based songs to go with a sermon or an emotional range of songs to create a mood, when we should be look-ing more carefully at the type of songs we are using and when to use them in order to facilitate the dialogical conversation so foundational to biblical worship. (Chap. 4 is dedicated to placing songs in worship.)

To enable music to function as sung prayer, take two steps. First, simply be aware of when a song of the church is written as a prayer. Many times we sing songs while completely unaware that we are praying while we sing. The easiest way to identify a song as prayer is to check to whom it is addressed. If the song is addressed to God, Jesus, or the Holy Spirit (by name, title, or metaphor), it should be considered a direct prayer. Most of the songs addressed to God tend to serve as petitions (asking God for some type of assistance as we worship). But remember that prayer does not consist of petitions or in-tercessions alone; praising God is prayer too. Sung prayer has many themes; therefore, the place to begin is to recognize that all songs directed to God are some type of prayer.

18. The daily office (also known as the Liturgy of the Hours) is an hourly rhythm of prayer that takes place during each twenty-four-hour day among both religious communities and individuals. The earliest Christians maintained the hours of prayer at the Jewish temple (see Acts 3:1). Over the centuries both cathedral and monastic times of daily prayer developed as a way to fulfill the apostle Paul's admonition to pray without ceasing (1 Thess. 5:17).

19. See the website Taizé, http://www.taize.fr/en.

20. Virgil C. Funk, introduction to *The Singing Assembly*, vol. 6 of *Pastoral Music in Practice*, ed. Virgil C. Funk (Washington, DC: Pastoral Press, 1991), v.

Second, if a song is truly a prayer to the triune God, let it function in the service as a prayer, not just as a song among others that seem to flow together to serve a different purpose. Place it in the liturgy so that the song plays a vital and intelligent role in the conversation. Is the prayer an invitation for God to be present among his people? If so, situate it near the very beginning of the service. Is it a plea for mercy? Let it be a part of the intercessions or prayer of confession. You get the idea. Contemporary worship services tend to employ a sung liturgy—at least for the first half of the service. Here's a challenge to contemporary worship leaders: examine the songs that are presently in rotation at your church and categorize them as to whether they are prayers, and if so, note the types of prayers they are. Then consider their placement in the song set(s) for the purpose of carrying the dialogue of worship as prayer. This adjustment alone could transform the experience of worship and help to capture the dialogical nature of biblical worship.

One dimension of sung prayer that has been neglected in many worship settings is that of **lament**. A lament is a biblical prayer form found throughout Scripture but especially represented in many of the psalms. In fact, there are more laments in the book of Psalms than any other psalm type.[21] Laments are prayers of complaint to God. While this prayer form is analyzed somewhat differently among scholars, it is characteristically composed of (1) an address to God, (2) a description of trouble or distress, (3) a plea for God to help, (4) a statement of trust in God, and (5) a promise to praise God or offer a sacrifice.[22]

Some worship leaders feel uncomfortable including songs of lament in worship for fear of darkening the mood. But the joyous praise so appropriate for Christian worship is not the only song fitting or needful as God's people gather. We live in a hurting world, and there is much pain in every community. To fail to name that pain and bring it honestly before God is to misrepresent the realities of the Christian life. Christians suffer too. Worship is the very place where we are welcomed to cry out to God. Where are the "crying out to God" songs of worship? Theologian Benjamin Wiker echoes the concern for balance: "What we tend to get is music appropriate to cheerfulness rather than joy, balm for scratches rather than deep wounds, songs of contentment rather than of peace which passes all understanding, music aimed more at giving us a bit of a lift on Sunday morning rather than drawing us into the

---

21. J. Clinton McCann Jr., "The Book of Psalms: Introduction, Commentary, and Reflections," in *The New Interpreter's Bible: A Commentary in Twelve Volumes*, ed. Leander E. Keck (Nashville: Abingdon, 1996), 4:644.
22. Ibid., 4:644–45.

perilous drama of salvation so we can make it through the week and the rest of life."[23] Some worship leaders seem fearful to recognize the hard difficulties of everyday life in worship "in an age that would rather soothe, if not anesthetize."[24]

On Tuesday, September 11, 2001, I discovered what many worship and music leaders discovered that day: our church was short on "crying out to God" songs. The horrific bombing of the Twin Towers in New York City rocked our nation's sense of equilibrium from coast to coast. At the time I was serving as the worship and music pastor at a large church. Like many churches across the country, our pastoral staff began planning a special service of worship for that very night, as well as for the Sundays immediately following. Many of us found that our congregational song repertoire was plentiful on praise and light on lament. A flurry of emails circulated around the country as leaders tried to assist one another. Where were the laments when you needed them? We learned a lesson that day.

To expand the possible songs of lament for corporate worship, begin by discovering those psalms that are identified as laments in Scripture. Simply consult commentaries or Bible study handbooks. Then, using various song indices, look for hymns and songs that are based on these very psalms. That will get things started. One of the hymns we chose for worship on 9/11 was "O God, Our Help in Ages Past," based on Psalm 90 (a communal lament).[25] A fine song from the contemporary worship tradition that "contribute[s] at some level to the meaningful expression of pain and suffering"[26] is Matt Redman's "Blessed Be Your Name" (based on Job 1:21). Another suggestion is to write or commission some new songs of lament for worship. If there is a gap, begin to fill it. Contemporary worship music offers very few examples of lament.[27] Why not adopt the psalmic form and encourage songwriters to follow the lead of worshipers from the ancient past to serve the present and foreseeable future?

Pastoral musicians understand that there is room among our many prayers for asking God the hard questions and receiving his assurance of help. The

23. Benjamin Wiker, "Music to Die For," *The Catholic World Report*, October 5, 2012, http://www.catholicworldreport.com/Item/1638/music_to_die_for.aspx.

24. Ibid.

25. Psalm 90 is categorized as a community lament by Richard J. Clifford, SJ, "Psalm 90: Wisdom Meditation or Communal Lament?," in *The Book of Psalms: Composition & Reception*, ed. Peter W. Flint, Patrick D. Miller, Aaron Brunell, and Ryan Roberts (Boston: Brill, 2005), 191.

26. Wendy J. Porter, "Trading My Sorrows: Worshiping God in the Darkness—The Expression of Pain and Suffering in Contemporary Worship Music," in *The Message in the Music: Studying Contemporary Praise and Worship*, ed. Robert Woods and Brian Walrath (Nashville: Abingdon, 2007), 90.

27. See ibid.

singing of laments recognizes that "honest worship will teach us how to worship God *through* our pain, in the *middle* of our suffering, in those lonely places of isolation and in the ambiguity of all the questions that begin with 'why.'"[28] Do not make the mistake of presenting the Christian faith as only joy-filled. Do not dismiss the people in every church who would benefit from praying the hard prayers in community as they worship. Songs of lament don't end in the depths of sorrow; instead they end with hope.

Sung exhortation. Many worship songs serve as inspiring songs of **exhortation** to fellow worshipers. The ministry of exhortation involves offering encouragement and edification to others. Singing songs in community is one vital way for this to occur. As we have seen, the worship of God is not only vertical (Godward) but horizontal (toward the community) as well. It is fitting and even necessary to sing *to one another*—an instruction Paul gives to the New Testament church (Col. 3:16; Eph. 5:19). He indicates that songs in worship can serve the community well in teaching and admonishing. To exhort is to encourage, strengthen, or embolden; to edify is to build up. Consequently, one of the vital ministries of congregational song "is to build faith, to increase hope, to exhort fellow believers in all matters of discipleship, to urge one another forward in our transformation in Christlikeness."[29] In discussing the various elements of worship, Paul makes it clear that everything that occurs must be done for the purpose of building up believers (1 Cor. 14:26).

Songs of exhortation most typically address other worshipers since their purpose is to edify. Members of the church call one another to faithfulness and fruitfulness as citizens of the kingdom of God. Music architects can identify songs of exhortation by noting to whom a song is addressed. If it is addressed to human(s) by human(s), then it is probably a song of exhortation. They will then be able to place it in the dialogue of worship where appropriate. Some songs may be best near the beginning of the service, such as "Come, Now Is the Time to Worship";[30] others might be more appropriate at the end of the service for sending one another out to bear witness to the good news ("Go, Make of All Disciples"[31]); still others may exhort believers to be faithful in their pursuit of holiness ("Take Time to Be Holy"[32]), and so on. Bear in mind that even though some songs serve a horizontal function, they do not diminish

---

28. Ibid., 90 (emphasis in original).

29. Constance M. Cherry, Mary M. Brown, and Christopher T. Bounds, *Selecting Worship Songs: A Guide for Leaders* (Marion, IN: Triangle, 2011), 14.

30. Brian Doerksen, "Come, Now Is the Time to Worship," 1998, Vineyard Songs (UK/Eire) (administered in North America by Music Services).

31. Leon M. Adkins, "Go, Make of All Disciples," 1964, Abingdon.

32. William D. Longstaff, "Take Time to Be Holy," public domain.

the God-focused nature of worship; God is well honored and glorified in the building up of believers.

Songs of exhortation are sometimes sung to one's self as a means of encouragement. The popular contemporary worship song "10,000 Reasons (Bless the Lord)"[33] is a perfect example, so also is the comforting classic hymn "Be Still, My Soul."[34] Last, sung exhortation may be directed to unbelievers; in this case the exhortation is to believe the word of truth and be converted. The twentieth-century gospel song "There's Room at the Cross for You"[35] is sung by believers to unbelievers. These songs, more popular among churches rooted in the various revivalist traditions, prayerfully plead for the lost who are present in worship to accept Christ as Savior and be born again.

Music accompanies the actions of worship in additional ways, such as giving personal witness, calling to action, announcing a prophecy,[36] and more. As pastoral musicians carefully think through the various ways in which music functions to accompany the primary purposes of worship, they will be better able to let each song serve the dialogue of worship. One caveat is in order here. While it is true that music accompanies worshipful actions, it is not "mere accompaniment" as Don Saliers points out: "Music that is wedded to liturgical actions and to the prayers of the assembly is never an ornament or a mere accompaniment to worship. Rather, music is intrinsic to the acts of proclaiming, praying, and enacting the mystery of the divine-human encounter."[37] In that case, music plays as vital a role as the actions themselves. The music is not separated from the actions but is a dynamic partner with them.

Music Accommodates the Dialogue of Worship

A second function of music is to help carry the dialogue of worship. Biblical worship is relational in nature; as such it is dialogical, for authentic relationship depends on communication. From the very beginning, the Creator and the creation were placed in dialogue with each other by God's design. God spoke humans into existence (Gen. 1:26), God spoke blessing upon them (Gen. 1:28), and God spoke of his provision for their every human need (Gen.

33. Jonas Myrin and Matt Redman, "10,000 Reasons (Bless the Lord)," 2011, Said and Done Music (administered by EMI Christian Music Publishing).

34. Katharina von Schlegel, "Be Still, My Soul," public domain.

35. Ira F. Stanphill, "There's Room at the Cross for You," 1946, Singspiration Music (administered by Brentwood-Benson Music).

36. For a thorough discussion of the prophetic role of music in worship, see J. Nathan Corbitt, *The Sound of the Harvest: Music's Mission in Church and Culture* (Grand Rapids: Baker, 1998), 81–110.

37. Don E. Saliers, *Music and Theology* (Nashville: Abingdon, 2007), 28.

1:29). Stunningly, God and the humans he created rendezvoused in the garden for personal conversation (Gen. 3:8–9). All creation speaks, proclaiming and celebrating the story of God (Pss. 19:1–4a; 148:1–10). The one true God, the God who created heaven and earth, established the created order to be in conversational relationship with the Creator. The God–human relationship has always been sustained with meaningful dialogue as evidenced in the Scriptures from beginning to end.

The dialogical nature of the God–human relationship forms the basis of corporate worship. The various episodes of worship in the Old Testament involve God and people speaking to one another, albeit often through an appointed leader serving as a mediator, such as Moses or David or one of the prophets. God spoke; people spoke back (see Exod. 19:3–25; 24:1–11; Josh. 24:1–28; Neh. 8:1–6; Acts 2:14–42; etc.). This very personal side of God, profoundly evident in the creation story of Genesis, is a remarkably distinctive feature of the one true God as opposed to the false gods of the surrounding nations. Likewise, Christian worship in the New Testament is characterized by dialogical qualities, as God in Christ is present through the Spirit to believers. All the aspects of New Testament worship—teaching, breaking of bread, prayers, fellowship—unmistakably portray the relational communion of God with people, people with God, and people with people. Paul's writings to the Corinthians assume the many dimensions of dialogical worship already at play (see 1 Cor. 11–14). The incarnational Christ himself is engaged in dialogical worship of the Father with his sisters and brothers in eternal worship (Heb. 2:11–13). Worship, at its most basic level—in principle and practice—is dialogical.

The essential components of the worship dialogue can be described as **revelation** followed by **response**. First is revelation. As in any relationship, someone begins a conversation; in so doing, a person and a purpose is revealed. In worship, God initiates the relationship through the self-disclosure of his person and purposes. In Scripture we see that God comes to persons first. God approaches, speaks, and anticipates a response from those to whom he speaks. God reveals God's self, nurtures the terms of the relationship through a variety of means, and communicates what is needed in order to fulfill God's kingdom purposes. The ultimate form of God's self-disclosure is in the person of Jesus Christ.

Next comes response. Once the conversation has begun, the participants respond in order to enter into dialogue. The parties engaged in dialogue are what define a conversation. Without a response, no conversation is really taking place. It takes more than one voice to produce a conversation. God doesn't shout directives from the heavens with no expectation of a response from the recipient(s). Instead, God's loving and interpersonal nature desires relationship. Even when God's harsh judgments are initiated, the goal is human response for the purpose of relationship. Christian worship is dialogical in nature because God desires relationship with people.

Music has facilitated dialogical worship in the church from ancient times to the present. Jeremy Begbie affirms, "On the one hand, *singing announced, and became a vehicle of, the presence of the Lord to his people.* . . . On the other hand, *singing served to articulate a response of the congregation to the Lord's presence with them.*"[38] Begbie affirms the conclusion of John Kleinig: "Singing, therefore, both 'proclaimed the Lord's gracious presence to his people at the temple and articulated their response to his presence with them there.'"[39] To say that music functions to carry the dialogue of worship is to say that the songs of worship can be either revelatory or responsive (or both). Sometimes our songs consist of words that intend to articulate the truth of who God is and also the message that God has spoken through the Scriptures. In other words, songs communicate the self-disclosed character of God. They explicitly describe, celebrate, proclaim, and praise the Holy One—and they do so on the basis of God's own gracious revelation to us as found in the written word (the Bible) and the incarnate Word (Jesus). Any song in any style that sets forth orthodox views of God, matters of faith, or objective Christian experience can be thought of as carrying the revelation part of the dialogical equation.

To help music architects identify revelation-type songs, here are a few simple characteristics. (Note: these are generalizations to help the reader be acquainted with the main principle, though there are exceptions and overlap exists.)

- *Revelation-type songs tend to be primarily objective.* Revelation-type song lyrics contain statements that are considered to be true, quite apart from how anyone feels about the facts. For instance, statements about God's grandeur are objective because the Scriptures portray God as glorious in transcendence (Ps. 19:1; Isa. 6:1; etc.). The fact that someone might not observe or appreciate God's grandeur doesn't alter the objective truth that grandeur communicates one aspect of God's nature.
- *They tend to be propositional in emphasis.* Propositional texts set forth something asserted as true that is then explained, elaborated on, defended, and so on. In essence, something to be accepted as true is "proposed" and explained in the song lyrics. Songs that carry the revelation part of

38. Jeremy S. Begbie, *Resounding Truth: Christian Wisdom in the World of Music* (Grand Rapids: Baker Academic, 2007), 65–66 (emphasis in original).
39. Ibid., 66.

the conversation major in statements of fact that are accepted as true by virtue of Scripture and orthodox belief.

- *They are rooted in scriptural allusion.* Since the primary source of revelation is the word of God, songs functioning in a revelatory manner will most often depend on words, ideas, metaphors, and so on, clearly linked to the Scriptures. Particular phrases, story lines, and images will spark the singer's imagination and ground the truth being expressed in the story of God.

- *They tend to be written in the third person; however, they may be personalized on occasion.* (For instance, creedal types of songs may use first-person pronouns in declaring, "I believe," yet the lyrics use exclusively objective statements of faith.) What makes a song revelation-oriented is the objective truth being communicated, not which pronoun is being used. That said, most objective songs make use of declarative statements that emphasize who God is rather than how one feels about who God is. Consequently, they are most often written *about* God or *to* God (as opposed to written about the singer).

While some songs carry the revelation part of a dialogue, others are written to carry the response part. Many worship songs serve very well as responses. A song should be viewed as a response when it tends to reply or react to what has been revealed. It gives the worshiping community an opportunity to express what the proposed truth means to them. Response songs are the "this is what it means to us/me" songs.

Here are a few general characteristics of songs that function as response (although songs are not always completely revelation or completely response):

- *Response-type songs tend to express more personal opinion related to who God is and what God has done.*

- *They tend to portray experiential witness of objective truths at work in believers' lives.*

- *They express intention to live in active obedience to the declared word of God.*

- *They appeal to God for help to live in accordance to the demands of the gospel.*

Essentially, response-type songs help a community to express what the proclaimed truths mean to them. The songs offer words we can sing in reply to what God has revealed.

The particular sequence—revelation then response—is extremely important. Worship begins with God's self-revelation. How can we respond to someone who has not yet spoken? How can we respond to something before it has been proclaimed? To begin in reverse—to begin with us responding to God before we have ever allowed God to reveal his divine presence and word to us in worship—is an error in theological and relational judgment. Is it possible that part of the angst some traditional worshipers feel when asked to participate in contemporary worship songs is that the placement of the songs in worship may seem counterintuitive? Many contemporary worship songs are response-oriented. To begin with worshipers and their desire to express themselves to God before acknowledging God's call to worship, before proclaiming that the triune God is present to and with the community, is a misrepresentation of biblical precedence and may be internally jarring. Order matters. God comes to us, God seeks us, and God calls us; we then respond to God's voice. Once the conversation is under way, worship songs help immensely to carry on the dialogue throughout the service.

Some songs will clearly be songs of revelation; others will be obvious response songs. Some songs combine the two aspects of dialogue. For instance, verses of Timothy David Hughes's "Here I Am to Worship," made popular by Chris Tomlin, present revelation-type of propositional truth in the verses, followed by response in the chorus: (verse) "King of all days, oh, so highly exalted . . . (chorus) And here I am to worship."[40] Gospel songs (also called revival songs and explained in chap. 7) often combine revelation and response.

While there will be challenges in determining how some songs function regarding revelation and response, simply keep two things in mind: (1) one feature will often predominate (go with what predominates), and (2) make sure you are aware of the normative rhythm of revelation/response, and work with it, not against it. Your congregation may not recognize exactly what is in play unless you acquaint them with this principle (which would be a great thing to do), but they may very well intuitively sense this natural order and benefit from it.

Because songs help to carry on the holy conversation of worship, they accommodate the journey of worship. They are especially helpful to prepare the people for the next action in the service or to move the actions forward as the service is fulfilled. The songs of worship give us the very words to converse with God from the heart, accommodating worship as the service progresses with its significant actions, fulfilling its ultimate purpose.

40. Timothy David Hughes, "Here I Am to Worship," 1999, Thankyou Music.

Music Accomplishes the Communal Ministry of Worship

We have seen that worship is dialogical in nature. Thus far it has been explained as primarily bidirectional. But worship is not *only* bidirectional. If it were, it could potentially be individualistic. Instead, the Scriptures are very clear that *three parties are actively involved in corporate worship*: God, individuals, and fellow worshipers. Worship is actually tridirectional in nature. Worship is always vertical (God speaking to the people and the community directing worship to God) and at the same time horizontal (the community in fellowship at worship). If worship is only vertical, only flowing in two directions (God to people/people to God), we risk becoming worshipers that operate independently. However, biblical worship is depicted as interdependent worship—worship that actually depends on the full participation and invest-ment of each member of the community while together. Mutual dependency among members of the body of Christ is a hallmark of Christian worship. Worship, then, is best understood to be tridirectional in nature. It flows in three directions at once: from God to the community, the community to God, and the community in conversation with its members.

Diagram 3.1
Tridirectional Singing

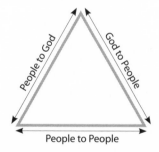

Singing is depicted in the Bible as tridirectional. We sing to God (Pss. 95:1; 96:1; 149:1; Eph. 5:19–20; etc.). When we do so, we address God directly. God also sings in our direction. God sings over us (Zeph. 3:17) and with us (the incarnate Jesus is described as singing praises with his brothers and sisters in the congregation [Heb. 2:12]). Some current songs depict God addressing believers in song. John Ylvisaker's contemporary hymn text, "I Was There to Hear Your Borning Cry," is a stunning example.[41] Finally, we sing to one

41. For a complete text of the hymn and related information, see John Ylvisaker, "I Was There to Hear Your Borning Cry," 1985, http://www.hymnary.org/text/i_was_there_to_hear _your_borning_cry.

another for the purpose of edification (1 Cor. 14:26; Eph. 5:19–20; Col. 3:16). In many songs the community addresses itself, for example, "Rise Up, O Saints of God!" by Norman O. Forness, and "We Are the Church" by Richard K. Avery and Donald S. Marsh. Begbie notes the prominence of the horizontal direction of songs in the early church, citing Paul's letter to the Ephesians: "There is singing 'to the *Lord*,' but in addition, the psalms, hymns, and spiritual songs are means of 'addressing *one another*' (Eph. 5:18–19) in edification, instruction, and exhortation. Indeed, much of what is regarded as hymnlike in Paul's writings is not directed immediately to God but is in the form of teaching or encouraging others (for example, Phil. 2:6–11; Col. 1:15–20)."[42] Begbie observes that "most of our hymnbooks and songbooks combine these two dimensions: the vertical (Godward) and the horizontal (to one another)."[43]

An erroneous teaching has emerged recently (and is gaining traction) in which worship is described strictly as vertical only. The conclusion is that songs must be only addressed to God, not to others. According to those promoting this extreme view, the basis for it is found in the book of Revelation where only songs to God and Christ are represented. Presumably, all the music of eternity is directed to God and therefore must be the model for the church now. This is an unfortunate viewpoint for it fails to take into account the clearly horizontal nature of worship, as expressed so emphatically in the New Testament.

A young worship leader, twenty-four years of age and wise beyond his years, insightfully shared with me his thoughts in an email exchange as to why such a viewpoint was scripturally problematic. His concerns included some profound observations. He reasons:

> First, if worship is only about me singing to God about God, there's not space for me to hear from God or to hear from my brothers and sisters. There's really no reason for me to even gather with the Body of Christ; I could just as well sing to God about God on my own at home. Second, in so-called "vertical worship" angels are seen as the best example for us to follow in worship. It is said that the highest and best worship is modeled by what the angels do: sing to God about God. But the angels are not our worship leaders; Christ is. And not only is Christ our worship leader, he is the means by which we worship. We should not seek to emulate the angels' worship; we should seek to emulate the submissive, sacrificial worship that Christ leads us in. Christ is the anointed one, not the angels. Third, and what concerns me most, is how specifically vertical worship seems to contradict the idea of singing God's story. Some vertical

42. Begbie, *Resounding Truth*, 70 (emphasis in original).
43. Ibid., 71.

worship proponents believe that the song of heaven is not a song of what Jesus has done or what he will do in the future. But even the angels do not sing to God without mentioning what he's done. In Revelation 5 the elders and four living creatures sing to the Lamb about his blood being the ransom for people from every tribe, language, people, and nation; they're singing about redemption, about the cross. . . . If we don't sing the whole story we are neglecting and discounting one of the most formative practices in the Christian walk.[44]

Well said.

John writes in Revelation that those gathered around the throne sing a *new* song (Rev. 5:9; 14:3)! Perhaps the songs sung at the end of time as we know it will be entirely different than those being sung in heaven now. It may very well be that our songs will be sung to God alone when the kingdom has come in its fullness (although it is also conceivable that we will continue to sing to one another of the joys of being in God's presence eternally). But until then, biblical worship is tridirectional in scope. As a young South African seminarian beautifully summed it up, "Music in worship has three purposes: to funnel the Word of God into our hearts, to express our love to God, and to edify believers."[45] Notice the three directions: God to community, community to God, and believer to believer.

The communal nature of worship music is vital to the pastoral musician's leadership. Music is a corporate offering of the worshiping community. *Music* is corporate because *worship* is corporate. As music serves the purposes of worship, it follows worship's lead. One of the most basic and necessary foundation blocks to lay for music in worship is to recognize music's corporate function within the gathered assembly. But what is meant by "corporate" and what are its implications?

The word "corporate" is derived from the Latin word *corpus*, referring to the human body. It suggests that a body has parts that interrelate in a cooperative manner so as to enable it to function for that which it was created. The apostle Paul beautifully employs the metaphor of the human body as an image of how the church should function overall (see 1 Cor. 12:12–27). When the church gathers for worship, it manifests one aspect of its functioning as the body of Christ. Paul applies the corporate nature of worship directly to music making in three of his letters. To the church at Corinth he supports the singing of hymns as a corporate feature of worship and suggests that various

<hr />

44. Aaron Hochhalter, "Vertical Worship," email message to author, February 24, 2014. Used with permission.

45. Esmarie Linde, "Music in Worship," lecture, *Evangelische Theologische Faculteit*, Leuven, Belgium, May 2014.

members will make a contribution in this way: "What should be done then, my friends? *When you come together*, each one has a hymn, a lesson, a revelation, a tongue, or an interpretation. Let all things be done for building up" (1 Cor. 14:26, emphasis added). Paul directs the Ephesians to "be filled with the Spirit, as you sing psalms and hymns and spiritual songs *among yourselves*, singing and making melody to the Lord in your hearts" (Eph. 5:18b–19, emphasis added). Similarly, when addressing the church at Colossae, Paul has the "one body" imagery in mind when he instructs the church to "sing psalms, hymns, and spiritual songs to God" (Col. 3:15–16). The sense of music in worship in the New Testament is very much a corporate affair—a contribution made by the people, among the people, to the glory of God.

To use the word "corporate" to describe worship is helpful and appropriate and, as we have seen, biblical. However, while we can say that worship is corporate, there is, perhaps, a better word to use—"communal." The word "corporate" emphasizes a functional relationship; in fact, Paul uses a form of the word to describe the body of Christ, equating the church with a properly functioning human body. But "communal" suggests a deeper emotional relationship—one that Paul describes elsewhere in the New Testament by using the Greek word *koinonia* when referring to the community of believers. *Koinonia* is translated into English using a number of possible words, including "partnership," "communion," or "fellowship." These words help to capture the special type of relationship worshipers enjoy as they make melody to the Lord in their hearts; it is a ministry they share in *partnership* as a result of Spirit-bestowed *fellowship*. Portraying music making as a communal offering, rather than a corporate activity (though it is not inappropriate to do so), may especially help today's worshipers grasp what is at stake here since we commonly use the word "corporate" in various contexts in American culture. We speak of corporate America (emphasizing business), corporate challenges (competitions in support of humanitarian efforts), or corporate funding (a company's financial backing of an endeavor). Notice that each of these suggests a functional relationship—involving the cooperation of people in order to get something accomplished. However, it is possible to operate corporately without experiencing true community. Plenty of coworkers cooperate when called on to do so but may not, at the same time, experience true fellowship.

By contrast, communal music making is all about fellowship and partnership with one another as the church seeks not only to offer songs to God but also to offer themselves in community as they do so. Singing in worship is not just an assignment that leaders make sure gets accomplished. Rather, it is the Spirit-filled fellowship we experience while offering our songs and ourselves to the triune God; it is a deep sense of partnership that goes beyond mere duty.

Worship is less about who participates in which aspect, ensuring that all the pieces of the liturgy get accounted for ("When you come together, each one has a hymn, a lesson, a revelation" [1 Cor. 14:26]) and more about the whole community *entering in fully to all aspects of worship* ("present your bodies as a living sacrifice" [Rom. 12:1]). The songs of the church are not the purview of the musical leaders or interested parties alone; they are the joyful action and vested interest of the entire community, which is in deep communion as it offers its musical worship to God and others.

Communal music making has several implications. First, it calls the church away from individualistic worship and toward unified worship, from independent to interdependent worship. Congregational singing is not intended as an opportunity for individuals to sing songs of personal devotion (individuals who just happen to be in the same room at the same time with other believers doing the same thing). A number of persons in the same space performing something simultaneously does not necessarily represent community. It is possible to close our eyes and tune out others around us for the sheer purpose of pursuing an intimate, personal experience with God, but that's not true corporate worship. While worship is *personal*, in the sense that God speaks to persons and persons respond to God in worship, it takes place in *community* when people as partners are offering shared songs in a given time and place. Interdependent worship takes place when believers understand that *each voice* ultimately contributes to the *one voice* of communication with God and others. Each song is gathered up and presented to the Father by Christ, who sings among us (see chap. 2). Interdependent worship is the church singing its songs with many voices in one accord.

Second, music making is participative rather than passive. Sometimes worshipers do not enter into the singing for various reasons. Perhaps they do not consider themselves good enough singers to join the song, or maybe they are not interested in music, or perhaps a Christian concert ethos has crept in: musicians up front sing enthusiastically (with the best of intentions) while worshipers watch and identify but do not participate vocally. Instead, worshipers appreciate the message of the music, but their vocal participation does not seem necessary or even invited. Passivity in music making can occur for any number of reasons. Astute pastoral musicians are needed to move passive worshipers to full participants in song. (Practical guidance for moving from passive to participatory singing is offered in chap. 10.) At the same time, there are occasions when worshipers truly *cannot* sing due to difficult circumstances; they have no will to sing and are unable to utter the words. At such times the community takes up the song and sings *for* the wounded sister or brother. This too is participative music making—perhaps at its best.

Third, presentational music plays its appropriate role in communal music making. **Presentational music** is music that is prepared in advance by one or more musicians to be presented on behalf of other worshipers for the glory of God. Most of the music offered in worship should be communally rendered. This practice is good and right. However, there is a place for music that is offered representatively. In many churches presentational music, sometimes referred to as "special music,"[46] has been eliminated in favor of congregational song exclusively. Yet presentational music has a role in communal worship as long as the emphasis remains predominantly on congregational singing. Perhaps a better term is "representational music"—songs or instrumental pieces that are prepared by qualified members of the community and then offered on behalf of the community, which represents the voices of the whole. It is understood that such music serves the same functions in worship as other songs sung by the group (proclamation, prayer, exhortation, etc.) but is simply voiced by prepared members. It is also understood at the same time to be edifying to one's fellow worshipers, inspiring them in their own offerings of praise and prayer. Have you ever heard someone eloquently say something and thought, *I wish I could have put it that way*? That experience is in keeping with presentational music. Presentational music should never be viewed as performance music—something that persons present primarily for the enjoyment of others—though it certainly may be enjoyed. Instead, it must be viewed as representative music that speaks for those assembled in order to enrich and enable and inspire their worship of God. Noted liturgical scholar James White summarizes the role of the choir (or other ensemble) in worship as having three possible functions: to sing *to* the congregation by sharing in the ministry of the word, to sing *for* the congregation in the offering of beauty, and to sing *with* the congregation in leading congregational song.[47]

Fourth, communal music making calls the church away from creating separate worship services based on various preferences and toward common services where the church is truly together as it worships. A prominent trend in many North American churches is to offer more than one primary worship service per week for the purpose of satisfying stylistic preferences. But providing services based on diverse styles does not call the church to sing the

46. While the idea is fine, the term "special music" is problematic for various reasons and should be avoided. It suggests that some music is better than others, or that music is performed for the benefit of others, or that the music is too performance-oriented, etc. For the purposes of written orders of worship, presentational music can be referred to simply by what it is—anthem, solo, instrumental meditation, etc.—or as a musical offering.

47. James F. White, *Introduction to Christian Worship*, 3rd ed. (Nashville: Abingdon, 2000), 114.

whole church's song—*together*! There is something to be said for a community that is willing to sing one another's worship songs, even if some songs are not the personal preferences of certain individuals. Communal worship is self-sacrificial. Being together and singing what is of value for other persons is more important than being apart so that each group is gratified. Harold Best argues the point with passion and clarity:

> To divide congregations into age groups, style groups and preference groups is to be semi- or even pseudocorporate. . . . It is ironic—worse, scripturally troublesome—to see local assemblies broken into groups, each doing their niche worship, for that is all it really seems to be. It is disheartening to think that church leadership has so succumbed to the secondary things about corporate gatherings that it feels constrained to go in this direction. If, for instance, a so-called traditional service and a so-called contemporary service were radically different in *every* respect, one could at least construct pro and con arguments based on internal consistency. But here's the rub: the divisions are primarily about music and musical style. This being true, worship is not really about the binding power of Jesus and his gospel but about something earthly, relative and transient.[48]

Best's solution to the dilemma is to remove music from the limelight and put Christ and his word in the center.[49] Communal worship is common worship; the community gathers around this kind of worship and with one voice offers its gift.

A final implication of communal music making is that the language of worship moves from personal to corporate references, from exclusive language to inclusive language. If we truly believe that we are a community at worship, we will move from fewer first-person pronouns to more corporate pronouns. "I" will become "we"; "my" will become "ours." If we believe the community comprises women and men, young and old, and people of all races, all economic and educational backgrounds, and all levels of physical or psychological capabilities, then we will use charitable language when speaking of our human relationships. "Mankind" will become "humankind"; "brothers" will become "sisters and brothers"; "children" will be used in acknowledgment of the young ones among us. These shifts are important because our use of language conveys what is in our hearts. Words matter. We must refrain from presuming that everyone understands what we mean when we use exclusive

---

48. Harold M. Best, *Unceasing Worship: Biblical Perspectives on Worship and the Arts* (Downers Grove, IL: InterVarsity, 2003), 74–75 (emphasis in original).
    49. Ibid., 75.

language. Perhaps they do not; make no assumptions. Why not be generous? Why not be gracious? Why not err on the side of God's love and goodwill?

Occasionally someone will argue that personal pronouns should be used prominently in the songs of worship because many of the psalms use personal pronouns. While many of the psalms do use personal pronouns, keep two things in mind: (1) the psalms often "weave together personal piety with corporate liturgy. . . . The Psalms are deeply personal and, at the same time, profoundly corporate";[50] and (2) though a singular voice is used, it is often understood to be a communal voice, given Israel's cultural view of society. The Middle Eastern understanding of community is pervasively communal. Mark Roberts notes, "Because the Psalms give voice to the faith of a community, they also support and strengthen communal dimensions of worship. . . . [T]he whole of the Psalms links the singular to the plural, the individual to the communal. Thus, the Psalms offer a crucial corrective to our tendency to write or use in worship only songs that express the 'I' but neglect the 'we.'"[51]

Similarly, the personal pronouns used in hymns are often understood to be representative of the whole congregation. For example, when Charles Wesley uses personal pronouns in his lyrics, "we can appreciate that the 'I' . . . may be Charles Wesley, or the singing self, or someone else singing . . . or the shared 'I' of a congregation singing."[52] Such openness of meaning is less obvious in much music written today where the "I" seems to explicitly portray the personal experience of the worshiper alone.

Music making in corporate worship accomplishes a communal ministry to God and others. It is a primary avenue through which the church can realize the multidimensional nature of its divine–human relationship.

Weakening the Foundations

Laying solid foundations for the use of music in worship is the most practical step that a pastoral musician can take. If the principles of ministering through music are true, we can expect that our music will make a solid contribution to worship. Unfortunately, there are possible threats to any foundation that is laid. Wise leaders will be alert to these threats and will prayerfully counter

50. Mark D. Roberts, "The Psalms and the Community of God," *Worship Leader* (January/February 2011): 22.
51. Ibid.
52. J. R. Watson, *The English Hymn: A Critical and Historical Study* (Oxford: Clarendon, 1997), 20.

them so as to protect the foundation. A few misconceptions and ill-advised practices are alive and well in worship leadership today. This chapter concludes by naming three of these threats: music making as idolatry, the use of secular music in worship, and confusing the power of music with God's actual presence.

Music Making as Idolatry

First, music making, like any other activity in worship, holds the real potential to become an idolatrous act. Idolatry is "the act of shaping something that we then allow to shape us. We craft our own destiny and then act as if it were supernaturally revealed."[53] Idolatry in the Old Testament largely consisted of the creation of physical figures that were worshiped.[54] These idols, fashioned from human hands, were then credited with divine power. God denounced such despicable behavior in the first commandment of the law given to Moses (Exod. 20:2–3); it was the greatest burden God carried for Israel as described throughout the Old Testament. Idol worship constituted unfaithfulness to the covenant; "[God's people] exchanged the glory of God for the image of an ox that eats grass" (Ps. 106:20). While idol creation and worship is mentioned in the New Testament, Best proposes that a broader view of idolatry is presented there: "Idolatry takes in everything that stands in the way of a direct, faith-substantiated life of continuous worship. . . . We are confronted with a pantheon of false gods that can range from something as quickly identifiable as the religions of the Greco-Roman culture to something as subtle and immeasurable as spiritual pride."[55] The apostle Paul strongly warned the church at Rome to watch out for wicked people who suppress the truth:

> Claiming to be wise, they became fools; and they exchanged the glory of the immortal God for images resembling a mortal human being or birds or four-footed animals or reptiles. Therefore God gave them up in the lusts of their hearts . . . because they exchanged the truth about God for a lie and worshiped and served the creature rather than the Creator, who is blessed forever! Amen. (Rom. 1:22–25)

53. Best, *Unceasing Worship*, 163. I find Best's ideas insightful and draw heavily from them here. See chap. 11, "You Shall Not Worship Me This Way: Worship, Art and Incipient Idolatry." I highly commend it to the reader.

54. Other preexisting entities were worshiped as well (e.g., the sun and stars). Even then, figures were often created to represent the object of worship, such as the Roman god Jupiter, the god of sky and thunder.

55. Best, *Unceasing Worship*, 164.

Music becomes idolatrous when we worship and serve the creature rather than the Creator—when we become more infatuated with the music itself or the musicians who perform it than we do with the object and subject of our worship—the triune God. It happens in any number of ways. What should we as pastoral musicians look for to challenge ourselves, and those we lead, to ensure a strong defense against the idolatry of music? Best offers four warning signs to help answer this question.[56]

1. *Whenever we assume that art mediates God's presence or causes him to be tangible, we have begun the trek into idol territory.* Attributing power to any particular type of music or the musical effectiveness of the leader is idolatry (shaping something that ultimately shapes us). Best warns, "When we are told by fellow worshipers that our music is actually making God more real, our repentance must be followed by corrective teaching."[57]

2. *Beauty and quality can become idols.* Beauty and quality in creation exist because God created first. All things made by God are both lovely and good. Because of this, beauty and quality are remarkable features worthy of our artistic pursuits in order to honor God. However, a pursuit of beauty and quality in order to satisfy the creature rather than the Creator is idolatry.

3. *We can easily make an idol out of the results we want our art to produce.* Music does not exist in order to create results; it has a higher purpose. Art forms may serve several purposes at once; they are largely offerings of the created to the Creator. Only God can give results.

4. *Style can be a golden calf.* We can make an idol out of any style of music by first creating it and then declaring its divine power. The insistence on accepting only one style of worship as relevant or powerful demonstrates a misunderstanding of God's nature as Creator.

There is one more critical thing to note regarding music as idolatry. The church was born into a place and time highly influenced by the ancient Greek civilization that surrounded it. Pagan ritualistic music of the Greek gods was regularly used to influence their deities. Music was thought to charm the gods and was used to earn their favor, or even to command their presence. Music served as a type of *epiclesis*, a Greek term meaning "to

56. Ibid., 166–69. I have quoted Best directly in italics (as in the original). The nonitalicized words are my brief interpretation of his assertions.
57. Ibid., 166.

summon."[58] Playing the right music at the right time was supposed to bring down the gods. The early Christians had to reject such pagan influences around them. Music isn't magic nor can it function on demand to control God. As Calvin Stapert notes, "Christian *epiclesis* [calling upon God to be present] is petitionary, not manipulative, and in a peculiar way it asks for what is already granted."[59] He observes that in the New Testament, "'Spirit filling' does not come as the result of singing. Rather, 'Spirit filling' comes first; singing is the response"[60] (see Eph. 5:18–19).

God had some pretty dramatic things to say to Israel about idols. There was only one thing to do with them: tear them down. As Jesus's disciples, we must take the threat of idol worship seriously. Whatever or whoever steals our love and adoration away from the One who is to be worshiped alone must be dethroned. Why? Because "idolatry is the chief enemy of the most fervently worshiping Christians, even to the extent that some of us may end up worshiping worship."[61]

Secular Music in Worship

A second potential threat to weakening the foundation of worship music is the inclusion of secular music in worship. This is a controversial topic in some churches. All truth is God's truth; in that sense, technically there may not really be a difference between secular and sacred, in that all of life is sacred. As humans made in the image of God, we enjoy common grace; God generously bestows creative giftedness to people, regardless of their spiritual credentials. In this respect, the line drawn between secular and sacred is somewhat artificial.

At the same time, there is some music that does not benefit the Christian corporate worship event, and may even detract from it. The argument for secular music in worship is typically based on the desire of churches to portray themselves as culturally relevant. The desire for so-called cultural relevancy is directly related to bridging the perceived gap between the church and those who are not acquainted with Christianity or the church (unchurched persons). Many leaders feel the need to create an environment that will provide connection and comfort so as to attract seekers. Often an appeal is made to historic precedence. A popular myth has circulated so widely as to be presumed true—that such

58. Calvin R. Stapert, *A New Song for an Old World: Musical Thought in the Early Church* (Grand Rapids: Eerdmans, 2007), 18.
59. Ibid., 19.
60. Ibid.
61. Best, *Unceasing Worship*, 163.

noted leaders as Martin Luther, and later John and Charles Wesley, used pub songs (drinking songs) for the purpose of evangelism. Not so. Both Luther and the Wesleys drew on many sources for tunes for their hymns, some of which were common folk tunes of the region, which were often in bar form—a simple structure of AAB (two parts to the song with the first part repeated). Unfortunately, "bar" form has been mistaken for "drinking songs." Two important things must be noted: (1) bar songs have to do with the structural form of the song, not songs associated with establishments for drinking, and (2) while Luther, the Wesleys, and others did draw from tunes written for purposes outside the church, they used the tunes for their thoroughly Christian hymn texts. (They did not sing common folk songs in worship.) This alone is not necessarily to say that secular songs should be excluded from worship; it is to say only that the practice cannot be argued from either Luther or the Wesleys.

The truth is, there has often been crossover in musical idioms between church and nonchurch settings. There may be occasional reasons to use music in worship that has roots outside the church, both in text and styling, but these reasons will not be so that we prove our viability in competing with secular art forms in the hopes of capturing a market share of unchurched people; instead, it will be for the purpose of worshiping the triune God. In other words, if music written for purposes other than the worship of God is programmed, it will be done so not to try to be *like* the culture but because we have discriminatingly borrowed *from* the culture to serve the true purpose of worship: bringing direct glory to God. If the music fails in this basic purpose, it is unsuitable for worship. Christian philosopher James K. A. Smith goes even further in expressing deep reservations about the secular influence on the delivery of music in Christian worship:

> In particular, my concern is that we, the church, have unwittingly encouraged [praise bands] to simply import musical practices *into* Christian worship that— while they might be appropriate elsewhere—are detrimental to congregational worship. More pointedly . . . I sometimes worry that we've unwittingly encouraged [praise bands] to import certain *forms of performance* that are, in effect, "secular liturgies" and not just neutral "methods." Without us realizing it, the dominant practices of performance train us to relate to music (and musicians) in a certain way: as something for our pleasure, as entertainment, as a largely passive experience. The function and goal of music in these "secular liturgies" is quite different from the function and goal of music in Christian worship.[62]

62. James K. A. Smith, "An Open Letter to Praise Bands," *Fors Clavigera* (blog), February 20, 2012, http://forsclavigera.blogspot.com/2012/02/open-letter-to-praise-bands.html (emphasis in original).

Here is where the heart of the argument lies: if we really claim that the central figure of worship is God in Christ and that we are gathered as believers to keep our covenant as God worshipers, it's difficult to ask the church to sing the world's song while gathered for another, primary purpose. It diverts and may even compromise our purpose. Christian worship cannot sacrifice its scriptural character and still remain biblically faithful. This is Robert Webber's concern:

> Obviously the church must speak to the culture. It only speaks authentically and with integrity, however, when speaking out of the story of God. The moment the church capitulates to the culture and speaks out of one or more of the culture's stories and not out of the story of God, the church loses its nature and mission and ceases to be salt and light to the world.[63]

This is not to say that all secular songs are bad and should not be sung by Christians. It is to say that they likely do not contribute to the worship of God, the God whose story we are singing when we gather together. The secularization of worship should be resisted.

Confusing the Power of Music with God's Presence

One last threat to mention is the inappropriate connection between worship music and God's presence. It is unscriptural to view worship songs as capable of initiating or guaranteeing God's presence. It is very easy to confuse the emotional power of music with the presence of God. The presence of God in the gathered community is an objective reality quite apart from what anyone might feel at any given moment. Is feeling an emotion required for the presence of the risen Lord among us to be true? Of course not. And what would happen if one believer intensely felt the presence of God while singing a song and the fellow worshiper next to her did not? Was God more or less present based on what was felt? And did music have the power to create or not create that feeling?

God in Christ is present through the Holy Spirit by virtue of the assembly. The risen Lord's presence is promised where two or three are gathered in his name (Matt. 18:20), not where two or three make music. Thankfully, God often graciously engages the music of worship as a means to experience the divine presence, but it is not a promise that is made to us categorically. Songs of worship cannot create, deliver, or otherwise command God's presence. We cannot sing down the presence of God. The presence is already real.

---

63. Robert E. Webber, *The Divine Embrace: Recovering the Passionate Spiritual Life* (Grand Rapids: Baker Books, 2006), 229.

Music is an element in worship, like other elements, that helps us to interact conversationally with the triune God who is present, but music must not be given power on our terms. We cannot say, "If we sing songs of worship we will be assured of God's presence." While "[God is] enthroned on the praises of Israel" (Ps. 22:3), this verse in no way promises God's presence through singing praises. "More important than our experience of Christ is the Christ of our experience," writes James Torrance.[64]

The possibility for weakening the solid foundation of worship music over music's perceived power may even be greater than we think. Several contemporary voices go further in sounding the alarm.[65]

> If in making music or listening to it I assume that faith will bring substance and evidence *to* the music, so as [to] make it more "worshipful," I am getting into real trouble. . . . I can make the mistake of coupling faith to musical experience by assuming that the power and effectiveness of music is what brings substance and evidence to my faith. I can then quite easily forge a connection between the power of music and the nearness of the Lord. Once this happens, I may even slip fully into the sin of *equating* the power of music and the nearness of the Lord. At that point music joins the bread and the wine in the creation of a new sacrament or even a new kind of transubstantiation.[66]

Music is a powerful gift from God to the church. Worship songs are vital—almost indispensable—as a means to communicate with God and others. However, as pastoral musicians, we must help leaders avoid too closely equating it with a delivery system for God's presence. We do have assurance that God is truly present in worship, but it is through the means God has designed; it is on God's terms, not ours.

Conclusion

To lay solid foundations for music in worship today is a big undertaking. However, music architects should not shrink from the task, for nothing could be more important than intentionally leading God's people in song in a manner that is intended by God. Music has a significant role to play in worship:

64. James B. Torrance, *Worship, Community and the Triune God of Grace* (Downers Grove, IL: InterVarsity, 1996), 34.
65. Some of these voices include Harold M. Best, James K. A. Smith, and the late Robert E. Webber; they are concerned about the possibility of music inadvertently being framed as a third sacrament.
66. Best, *Unceasing Worship*, 30 (emphasis in original).

to facilitate the proclamation and celebration of God's story. To fulfill that role, music accompanies, accommodates, and accomplishes God's purposes for worship. This chapter has laid out very practical steps for worship leaders to help worshipers engage in music that gives glory to God.

Key Terms

exhortation. To encourage, strengthen, or embolden.

lament. Prayer of despair, frustration, and/or complaint to God.

presentational music. Music prepared in advance as an act of worship to be presented on behalf of other worshipers.

response. The reply to God-initiated revelation; expresses the meaning of revelation to believers.

revelation. God discloses his person and purpose; constitutes revealed truth.

To Learn More

Begbie, Jeremy S. *Resounding Truth: Christian Wisdom in the World of Music.* Grand Rapids: Baker Academic, 2007.

Best, Harold M. *Music through the Eyes of Faith.* New York: HarperCollins, 1993.

Corbitt, J. Nathan. *The Sound of the Harvest: Music's Mission in Church and Culture.* Grand Rapids: Baker Books, 1998.

Kroeker, Charlotte, ed. *Music in Christian Worship.* Collegeville, MN: Liturgical Press, 2005.

Pass, David B. *Music and the Church.* Nashville: Broadman, 1989.

Woods, Robert, and Brian Walrath, eds. *The Message in the Music: Studying Contemporary Praise and Worship.* Nashville: Abingdon, 2007.

Engage

Take practical steps to discover how songs are functioning in your setting in order to promote the primary role of music in worship, which is to proclaim and celebrate God's story.

1. Make a list of the twenty-five most recently sung songs in your church. How would you identify each one by function? (Choose from these four

functions: proclamation, praise, prayer, or exhortation.) Do you see balance or imbalance? If the functions appear to be imbalanced, how could you improve?

2. Looking at the same list of twenty-five songs, decide if each one is primarily revelation or primarily response. Does either revelation or response tend to predominate? If so, make a list of some possible additional songs to round out the sung dialogue.

3. Does your worship service ever include presentational music? If so, look back over your orders of service. How has it typically functioned? How could it best function?

4. What do you see as possibly weakening the foundation of biblical worship in your community, currently or in the future: music making as idolatry, the use of secular music, confusing the power of music with God's presence, or other (something not mentioned)? Write a brief prayer asking God's Spirit for power to resist the force that could threaten music's biblical purposes. Share your prayer with another leader in your church.

4

Selecting Songs for the Movements of Worship

Creating Logical Flow

Explore

Before reading this chapter, discuss the following questions with someone involved in the music ministry of your church or organization. Or find a friend who shares your interest in worship music and discuss these questions with him or her over a cup of coffee or an online chat. Think about your worship service and the importance of placing particular songs in particular places for particular purposes.

1. When songs are selected for a particular worship service, how is the order of the songs determined?
2. How often does the order of songs depend on practical considerations (e.g., musicians' ability to modulate between keys, the desire to vary tempos or create "flow," etc.)?
3. To what degree does the functionality of each song enter in (e.g., considerations related to the direction of the song [toward God, toward self, or toward others] or whether it is praise, prayer, exhortation, etc.)?
4. Do most of the songs happen consecutively in the service in song sets, or are they interspersed throughout the service? Explain why your church takes the approach it does.

Now that you have begun to reflect on placing songs within the order of service, read the rest of the chapter to consider the importance of finding the best place for particular songs in worship.

Expand

When friends meet for a conversation, there is often a logical flow to the dialogue. Phrases are exchanged that naturally unfold and make perfect sense. Friends begin by greeting one another, making small talk about the weather or what they have been up to. Then they probably move on to a topic or two of real significance before saying their good-byes and wishing one another well. It would seem odd to begin with the good-byes or to jump into deep issues before catching up. Conversations just seem to unfold in movements that flow together into one significant dialogue based on relationship.

Like human conversations, worship is a type of dialogue based on relationship. In the previous chapter the Christian worship service was presented as essentially a dialogue between God and people. As such, a holy conversation takes place. This very special dialogue, like human conversations, should naturally unfold in a logical way that makes sense to those who are involved in the relationship. The purpose of this chapter is to help worship music architects understand the importance of placing each and every song in an appropriate location within the service so as to maximize its function in the God–human dialogue. To accomplish this, we will first need to explore the significance of the worship form in general, looking at particular models for the overall movements of worship—the big structure of the service. As we do so, we will compare options for employing songs within the service. Whether churches use "song sets" or weave songs throughout the various parts of the liturgy, the leader must consider how songs help to carry the conversation. This chapter also includes very practical steps for placing songs within the service.

The Importance of Dialogical Movements in Worship

Have you ever been involved in a conversation that seemed to have no direction? Perhaps it consisted of random topics that were all over the map; it was difficult to see how one thought led to another. If so, you probably found it disconnected and confusing. It can be pretty frustrating if there seems to be no logical order to the ideas that are being expressed. However, when a conversation is easy to follow and one part leads to another in sensible and meaningful ways, real communication happens.

From its beginning, Judeo-Christian worship has unfolded in such a way that certain patterns became normative. In the case of the Old Testament, the patterns were directives given by God. For instance, as Jewish worship developed in the wilderness and later in Jerusalem, God was quite specific about what should take place, who should lead, and the order of events. Moses, David, Solomon, and other leaders throughout the centuries were given particular commands by God concerning the meeting between God and his covenant people. Following God's directives for the ordering of liturgical events was one way to demonstrate love and respect to the Almighty. There were also consequences for failing to do worship God's way (e.g., see Num. 16:1–50).

The New Testament church likewise had its patterns for worship. These begin to emerge as early as Acts 1, where prayer is seen as the primary feature of the gathered community following the ascension of Jesus. Some of the patterns for worship seem to be prescribed by the apostles; others are described as recommended practices. Together, they formed the normal pattern of Lord's Day worship among the earliest believers. The apostle Paul spent a large portion of one of his letters to the Corinthian church concerning matters related to worship order (see 1 Cor. 11–14). He was very straightforward in his passionate conclusion that "all things [in worship] should be done decently and in order" (1 Cor. 14:40). As was the case in the Old Testament, order was a means to demonstrate love and respect for God and others. The ordering of worship either enabled or hindered the relationship.

Corporate services of worship need to have a natural and understandable order so that real communication is enhanced and relationships are enriched between God and people and between fellow believers. This chapter, when addressing the order of worship, will refer exclusively to the large movements of worship—the overall structure of a service with several primary "zones," if you will. *It is absolutely essential to realize that the ordering of worship into large sections has nothing to do with worship style.* It has everything to do with relationship. A biblically based, intentional framework for the worship dialogue can be carried out in any number of styles. Consider this: human conversations often carry the same overall sequence (as mentioned earlier), yet they vary greatly in dialect, accent, choice of vocabulary, mannerisms, and colloquialisms. In short, the conversational style varies while the logical sequence is maintained. This chapter does not address the micro-ordering of worship (where to place the offering, the prayers, the testimonies, etc.). Each community can make those decisions once it understands the sensibilities of the larger structure of the conversation.

An organizational framework for a worship service is not only valuable it is also necessary. All worship services have an order to them. Even so-called free worship, valued by many communities, has form to its worship. There is a general pattern that develops, whether intentional or not, in every worshiping community. The question will not be *whether* there is form but how *intentional* the form is. Worship leaders should not be suspicious of form. Form is the worshiper's friend; it provides a guide for the worship conversation to fulfill its God-given purposes. The shape of the liturgy (remember, this is a style-neutral term) is more than the order of a service; it is "the animating principle."[1] Form doesn't, in and of itself, threaten to make worship lifeless. Form can actually animate the worship in a particular place and time. Good worship will draw on a deep structure that undergirds the actions. Good structure does not draw attention to itself but goes relatively unnoticed. It is there to support the actions of the liturgy but does not constrict it. It breathes with the participants as the dialogue unfolds. Deep structure is different than surface structure.[2] Deep structure runs underneath to provide a secure foundation for the dialogue; it is unchanging. Surface structure consists of the many particular decisions made for ordering various elements of worship. Surface structure changes often, perhaps even weekly to some degree, as a prayer is offered here or a Scripture reading there—whatever is needed to carry the dialogue for the day. Yet underneath it is a foundation that gives worship a sense of stability even while variables exist.

While visiting a Christian university recently, a group of young emerging worship leaders were eager to talk about worship structure. One of them asked, "Do you think that the people will know when there is an overall structural pattern to worship? And does it matter if they recognize it or not?" Great questions. I answered that worshipers will probably intuitively feel the sense of security and logic in worship that form offers, even if they cannot identify that a regular, intentional pattern of worship exists. It would be a good thing to disciple people as to what to expect in worship and to help them see how to make the most of the corporate experience. But whether they get it or not, good structural form is there to guide them as they are carried through the parts of a good conversation with God. Think of structure like a river. A river's undercurrent moves the river along while the surface waters take on their own noticeable patterns—at one place they gurgle over a fallen log, and in another they seem to lie calm and still. We don't see the undercurrent; we just see its effects. Good form is like that: we don't see it; we just experience

1. Melanie C. Ross, *Evangelical vs. Liturgical? Defying a Dichotomy* (Grand Rapids: Eerdmans, 2014), 6.
2. Ibid. I borrow Ross's terms "deep structure" and "surface structure" while offering my own thoughts.

its effects. Deep structure runs like the undercurrent of a river; surface structure ebbs and flows according to the variables we create with the micro-order. Worship form was never designed to be restrictive; it is there to give direction while at the same time accommodating the moment-by-moment currents that happen. We shouldn't carry form; rather, we should let form carry us. Music architects work *with* form rather than against it.

Form in worship has meaning at both levels mentioned above—the surface structure and the deep structure. First, order takes on meaning through the actions of the surface structure. Order on paper is lifeless; it is simply a plan. Order enacted through the elements of worship comes to life. The meaning of the form is defined in the *doing* of worship. The infinite number of possible worship elements and their arrangement allows music architects to fashion a conversation appropriate to their context. While some order for corporate worship must be chosen and employed in each worshiping community, it is never order for order's sake. Rather, order is chosen and employed to gracefully and convincingly help a community to succeed in dialogical worship.

Second, the deep structure of the worship form itself holds meaning. The large form we employ for worship is a symbol of a greater reality. Perhaps you have heard it said that the medium is the message.[3] That's why forms may not be randomly chosen. They are not neutral in their message. The medium (form) expresses the message (content) as the two operate symbiotically. While both play a role, they play it together. Form and content organically merge in such a way that the distinct power of either one goes relatively unnoticed, resulting in a greater impact beyond what either one could achieve on its own. Worship's structural form is not utilitarian in nature; it is not a tool through which something else is achieved. Rather, the form is a vital part of the process of the event itself. Worship is an event with a shape.

The DAKASTUM (Danse Kanoon du Secteur Ntumplefet) dance association from Yaoundé, Cameroon, graphically demonstrates the idea that meaning is found in the form.[4] Concentric circles of singers and dancers sway and move around a center circle of drummers, but the movement does not consist of random acts of inspired individualistic expression—far from it. Rather, the intricate, sophisticated blend of dance and song expresses meaning as form merges with content. Form holds meaning. Every culture employs a certain order to their worship, an order with both deep structure and surface structure. Music architects must be aware of the power of the form so that songs can be well placed to enliven and enrich the conversation.

3. "The medium is the message" was an idea made popular by Marshall McLuhan in *Understanding Media: The Extensions of Man* (Cambridge, MA: MIT Press, 1994).

4. Brian Schrag, "DAKASTUM Movement," Yaoundé, Cameroon (Ethnomusicology and Arts Group, SIL International, 2002), Vimeo, http://vimeo.com/34906424.

Biblical Models of Worship Structure

Recognizing the need for effective form in corporate worship is one thing; choosing an appropriate form for one's community is another. How do leaders go about giving shape to the holy dialogue? Is one form as good as another? Should the form change fairly often in order to keep things fresh? These are important questions. No particular form for corporate worship is mandated in Scripture. However, there are several biblical paradigms that could prove useful in ordering worship. I will present three biblical models of worship structure that are used widely in today's church: the Isaiah 6 Model, the Tabernacle Model, and the Gospel Model (Fourfold Order)—the last of which I suggest holds particular potential for a robust experience of worship. As each model is explained, practical suggestions are made for placing worship songs within the form so as to maximize the potential of dialogical experience.

The Isaiah 6 Model

One order of worship is based directly on Isaiah 6:1–13. A sequence of worshipful events transpires during a vision involving God and the prophet Isaiah as outlined here.

- God approaches and reveals his glory (vv. 1–2). God initiates an encounter by disclosing his divine presence. Implication: in worship we begin by acknowledging God's presence.
- Worshipers are aware of God's holy presence (vv. 3–4). Praise surrounds God's presence. Implication: worshipers join the eternal song of the cosmos in singing of the glory of God.
- Worshipers are aware of human unworthiness (v. 5). A true vision of God's holiness results in despair as the discontinuity between the divine and the human becomes painfully apparent. Implication: we offer a prayer of confession of sin.
- God cleanses the worshipers (vv. 6–7). God faithfully provides forgiveness to allow for ongoing participation in the experience of worship. Implication: we receive assurance of God's forgiveness.
- Worshipers yield to God's presence (v. 8). Worshipers offer themselves in a yielded state to God's will. Implication: worshipers present themselves as ready to hear the word of the Lord.
- God speaks (v. 8). God inquires, "Whom shall I send, and who will go for us?" Implication: worshipers listen to the word of the Lord.

- Worshipers respond (v. 8). The only appropriate response to God's inquiry is surrender: "Here am I; send me!" Implication: worshipers surrender themselves to God's will while remaining in God's presence.[5]
- Worshipers are sent (v. 9). God commands Isaiah to "Go!" Implication: worshipers are sent out with God's message by his command.

The Isaiah 6 Model has several strengths: it is God-focused from the outset; it is highly dialogical in nature; it moves consistently from revelation to response; it is personal and relational; and it is producible in any number of worship styles. A deficiency is that it does not account for critical New Testament features such as the regular celebration of the Lord's Table (though one might argue that this could be included in the response of surrender).

Diagram 4.1
The Isaiah 6 Model

The Tabernacle Model

Another popular model of present-day worship is referred to as the Tabernacle Model.[6] Especially popular in charismatic/Pentecostal circles,[7] this model is based on the physical structure of the tabernacle and temple during

---

5. For a thorough explanation of the difference between the response to the word vs. the sermon application, see Constance M. Cherry, *The Worship Architect: A Blueprint for Designing Culturally Relevant and Biblically Faithful Services* (Grand Rapids: Baker Academic, 2010), 99–100.

6. Various terms are used for this model including Tabernacle, Temple, Temple Courts, etc. The most common is the "Tabernacle Model," which I will use throughout this chapter. While there were differences in architectural layout between the tabernacle and the temple, the system of courts and holy areas were similar, hence the interchangeable use of the terms.

7. "The Style of Contemporary Worship" (Article 196), in *The Renewal of Sunday Worship*, vol. 3 of *The Complete Library of Christian Worship*, ed. Robert E. Webber (Peabody, MA: Hendrickson, 1993), 213–14.

certain periods in Israel's history as described in the Old Testament. God, the master architect of both the tabernacle and the temple, specified that the physical structure would consist, broadly speaking, of three primary sections—the outer court, the inner court, and the sanctuary with the Holy of Holies—with gates leading to various sections.[8] God's plan specified that access to each area be restricted to certain people and that special actions be carried out in each area by particular people. The outer court (the Court of Israel) was open to the general population of Jewish citizenship, both women and men, who were ceremonially clean; it was also open to gentiles.[9] The inner court was open strictly to the priests and the Levites as they carried out their God-given duties. And the Holy of Holies was open only to the high priest, yearly on the Day of Atonement.[10]

The architectural design of the Old Testament tabernacle becomes a metaphor for the progression of worship. Just as ancient Jewish worshipers journeyed from Jerusalem's outskirts into the outer court, the inner court, and finally into the Holy of Holies, so believers today are encouraged to make a similar, spiritual journey of worship. Through the use of a very intentional progression of songs, worshipers "sing their way" from the outer court to the Holy of Holies. While the Tabernacle Model most often begins with songs designed to help the people enter the gates of worship into the outer court, one could argue that ancient temple worship began long before arriving at the outer court: Psalms of Ascent (e.g., Pss. 120–134) were sung as pilgrims journeyed from their homes throughout Palestine to keep the required festivals or to pay their vows. Nevertheless, songs of general praise and celebration are typical of outer-court worship—songs that simply rejoice in worshipers being called into God's presence—songs rooted in phrases from the Psalms: "Make a joyful noise to the LORD, all the earth. Worship the LORD with gladness; come into his presence with singing" (Ps. 100:1–2) and "bring an offering, and come into his courts" (Ps. 96:8b). Next, worship in the inner court becomes more focused on God, as worshipers sing songs *about* God,[11] emphasizing God's character and nature. Finally, the congregation is led into songs considered appropriate for the Holy of Holies—songs directed *to* God, songs that encourage more personal expressions of love and adoration. The

8. It is difficult to refer to the layout of "the temple" when as many as three edifices were built/rebuilt over centuries. Nevertheless, the sections referred to by proponents of the Tabernacle Model are speaking of the courts and gates in a very general way—areas that would have been common to the tabernacle and all the temple structures.

9. Arthur E. Cundall, "Tabernacle, Temple," in *Baker Encyclopedia of the Bible*, ed. Walter A. Elwell (Grand Rapids: Baker, 1988), 4:2018.

10. Ibid.

11. "Style of Contemporary Worship," 213–14.

Tabernacle Model is based on a journey toward God, with the end goal of experiencing moments of intimacy with God. After several songs "in" the Holy of Holies, the congregation is presumed to be ready to hear the preaching/teaching of the day, and the service moves on.

The Tabernacle Model has the advantage of conveying that worship always progresses *from* → *through* → *to*, that worship is, in fact, a journey. It is also a model that wisely acknowledges that people need preparation to encounter the living God. At the same time, this model has its challenges: (1) It is not innately conversational in nature; the form doesn't intentionally invite a God–human dialogue, although that may occur as a by-product of the particular songs in the extended song set. (2) Some of the biblical foundations are thinly laid for correlating physical structures of the temple with a particular worship progression. For instance, the model depends on Psalm 100:4 ("Enter his gates with thanksgiving, and his courts with praise") and a few similar passages as the basis for stages of worship, but the model seems to disregard the use of parallelism (a poetic device employed extensively in Hebrew poetry) in this verse. Parallelism is used to repeat one idea; it is not intended to suggest a literal sequence of events.[12] To "enter his gates with thanksgiving" is another way of saying to "[enter] his courts with praise." The main point that is being made scripturally is that coming to the temple for worship is a joyful event. (3) The Tabernacle Model really provides the structure for only one part of the worship service, the gathering of the people before God. Consequently, it does not guide the music architect in matters concerning the whole service. (4) The model leans toward the individualistic side of worship as it progresses to moments of greatest intimacy. The purpose of intimacy in the Holy of Holies is to help individual worshipers commune with God on a deeply personal level. In the company of like-minded worshipers, individuals seek a special, interior, satisfying encounter with God. While virtually everyone would agree that a meaningful encounter with God is wonderful, using this model may tend to result in worshipers experiencing *simultaneous* worship but not necessarily *corporate* worship. (5) Last, music is forced to function sacramentally; that is, particular types of songs are sequentially programmed with the hope that certain emotions and results are achieved (a feeling of affection and experience of closeness, for example). Such experiences in worship are special and valued when they occur. But musical sequencing cannot, of itself, produce an encounter with God. Only the Holy Spirit can do this and regularly does so quite apart from our own strategies.

12. Brian Wren, *Praying Twice: The Music and Words of Congregational Song* (Louisville: Westminster John Knox, 2000), 217.

There are strengths, as mentioned, to both the Isaiah 6 Model and the Tabernacle Model. In mentioning their weaknesses I intend in no way to dismiss either one as inappropriate for ordering corporate worship. Wise music architects must simply be aware of the formational power of any form used because, as I have tried to show, the form also communicates something. These two models are rooted in biblical imagery, which is a big plus, making them viable options for ordering worship. Let's explore one more model that may hold some real advantages for the Christian leader who is searching for a more comprehensive framework that brings the New Testament message to bear in the form itself.

Diagram 4.2
The Tabernacle Model

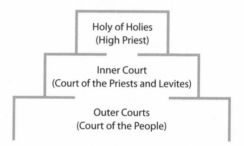

The Gospel Model (Fourfold Order)

One last deep structure to explore is the Gospel Model. This historic model has traditionally been referred to as the "fourfold order" of worship; however, I will call it the "Gospel Model" for reasons that will become clear. There are some profound features of the Gospel Model that set it apart from the two models described above. The primary feature that commends this model is its structural flow, which is itself a narrative of God's story. The *medium* is the *message*!

The most significant reason to consider the Gospel Model is that its sequence of movements constitutes a narrative—the narrative of God's astounding actions from creation to re-creation. This narrative is *the* metanarrative of reality that is true and therefore completely dependable. The word "gospel" (*euangelion*) is translated as "the good news."[13] This good news consists of all God's remarkable activity, from the beginning of time when God created

13. W. E. Vine, Merrill F. Unger, and William White Jr., eds., *Vine's Complete Expository Dictionary of Old and New Testament Words* (New York: Thomas Nelson, 1985), s.v. "gospel."

the heavens and the earth (Gen. 1:1) to the end of time when the petition of believers to "Come, Lord Jesus!" will be answered (Rev. 22:20). The good news consists of God's story that reaches its climax and is centered in the person and work of God's Son, Jesus the Christ. The gospel is the story of all that God has done, is doing, and will do for the sake of his glorious creation, as redeemed by the Son. As the reader will soon see, the movements of the gospel story, as a deep structural framework, dramatically tell God's story, providing a foundational narrative for the worshiping church.

Choosing the Gospel Model for the church's deep structure of worship *is one way to proclaim the gospel*. Bryan Chapell endorses this approach enthusiastically: "The liturgy of the church—the structure of our worship—does more than simply alert people what hymn or prayer should come next. Just as preaching represents the gospel in word, and as the sacraments represent the gospel in symbol, so also the liturgy represents the gospel in structure."[14] Chapell challenges contemporary leaders:

> Worship cannot simply be a matter of arbitrary choice, church tradition, personal preference, or cultural appeal. There are foundational truths in the gospel of Christ's redeeming work that do not change if the gospel is to remain the gospel. So, if our worship structures are to tell this story consistently, then there must be certain aspects of our worship that remain consistent.[15]

Daniel Stevick goes even further: "So integrally are these liturgical forms the enactment of the Christian message that churches which drop some of them, but which seek to hold to that central message (as many Protestant groups have done), eventually must painfully and joyfully rediscover them."[16]

The Gospel Model is rooted in Scripture, ancient apostolic precedence, and continuous historical use. It is not a humanly conceived order of worship, although the church along the way has shaped it. Its most basic, primary movements—Word and Table—are immediately seen in the practices of the earliest believers, as early as the description of Pentecost. (Note: The names of each of the movements from this point on will be capitalized to help the reader easily see them as the sections of the fourfold order.) Luke, reporting on the phenomenal day of Pentecost, describes the newly birthed Christian church: "They devoted themselves to the apostles' teaching and fellowship,

14. Bryan Chapell, *Christ-Centered Worship: Letting the Gospel Shape Our Practice* (Grand Rapids: Baker Academic, 2009), 118–19.

15. Ibid., 85.

16. Daniel B. Stevick, *The Crafting of Liturgy: A Guide for Preparers* (New York: Church Hymnal Corp., 1990), 18.

to the breaking of bread and the prayers" (Acts 2:42). Rather than listing four equal or random items, this verse shows that worship has two major emphases: the apostolic teaching (in the context of fellowship) and the breaking of bread (accompanied by prayers).[17] Central to the emerging practice of corporate worship was the apostolic teaching (Word) and the breaking of bread (Table). In fact, this commitment to Word and Table began to define the new community at worship.[18] As will be explained below, the early church promptly developed **rites**—gathering rites and sending rites—for worship, which consistently framed the central acts of Word and Table.[19]

The scriptural roots for the Gospel Model are also seen in many instances of God–human encounters throughout Scripture, in both the Old and New Testaments—so much so that the consistency of the flow of dialogue on these many occasions provides a convincing rationale for ordering worship in the same way. F. Russell Mitman, in his significant book *Worship in the Shape of Scripture*, points to numerous narratives of divine–human encounters that portray the familiar fourfold order, such as Moses's experience at the burning bush (Exod. 3:1–4:17), Mary's visitation by Gabriel (Luke 1:26–38), Jesus's feeding of the five thousand (Matt. 14:13–23 and others), and Isaiah's vision (Isa. 6:1–9a).[20] Many more than these examples abound in the Bible, including Peter's vision of unclean animals (Acts 10:9–23), Abraham's near sacrifice of Isaac (Gen. 22:1–19), and Zechariah's vision announcing the birth of John (Luke 1:8–21, 59–79). Each encounter moves through phases consisting of God's approach, God's message proclaimed, an eventual positive response of surrender by the recipient of the message, and an immediate action on the part of the person to obey God's instruction. No one can claim, of course, that every God–human encounter in Scripture follows this clear pattern; even if it did, there is no forthright command to fashion Christian worship using this deep structure. Nevertheless, with such a consistent pattern of divine–human conversation seen in Scripture, it suggests a normative approach—even a solid rationale—for seriously considering this pattern for the divine–human encounters of corporate worship.

In addition to Scripture, ancient documents demonstrate that the early church consistently employed the Gospel Model in its organization of Sunday

17. Because of the placement of the comma after "fellowship," this verse lists two major items rather than four smaller items.

18. Simon Chan, *Liturgical Theology: The Church as Worshiping Community* (Downers Grove, IL: InterVarsity, 2006), 64.

19. Ibid., 63.

20. F. Russell Mitman, *Worship in the Shape of Scripture*, rev. and updated ed. (Cleveland: Pilgrim Press, 2009), 43. This book makes a considerable contribution to any discussion regarding the ordering of Christian worship.

worship. The earliest of these documents, *First Apology* of Justin Martyr (mid-second century in Rome), clearly outlines the Gospel Model: the people assemble, the word is read and preached, the bread and wine are received, and a plan of action is undertaken to care for those in need.[21] Other early documents indicate faithfulness to this initial outline as well. The fourfold order became standard and has been used throughout the centuries; it remains in use to this day as a "basic structure that has evolved in the worship life of the Christian community over the centuries and that shares a common shape regardless of the uniqueness of particular denominations and local church practices."[22]

The Gospel Model has four essential, large movements that occur in a specific order. It unfolds as a very natural, conversational pattern. However, in this case the order is not designed to lead to a particular emotional result or state of worship. Instead, it leads to God's mission in the world. The pattern consists of the Gathering, the Word, the Table/Response, and the Sending.[23]

The Gathering. First, the community gathers in response to the call of God. On the first day of the week, in memory of the day of the resurrection, early Christian worshipers greeted one another, affirmed and welcomed God's presence through Christ, and invited God's blessing. They prayed and sang songs of devotion and faith. The Gathering emphasizes that God initiates worship, that *God* gathers *us*; therefore, we come in response to God's desire and will. The Gathering collects us as the family of God and unifies us to serve God's purposes in worship. It also prepares us to hear the word proclaimed. In the Gathering, God summons his covenant people, who come at his gracious invitation.

The Word. On being gathered, we are addressed by God through Scripture reading and the proclaimed word of God (the sermon). The Word is a time of attentive listening to the Lord. The preacher proclaims a message, "Thus saith the Lord," while devoted followers of Jesus lean into the message for the day. The Holy Spirit dynamically inspires the hearing of the word, even as the Spirit inspired the writing of the word. During the Word, God directly speaks to the community.

The Table/Response. The word of God always demands a response. It is unthinkable to have been addressed by God and then walk away from the

21. Geoffrey Wainwright and Karen B. Westerfield Tucker, eds., *The Oxford History of Christian Worship* (New York: Oxford University Press, 2006), 50.

22. Mitman, *Worship in the Shape of Scripture*, 37.

23. For a detailed explanation of the fourfold order, see Cherry's *Worship Architect*, chaps. 4–8.

encounter without carrying out our part of the conversation. A dialogue requires at least two parties: in this case, God and people. For the majority of centuries of Christendom, the Table of the Lord was the weekly response to the word. Believers responded by joyfully offering themselves anew in surrender while feasting on the bread and wine that would sustain them to live holy lives. Today, Communion is not offered weekly in many Protestant churches. Still, music architects must plan for appropriate alternative ways for the community to joyfully offer themselves anew in surrender by carefully selecting worship elements that serve as vehicles of response to God.

The Sending. The parting of the community is not just a businesslike dismissal; it is a vital conclusion to an appointed meeting with God. The Sending consists of the powerful commissioning of the community to serve God and others. It is the missional thrust that connects the hearing of the word and the doing of the word (James 1:22–25). Jesus commissioned his disciples on the evening of the resurrection with his peace and his authority saying, "'Peace be with you. As the Father has sent me, so I send you'" (John 20:21). Worshipers receive the blessing and empowerment of God through final acts of worship—singing, benediction, exhortation, announcements related to service, and so on. Even as it is God who calls us to worship, it is also God who sends us from worship.

The most important feature of the fourfold order of Gathering, Word, Table/Response, and Sending is that *the order itself is the Gospel message*! The good news is this: God seeks us, approaches us, initiates a relationship (Gathering); God speaks the message of salvation, proclaiming the redemption available in Jesus Christ (Word); God awaits a response of personal surrender, for the one apart from God to say yes to God's offer of salvation (Table/Response); and God sends us to go and make disciples, providing for orphans, widows, prisoners, and all who need loving care (Sending). God seeks; God speaks; God awaits; God sends. These very four movements of the Gospel Model not only *depict* divine–human encounters in the Scriptures, but they also *announce* the story of God. To be clear, we are not saying that every service is overtly evangelistic in its intention; rather, every service benefits from embodying the gospel in its form. Will worshipers pick up on this? Maybe not explicitly, unless as pastoral musicians we tell them; however, they will likely implicitly feel the rightness of the flow, and in its repeated use will sense the undergirding of truth. "The liturgy is so bound up with the Gospel itself that the structures of liturgical life are the structures of redemptive life."[24] Occasionally worship leaders worry that using any form

24. Stevick, *Crafting of Liturgy*, 18.

for an extended period of time will lead to dullness, boredom, and routine. But consider that "for the individual believer, these [Word and Table] are forms that stand in such vital relation to the Gospel itself that one only tires of them when one tires of it."[25]

The Gospel Model holds the most profound opportunity for divine worship. Brian Wren summarizes it well: "In place of a temple procession, Christian tradition offers another journey with a compelling narrative, leading not to a temple, but to a table."[26] The Gospel Model ultimately moves us to the Great Commission, not to personal intimacy, as precious as that is. It is focused outward, not inward. The gospel narrative of worship leads us "to love one another, welcome strangers, love our enemies, treat family members with care and respect, stand with the downtrodden and dispossessed, and spread the good news of Jesus Christ."[27] Mitman suggests that "'to be continued' might be the epilogue printed each week at the end of the order of service . . . [for] the conversation is to be continued the next time the community gathers again for worship."[28] In between are the days and hours that the dispersed assembly lives as true disciples of Jesus Christ until they are gathered in the presence of their risen Lord for worship in community once again. Godly worship is an uninterrupted cycle of corporate and individual self-sacrifice.

The strengths of the Gospel Model are noteworthy: (1) It is a model that is thoroughly relational in ethos and movement. (2) Its dialogical nature favors interpersonal interaction. (3) It facilitates the appropriate dynamic of revelation/response, especially in the sequence of Word/Table (macrolevel), while remaining extremely flexible for creating many revelation/response moments throughout (microlevel). (4) It leads forward into mission; Lord's Day worship prepares the community for worship 24/7. (5) Most of all, the fourfold order of Gathering, Word, Table/Response, and Sending depicts the very movements of the Christian gospel. The narrative structure is yet one more way to proclaim truth. Structure tells stories too.[29] The challenge of the Gospel Model is the inconsistency with which the Table of the Lord is offered among Protestants. To maintain the dialogical character of corporate worship, some other response to the word becomes necessary.[30]

25. Ibid., 21.
26. Wren, *Praying Twice*, 221.
27. Ibid., 219.
28. Mitman, *Worship in the Shape of Scripture*, 36.
29. Chapell, *Christ-Centered Worship*, 15.
30. For a detailed explanation of the alternative response to the Word, see Cherry, *Worship Architect*, chap. 7.

Diagram 4.3
The Gospel Model

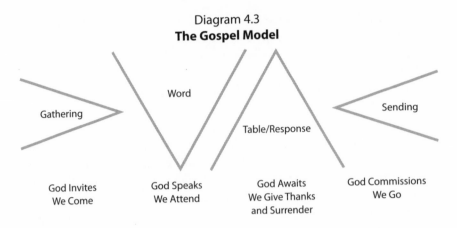

Gathering	Word	Table/Response	Sending

God Invites	God Speaks	God Awaits	God Commissions
We Come	We Attend	We Give Thanks	We Go
		and Surrender	

Avoiding Inadequate Models

Worship leaders beware: not all models are created equal; not all of them are appropriate to drive the God–human event of corporate worship. The order of worship is not neutral if the medium is the message. Each structure itself *will* communicate something. Therefore, music architects are not free to impose just any order in an attempt to break from classic, scripturally driven models.

Two examples, one somewhat older and one very new, may serve as illustrations of inadequate structures for Christian worship. The first I will call the Revivalist Model. The highly influential nineteenth-century pastor-evangelist Charles Finney adapted the service model used for revivals during the settlement of the American frontier to create a new *ordo* for worship in local churches. In so doing, he significantly altered the purpose of worship from the believers' appointed meeting with God to using worship to call the unconverted to salvation. Saving souls became the singular purpose of worship. Finney's threefold order of service consisted of (1) preliminaries (extended time of spirited congregational singing, testimonies, dramatic vocal solos, inspiring instrumental performances, etc.); (2) fiery preaching; and (3) public altar calls urging sinners to make immediate, personal decisions for salvation. He applied the practices of frontier revivalism in America to urban church settings. It greatly affected worship across denominational lines then and to this day.

While many evangelical churches have now departed from this weekly practice as other church growth tactics have influenced their worship order, it is still used today in many places where public altar calls are offered at the end of every service. The purpose of corporate worship was altered for pragmatic reasons. The departure from the biblically rooted, historical, ecumenical Gospel Model of God's covenant people in deep, corporate communion with God gave way to worship as evangelism. Evangelism became focused inside the church rather than outside the church. The origination of the threefold order (preliminaries, preaching, and public altar calls), with its roots in American revivals held outside local churches, serves parachurch evangelistic thrusts very well, as the revivals of Dwight L. Moody, Billy Sunday, Billy Graham, Greg Laurie, and others have proven over several centuries. The souls converted as a result of evangelistic crusades such as these are cause for wonderful celebration and joy. However, with the shift toward evangelistic goals for worship, Americans have inherited "program worship"—inspirational singing and preaching that is more presentational in nature than participatory in nature.[31] A different purpose is served in the Revivalist Model than the models mentioned earlier in this chapter. The Isaiah 6 Model and the Gospel Model end with "Here am I, send me," as believers are commissioned to do evangelism in the world; the Revivalist Model ends with "Here you are, come to me," leaving evangelism resting largely in the hands of the preacher, while congregants serve a supporting role. It is crucial to note that evangelistic preaching and public calls for repentance are perfectly fitting for corporate worship, especially when the scriptural passage(s) for the day calls for this type of proclamation and response, when a preaching series focuses on evangelism, or when special emphases are appropriate given the season of the Christian year. But to adopt the threefold order as the default mode and expect it to undergird dialogical worship is asking it to do something it cannot really do. Normally this order is inadequate to fulfill the biblical purposes of corporate worship. One might ask, if the Sunday service is given over to evangelistic purposes, when does the church assemble to truly worship?

A second example of an inadequate structure for worship has developed very recently in one evangelical megachurch and is being taught to other church leaders. The worship leader who originated this model refers to it by a particular name; however, for our purposes this model will be referred to as the "Works Model" so as not to identify it with any church or leader. The Works Model consists of three levels of engagement with God whereby the worship leader takes worshipers on a journey of body, spirit, and soul. This journey is portrayed as moving downward from surface level (body), to deeper level (spirit), to deepest level (soul) in experiencing God. The first layer engages the body by simply singing songs that are conducive to movement—clapping, swaying, dancing—songs that call on the physical body to

31. For a detailed explanation of program (or presentational) worship vs. participatory worship, see ibid., 269–70.

participate. The leader urges worshipers to surrender themselves to a greater degree to God's will in order to move to the next level: "spirit worship." Here songs of a more reflective nature are provided for worshipers to engage their spirits. Eventually, if the worshipers are willing to surrender all in complete abandon to God, they can reach "soul worship"—a moment of union with God. If the individual worshiper does not surrender enough, reaching soul worship can tragically be blocked. All three worship states are accomplished through the personal surrender of individuals and accompanied by certain song types that are intentionally chosen to help move worshipers from surface to deep experiences of God.

At face value the Works Model seems to resemble the Tabernacle Model, but the approach is vastly different, and the two models should not be confused. The Works Model is based on several erroneous assumptions. (1) Worship is "achieved" by the individual worshiper rather than received as a gift to the church from God. We never arrive at a certain experience of worship based on what *we* accomplish but what God in Christ has accomplished. Worship leaders overtly pressuring worshipers for greater and greater personal surrender in order to meet God at the "deepest level" is simply unscriptural. (2) One cannot separate body, spirit, and soul into neat packages—a notion more akin to gnosticism than Christianity. We are holistic human beings created in the image of God. As such, we are unified in all aspects of our humanity. We do not move from one dimension of our being to another in worship or any other endeavor. (3) The weight of helping worshipers arrive at the deepest "soul" level of worship is placed on the shoulders of the worship leader, who must incite worshipers until they are willing to surrender themselves fully at the appointed moment or they will not experience union with God. That is an impossible burden for any worship leader to bear. (4) Last, this model is largely individualistic in nature. While it is true that worshipers are located in one place at one time, the emphasis is on individual persons reaching soul worship. It is hoped, of course, that everyone present will reach the deepest level, but it all depends on how much surrender occurs within each individual. The verbal admonitions by the worship leaders are primarily directed toward persons rather than to the church.

At the risk of sounding harsh, this model has more in common with certain ancient pagan religions still practiced today than with Christianity. Worship can never be earned. Worshipers most certainly should prepare for worship and offer themselves in sincere worship, but worship is to be received not achieved. The manifest presence of God is something that occurs on God's terms and in God's time, not because we have followed a prescribed pattern, whatever that may be.

The purpose in providing examples of inadequate models is not to indict anyone but to raise the music architect's consciousness concerning weak or even false structures for worship. Better theological reflection must take place within the church. Just because Christians may posit particular approaches to worship, though innocently and sincerely intended, we cannot afford to accept these methods merely on the basis that a Christian leader has developed it. After all, the medium is the message.

Approaches to Placing Songs in a Worship Service

So here we are. We are music architects, expected not only to select songs suitable for our local church services but also charged with placing each song in the service to enable communication with God and one another. The matter of evaluating the quality of each song on its own merit is the topic of the next chapter. For now we are concerned with the practical aspect of placing songs in the order of worship. There are two primary approaches common today: song sets and interwoven songs. Either of them can be effective when the music architect understands and implements song choices well. Both approaches depend on understanding the various functions that songs play in worship, such as praise, petition, exhortation, and so on. (See chap. 3 to review the functional nature of worship songs.) Let's look at each of these approaches in turn.

Song Sets

One very popular use of songs in worship is for several songs to appear consecutively, referred to as "**song sets.**" This term is borrowed from the entertainment industry where it is used in relation to various types of performances of music, comedy, short dramatic skits, variety shows, and so on. Between various entertainment sets are intermissions or alternative performing groups that create interest in programming and provide a break for the primary artists. The term "sets" is used widely in musical concert settings. Currently, many churches employ song sets in worship—back-to-back songs that flow directly from one to the next. In between these are other necessary acts such as the offering, announcements, video testimonies, and so on.

Song sets appear most commonly in the contemporary worship style. As contemporary worship has developed over many decades, it has become music-driven with extended times of singing. Several different worship structures have emerged among contemporary worshipers such as the Twofold Model (an extended time of singing followed by an extended time of teaching), the

Five-Phase Model made popular in the Vineyard Movement,[32] and the Tabernacle Model. Many centuries ago, the entire liturgy was sung. It still is, in some places. Leading up to the Reformation, the Mass was sung by clerics and professionally trained musicians. In their passion for the priesthood of all believers, Martin Luther, John Calvin, and other Reformers decreased the amount of clerically performed song while increasing congregational song. This move effectively reduced the percentage of the service that was sung, which has continued to influence most Protestants to this day. In some respects the extended singing so typical of Pentecostal, charismatic, and evangelical contemporary services is recapturing the "sung liturgy." Though not intentionally attempting to recover a lost liturgical practice, they have simply discovered that what can be said can be sung.

Many times the order of the songs in a set is arranged for pragmatic reasons or according to miscellaneous factors. The order may be rather randomly determined by such things as currently popular songs, attempts to create a mood, the theme of the day, the personal preference of the leader, the ability of the musicians, smooth modulations between keys, and more. There are always multiple factors that legitimately enter into song placement. However, *the primary consideration for the placement of songs within any set is the narrative that is being sung.* If worship tells God's story and if worship is dialogical, songs must appear in a logical sequence that provides a coherent narrative and a conversational purpose at the same time. Most often in current practice, song sets are used for an extended time of singing at the beginning of the service, though some churches also program a set following the sermon as a type of response to the Word.

Placing songs within a song set requires special considerations of purpose, function, direction, flow, and story line.

Purpose

Worship music architects must understand the *purpose* of each section of the service. As we have seen, the purpose of the Gathering is to help the congregation respond to God's invitation to be in his presence, to unite believers as the body of Christ, and to move worshipers toward readiness to hear and receive the word proclaimed. Songs in the opening set must fit these purposes, regardless of the model being used. Music architects should choose songs that speak of God calling us to worship and our response to that call, songs that celebrate the presence of Jesus Christ in the worshiping

32. "Style of Contemporary Worship," 212–13. The five phases consist of invitation, engagement, exaltation, adoration, and intimacy.

community, songs that acknowledge the special communal bond of believers, and songs that recognize the worldwide—even cosmic—nature of our praise and worship. Since song sets vary in length, the music architect will need to consider how much is accomplished in each set. If the Gathering consists of one long opening song set (as is the case in the Tabernacle Model or other similar models), it will accomplish most or all of the purposes of the Gathering in relatively continuous song. If the Gathering consists of two song sets of moderate length, each one has its own purpose—the first focused on entering into God's presence, the second on leading worshipers toward quiet reflection and attentive listening as the service of the Word is approached.

When the purpose of Gathering is unclear in the minds of the leaders, disorder of songs occurs. For instance, to begin with a song about worshipers offering their response to God before allowing God to reveal his presence among the worshiping community is disorienting. One currently popular worship song actually begins with asking *God to respond to us*. That's backward. God most certainly responds to his children, but that is not to be the *first* action of worship. Worship is a spiritual discipline in which we begin with God's revelation of his Being to which we respond in gratitude and humility.

Function

Music architects must understand the *function* of each song. Refer to your findings from "Engage" at the end of chapter 3. Using the functions of each song in your church repertoire, start to place each song in the Gathering according to its function. If a song is an invitation to worship, it goes at or near the beginning of the set; if it's a prayer for forgiveness or mercy, it goes a little later to serve as a prayer of confession; if it is a song asking for the word to speak to us, it comes near the end of the song set(s) as a final song of preparation to hear the word, and so forth. You get the idea. Music architects will be amazed at how effective this type of planning will be in enabling dynamic worship.

Direction

Remember that every song has *direction* in that it addresses someone—God, others, or self. Identifying who is being addressed in song is a great way to help you with conversational worship. Place songs in sets in order to help carry the dialogue. This does not mean that each song has to literally alternate in direction back and forth, but we should be aware of who is being addressed so that there is logic and intentionality as the service unfolds. Attending to this detail can spare worshipers from imbalance and from one party overtaking

Diagram 4.4
The Direction of Songs

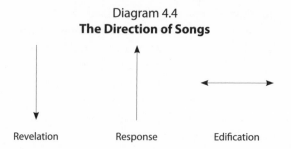

Revelation   Response   Edification

the conversation (like worshipers doing all the talking!). Check to see if the
direction of the songs seems to make sense for each service.

Flow

Each movement of the worship service, regardless of which form you have
chosen, has its own unique character. Select songs that help the *flow* of the
particular movement in its overall progression. Sections of worship are not
static; they move between points of engagement as the conversation is advanced. In placing songs within sets, pay attention to the type of song needed
as a certain movement begins and draws to a close. For example, when using
the Isaiah 6 Model, majestic songs are a good choice as the first movement
begins; these are followed with praise songs and then on to confession. There
are subtle shifts in the tone of the conversation that song choices help to carry
out as each movement serves its purpose and flows on to the next.[33]

Story Line

The ordering of songs in song sets contributes to the *story line* that proclaims
the narrative of God. The work of Jesus Christ is dynamically told when the
church observes and celebrates the Christian calendar throughout the year.
Songs should make clear what aspect of the story is observed on a given Sunday.
Are we reflecting on the incarnation? Then sing songs that tell of the mystery
of God becoming human. Are we celebrating the arrival of the Holy Spirit
to the church on the day of Pentecost? Let people sing songs of thanksgiving
for this miraculous Gift. The true metanarrative known as the story of God
is told through carefully placed songs in seasons of the church's faith.

Purpose, function, direction, flow, and story line: by now it may seem that
there is a lot to consider when placing songs in the order of worship. It's true

33. I am intentionally using the word "tone" as opposed to "mood." It is natural to let the
tonalities, tempos, rhythms, etc. of songs *express* worship, which is quite different than willfully
creating a particular mood for *effect*.

that several factors require our attention, but try not to get legalistic or technical about it. Simply hold these things in balance while not feeling pressured to create some perfect scenario. You will find that once you have thought about each aspect, songs will most often fall into place without forcing the issue. Play around with the order of songs, keeping these five features in mind, and you will do well. The worship service will certainly be a much richer experience for your people than if you gave no thought to these important matters.

When using extended song sets (rather than interwoven songs), music architects need to do an additional level of assessment. Not only must each individual song be evaluated for its congregational worth but also the *entire set must be evaluated* on whether the consecutive songs achieve the fullness of the liturgy. Do they narrate the service? Do the songs collectively achieve the purposes of the entire movement? Is there a dialogical progression? Do the songs in the sequence move worshipers *from → through → to*? Here's a practical step to begin. Go back and look at your song sets from the past three months. How well have you done? Where might you make changes? Try to improve one aspect of the song set narrative at a time. Prayerfully take thoughtful steps forward until your song sets truly become the narrative they should be.

Interwoven Songs

A second, very common approach to placing songs in worship is interweaving songs throughout the entire service to fulfill specific purposes. Since the Reformation, this has been the most common approach among Protestants. (The current practice of using song sets in contemporary worship services and the "song service" that developed during the American frontier revivals are, historically speaking, recent developments that have influenced a number of Protestant groups today. Still, the majority of Protestant services take the interwoven approach.)

With the interwoven approach, individual songs are employed throughout the service in a number of ways to contribute to the overall liturgy. Let's return to the discussion of chapter 3 where we discovered that music accompanies, accommodates, and accomplishes worship. Because each song has a primary function, it is chosen and placed intentionally to fulfill its purpose as it serves the liturgy: a song acknowledging God's presence in worship helps to serve the call to worship; a song that invites the Holy Spirit to illumine the reading of Scripture is a prayer of illumination; a song that is a benediction concludes the service; and so forth. (Remember, anything that can be said can be sung.) Each song is set much like a jeweler places precious gems in a beautiful jewelry piece so that it adds to the overall magnificence of the piece. In this manner, songs are positioned throughout the service as acts of worship to accompany the service.

Another way that interwoven songs are employed is in dialogical partnership with spoken or symbolic acts of worship that surround them; in this way music accommodates the conversation. Because revelation/response is both a large-form (macro) feature and a "minidialogue" (micro) feature of worship, particular songs are extremely effective when partnered with neighboring acts of the worship conversation. For example, traditionally the Psalter lesson provides commentary on the Old Testament lesson;[34] when the Psalter lesson is sung (a wonderful practice given that the psalms were written to be sung), it forms a partnership with the Old Testament lesson. This becomes its own unique moment of revelation/response within the service. When there is a sung call for the offering, followed by the symbolic presentation of gifts, a spoken prayer of dedication, and a sung response (e.g., "The Doxology"[35]), music has partnered with spoken and symbolic acts to create a meaningful unit of the overall conversation. Songs interwoven throughout may beautifully serve in leading toward a worship action, interpreting a preceding action, or emphasizing a particular act of worship by embellishing it. In these ways and others, worship actions are advanced dialogically through congregational singing.

Finally, the interweaving of songs throughout the whole service helps to accomplish a sense of communal ministry. Singing songs that are multidirectional in address (to God, to others, to self, etc.) really assists in the relational feel of the service. There is nothing quite like hearing the community sing together. When songs are sung from the beginning of the worship service to the end, the communal ethos is sustained. Singing together truly advances a sense of unity and oneness in purpose.

Conclusion

Placing songs in the order of worship is a critical skill to be developed by the music architect. The overall worship order is set first; the songs help to fulfill the order. The placement of songs will either help or hinder the greater

34. *The Revised Common Lectionary: The Consultation on Common Texts* (Nashville: Abingdon, 1992), 11.

35. Although there are many forms of doxologies, Thomas Ken's stanza from a longer hymn, paired with Louis Bourgeois's tune "Old 100th," has come to be referred to as "The Doxology" due to its sheer popularity throughout the centuries.

purposes of worship. When done well, the whole service has the potential to be more spiritually forming: "When the song is bent around the *ordo*, when its words and rhythms gather a people to do the central things, such song may be our finest means of formation."[36] However, when the *ordo* is bent around the songs, its message may be lost and the narrative of worship compromised. As one of my students notes, "Worship songs reach their full potential when they say the right thing, in the right place at the right time."[37]

Key Terms

ordo. Latin for "order"; used often to refer to the order of service.

rites. Generally refers to actions, words, gestures, and so forth that make up the content for the order of service.

song sets. Organizing a series of worship songs consecutively as a segment of public worship.

To Learn More

Chapell, Bryan. *Christ-Centered Worship: Letting the Gospel Shape Our Practice*. Grand Rapids: Baker Academic, 2009.

Furr, Gary A., and Milburn Price. *The Dialogue of Worship: Creating Space for Revelation and Response*. Macon, GA: Smyth & Helwys, 1998.

Mitman, F. Russell. *Worship in the Shape of Scripture*, revised and updated. Cleveland: Pilgrim Press, 2009.

Stevick, Daniel B. *The Crafting of Liturgy: A Guide for Preparers*. New York: Church Hymnal Corporation, 1990.

Engage

Now answer these questions and try your hand at arranging songs for a worship service.

1. How would you describe the "deep structure" of your present worship service?

36. Gordon W. Lathrop, *Holy Things: A Liturgical Theology* (Minneapolis: Fortress, 1993), 124.
37. Paul Sunderland, "The Language of Our Songs in Worship" (class paper, The Robert E. Webber Institute for Worship Studies, Jacksonville, FL, May 15, 2014), 4. Used with permission.

2. Which one of the three large form models explained in this chapter (the Isaiah 6 Model, the Tabernacle Model, or the Gospel Model) comes closest to representing your current practice?
3. Working with one of these three models, try arranging songs into an order that carries out the form. Feel free to use either the song set or the interwoven approach. The main thing to consider is the worship conversation that each model is trying to encourage.
4. Return to your list of twenty-five songs from the "Engage" section in chapter 3. This time, look carefully at the direction of the songs your church sings the most. Mark each song using arrows as suggested in diagram 4.4 for a quick reference.

5

Evaluating Worship Music

Creating a Canon of Song

Explore

It seems that everyone has an opinion about songs that should be sung in worship. We all have our likes and dislikes. However, it would be very inefficient (and ill-advised) to assign the weekly worship song selection process to all members of a local church. In every community, some person or group is made responsible for choosing which songs will or will not be sung in worship. Who chooses the songs? And what process is appropriate to use in making these determinations?

Before reading this chapter, think about the process your church uses for selecting worship songs. Consider these questions:

1. Who makes the weekly song selections for corporate worship in your church?
2. What criteria are used for determining the appropriateness of the songs sung in your community?
3. Is there a written set of approved criteria for these songs?
4. What type of training (theological, musical, pastoral, etc.) is expected of those who choose the songs?
5. Do the persons involved represent various aspects of ministry in the church?
6. Do the persons involved represent a diverse combination of regular participants?

7. Is there a record kept of how often each song is sung?
8. Is there long-range or short-range planning for placing songs in or out of rotation?

Now that you have begun to consider the process presently used for selecting songs at your church, read the rest of this chapter to gain insight for strengthening the process.

Expand

"Does it really matter?" one of my students asked one day in class. One of his peers had noted that the title "Lord" was used differently in certain songs and had asked if "Lord" referred to God or Jesus. Classmates chimed in with their perspectives. As they did so, other questions rose to the surface. "Does the song have to refer to God by name at all? After all, we know to whom we're singing." "Why aren't there more songs addressed to the Holy Spirit? Or songs that mention all Persons of the Trinity?" Someone else expressed, "If my intentions are right, I don't have to be specific; I'm just singing my love to God. God knows who I mean." It was an invigorating conversation. Discussions such as these, and many more like them, are raised among worship leaders today. Behind the questions are very significant assumptions about God, the church, Christian discipleship, community, and local culture. The consensus in the classroom was that most of these things *do* matter and that the issues surrounding the songs a worshiping community sings are a big deal. We just need a way to sort it all out.

One of the most important questions any music architect will ask is this: "What kinds of things should be considered to determine if a song is appropriate to use in my worshiping context?" Leaders may disagree about what these criteria should be, but we all benefit from becoming more thoughtful and prayerful about the songs we choose. That is the goal of this chapter—to encourage leaders to *clarify* the rationale used for song selection, to intentionally *develop* their canon of song, and to *evaluate* the overall balance of songs used in their local congregation. Clarify, develop, and evaluate: this is the wonderful opportunity set before us now.

Clarifying the Rationale for Song Selection

Let's start at the beginning. Should worship music even be evaluated? Some people say no. I remember a student in a graduate class insisting that it was improper to critique worship music. He rejected the idea of rating songs according to their theological, lyrical, or musical qualities because all art is from God. The irony was that he is a professional artist who regularly submits his work to art shows to be evaluated competitively. Some leaders have real reservations about discounting any song for worship regardless of how weak it may seem to be. Some do not feel comfortable dismissing anything of a religious nature; it just seems unspiritual. It's risky too. What if God inspired the song? Who are we to stand in God's way? This kind of internal argument is very common. The truth is, every leader already makes judgments about the music of worship. The question is not whether songs are evaluated but what we will use as a measure for evaluation.

Songs must be assessed for their authenticity and value in Christian worship. The stakes are very high for several reasons. First, worship songs form us (or de-form us). The words we sing contribute to the faith that is forged in us (see chap. 11). The power that our corporate songs of faith possess pours into us, helping to mold us as devoted disciples of Jesus Christ. They encourage us to love the Lord our God with all of our hearts, souls, minds, and strength. As we sing, we become coparticipants with God in our spiritual formation. Second, songs must be assessed because, as leaders, we are accountable to God for the spiritual formation of God's people. God has entrusted music architects with the same degree of authority as one who writes the Christian education curriculum for the church, or the preacher who delivers the word of God. "Pastoral musicians have the important and terrifying priestly task of placing words of sung prayer on people's lips. . . . [They] have the holy task of being stewards of God's Word."[1] There are no throwaway songs in worship. Each one potentially contributes to or detracts from the singers' formation. "When it comes to matters of spirituality and faith, we are what we sing."[2]

Given the high calling on leaders to evaluate all the music of corporate worship, a rationale is needed for judging the songs under consideration. To accept our holy duty is one thing; to implement it well is another challenge. The criteria one uses for evaluation is extremely important, for the *means* through which we make our decisions must match our *goals* for worship. It is critical that the criteria for assessing songs is directly related to our ultimate goal: engaging in scriptural worship.

1. John D. Witvliet, *Worship Seeking Understanding: Windows into Christian Practice* (Grand Rapids: Baker Academic, 2003), 232.
2. Ibid., 231.

Judging worship music occurs any time a song is selected for the community to sing. A few fairly prominent approaches have emerged for song selection today. These lines of reasoning include the following examples.

- *We will sing a song because it works.* This is the pragmatic approach. When asked what "works" means, the answer often has to do with a felt response. If the song achieves a certain result for which the leader is searching, it works and is therefore included in worship.
- *We will sing a song because it's popular.* This is the relevance approach. There is a mystique that if a song has become well known among a wide fan base, then it is considered worthy to be sung in corporate worship.
- *We will sing a song because I like it.* This is the personal preference approach. Leaders sometimes succumb to the temptation to put songs in rotation on the basis of their own fondness for a given song or artist.
- *We will sing a song because God inspires it.* This is the spiritualized approach. Leaders sometimes assume that every song using Christian words must be inspired by God; therefore, they are hesitant to lay them aside.

Caution is in order for each of the above rationales. First, be cautious in choosing a worship song simply because it works in the pragmatic sense. This tactic can lead to crossing the line into manipulation, something to be avoided at all costs. We acknowledge that some songs have a track record of being pretty powerful in the worship setting, but when we intentionally call for them so as to produce certain results or to set a particular mood, we default to pragmatism. Use songs instead because they serve the purpose of the liturgy rather than serving their own purposes (see chaps. 3 and 4). The songs chosen may, indeed, affect worshipers, but this should be the result of the leader's integrity in letting the music serve the liturgy.

Second, be cautious in singing only what is currently popular in order to prove that your church is relevant. Popularity doesn't make a song bad but neither does it make it good. Popularity is fickle; it's a moving target based on perceptions and marketing strategies. Popular songs are often transient; they pass in and out of use relatively quickly. Relevance has to do with meaningfulness, not necessarily popularity. Many songs that are meaningful to worshipers of all ages fail the relevant test if they are not among the top ten songs currently sung on one's continent today. Also be cautious about typecasting. Once you suggest that something is "popular," the question becomes, popular with whom? Popularity defies category. Sometimes we wrongfully assume that all persons of a certain demographic prefer only one type of music. If we do our homework, we may find otherwise.

Third, be cautious in letting your own preferences dominate your musical choices. We all have our favored styles, to be sure. But the servant leader is called to lay aside his or her desires, if necessary, for the good of the community. Am I willing to learn someone else's song? Can we all sing one another's song? Beware of the temptation to control your church's repertoire according to your partiality. Worship should not be viewed as an opportunity to satisfy our own desires. Humility is a virtue.

Finally, be cautious in assuming that Christian words automatically mean divine inspiration. This is a tricky one. Trying to determine what is inspired by God is a messy and subjective process.[3] There is very little objective means of knowing what is truly inspired by God for corporate worship; it is all but impossible to know. Consider two things. First, not every song that uses religious lyrics was divinely inspired for the purposes of corporate worship. There are many reasons that Christian songs are written, including for income or notoriety. Some so-called Christian songs are even written by nonbelievers for other purposes and inserted into corporate worship on the basis of their religious vocabulary, obscure as it may be. (I read of a church that sang the popular 5th Dimension song "Up, Up and Away"[4] on Ascension Sunday.) Second, no church can possibly sing all that *is* inspired by God, so there is no reason to feel obligated to use God's inspiration as a rationale. Occasionally anxiety can take over. One reasons, "If God gave the artist the song, perhaps we will miss the blessing God wants us to receive if we overlook it." Don't be paralyzed by the "what-ifs." In ministry, one can go crazy with second-guessing. While God may inspire Christian songs in general, that does not obligate the leader to consider each one of them appropriate for corporate worship.

The types of rationales mentioned above lie on the weaker side of reasoning for accepting songs in worship. Instead, choose songs based on a better rationale; this process may lead to some of the same selections, but the selections will be made for better reasons. To arrive at stronger rationales for evaluating worship songs, consider these alternative criteria. (Note that these criteria relate to the role and functions of music in worship explained in chap. 3.)

3. I am not arguing that some works of art are uninspired in the general sense. Because God creates, humans create—whether Christian or not. In this sense, there is a level of divine inspiration at work whenever art is created. However, what is normally meant by inspiration in this case is the claim that a song was the result of a moment when God was directly and providentially at work in giving birth to it for God's future holy purposes.

4. Jimmy L. Webb, "Up, Up and Away," 1967, Soul City Records; made popular by The 5th Dimension.

- *We will sing this song because it helps to tell the story of God.* This is the purpose-driven approach. Music's primary role is to facilitate the proclamation and celebration of the story of God and our place in that story. Ask: Does this song contribute in an obvious way to what God has done, is doing, and will do from creation to re-creation?

- *We will sing this song because it helps worshipers to fully participate in the God-given ways called for in Scripture.* This is the engagement approach. Music gives worshipers ways for various worship actions to be sung instead of spoken, thereby engaging them at multiple levels; it helps to make worship dialogical, thereby capturing the conversational nature of the meeting between God and people; it also enables interdependent worship by encouraging true interpersonal relationship between God and fellow believers. Ask: Does this song enable worshipers to be full participants in the action of the liturgy?

- *We will sing this song because it responsibly represents our Christian faith tradition.* This is the discipleship approach. Songs give us the way to declare the truth of the gospel; they also offer us the opportunity to express what our "tribe" of the family of God believes in particular (our denominational beliefs). Ask: Does this song contribute to our understanding of the Christian faith?

Our first step in evaluating worship songs has been to think through our rationales for determining their merit on a case-by-case basis. Yet the benefit reaches far beyond assessing individual songs. The ultimate purpose is to arrive at a body of song that is truly suitable for worshipers in one's context over time. Let's now take a look at what this means.

Developing a Canon of Song

Every church has a song repertoire—a collection of known songs that provides the starting place for its choices for worship from week to week. It may be official or unofficial, but each community has a group of go-to songs when planning worship. The songs in the collection shift over time. Depending on the rate of change with which songs are added or deleted, a community's core group of songs can change very slowly (many years) or quite quickly (only months or even weeks), especially given that the shelf life of new songs used today can tend to be rather brief. Some churches have only a few songs in rotation at a given time; others have many. Sometimes the repertoire is contained in a published denominational hymnal; other congregations have created their own local songbook. Sometimes the repertoire is simply the list of songs found in Christian Copyright Licensing International,[5] or leaders create their own database of digital audio files that they consult for their weekly choices. A canon of song can be as flexible as a list of songs on a cell phone, or as inflexible as a published list of hymns that cannot be changed without pastoral approval. Whether on a scribbled list stuffed in a guitar case or neatly entered in a worship software program, somebody's got a list of songs that are in current circulation in the church he or she serves. That is the church's canon of song.

A **canon of song** is a body of song that has been vetted and authorized for use in the worship of a given Christian community. The English word "canon" is from the Greek word *kanōn*, referring to a wooden measuring stick or rule—an instrument that helps to set the criterion for ruling between things. The word came to mean that which was measured or ruled.[6] As an example, the Holy Bible is referred to as the canon of Scripture—our rule of faith. By faith, Christians believe that the Holy Spirit directed persons to spiritually discern sixty-six books for inclusion in the Old and New Testaments from among many writings. The books that were officially accepted by the church fathers as uniquely inspired were admitted to the collection. Once a book became canonical it was accepted as uniquely authoritative. Similarly (though without the same level of inspiration and scrutiny), authorized individuals, be they a hymnal committee or a team of staff members at a local church, sift through an abundance of songs to determine which ones should be approved for the worshipers under their care. Authorization may be formal (a committee is officially established and charged with the task of formulating a body of song) or informal (a leader is asked to supply songs for Sunday's order of service). Either way, someone becomes the gatekeeper. What is allowed is placed into worship; what is disallowed is not sung. However it happens, when someone authorizes songs for use in worship, that person has effectively created a canon of song.

How can music architects learn to make such important decisions with confidence? How can they ensure the use of proper rationale? They must

5. Christian Copyright Licensing International (CCLI; http://us.ccli.com) is a licensing group that provides permission for use of a large body of songs, mainly contemporary in styling. A list of songs based on popular use serves as a repertoire database for many congregations. Other licensing groups also exist, but CCLI is currently the most well known.
6. Elio Peretto, "Canonical-Canon," in *Encyclopedia of Ancient Christianity*, ed. Angelo Di Berardino (Downers Grove, IL: InterVarsity, 2014), 1:417.

become persons of prayerful discernment and wisdom. Leaders can learn the art of discernment.[7] The English word "discern" is from the Latin *discernere*, which means to separate, divide, or distinguish between. To discern means to see distinctly, to separate from surrounding objects.[8] In this case discernment refers to the spiritual perception needed to create a canon of song for worshipers. Leaders can learn to separate the best of available songs from the poor ones, the strong from the weak, the wheat from the chaff. Their willingness to thoroughly examine the possibilities while fully submitted to the Holy Spirit's guidance will yield trustworthy results. When the Lord appeared to Solomon and offered to grant him a request, Solomon asked for discernment on behalf of those under his care: "Give your servant therefore an understanding mind to govern your people, able to discern between good and evil; for who can govern this your great people?" (1 Kings 3:9). Solomon's request pleased the Lord (v. 10), and it was granted. God will grant our request for wisdom as well. The apostle James assures us, "If any of you is lacking in wisdom, ask God, who gives to all generously and ungrudgingly, and it will be given you" (James 1:5). Judicial perception is ours for the asking. Discernment is best done in community, so include others in the process. Divine wisdom will guide music architects in creating a canon of song that is pleasing to God.

A canon of song is not only necessary for theological or artistic integrity in worship; it is also critical in establishing community. When a certain population of people shares a common body of song, bonds are established. The songs help to form corporate identity, and singing them as a group nurtures fellowship. Singing aloud together the songs in which a community finds meaning helps to establish a commitment to the community and its identifying features; at the same time, it is an affectionate act. Spirit touches spirit. The great tradition of corporate singing in Wales is a wonderful example. There, communal singing is a national pastime. From large crowds attending rugby matches to the *Gymanfa Ganus* ("singing festivals")[9] in chapels dotting the landscape, the Welsh have expressed their sense of nationalism by robust corporate singing. Feelings of social unity are very real in those moments. Shared musical heritage is important. *New York Times* columnist David Brooks raises concern over the societal fragmentation that occurs when Americans develop individualized canons

7. While discernment is one of the spiritual gifts mentioned in Scripture (1 Cor. 12:10), it can also be developed in leaders.
8. *Webster's New Universal Unabridged Dictionary*, 2nd ed. (New York: Simon & Schuster, 1983), s.v. "discern."
9. *Gymanfu Ganu* is Welsh for "festival for sacred song."

of song.[10] The iPod culture affords us the capabilities to create our own personal playlists, but at what cost? Brooks suggests that with the ever-increasing range of musical styles enjoyed today and the resulting array of market niches, we are at risk of losing "a common tradition that reminds [us] that [we] are inheritors of a long conversation."[11] North Americans used to know and sing a canon of popular song. Not so much anymore. Singing the same songs together fosters community.

Developing a canon of song is essentially a call to integrity of repertoire. Integrity refers both to being honest and to being whole. We have integrity if we are honest, if the person we portray ourselves to be is the person we truly are. Integrity is also related to the word "integration." We have integrity if we are an integrated person; that is, if the various aspects of our life relate to one another in meaningful and holistic ways. To integrate is to thoughtfully combine disparate parts for the purpose of personal congruency. Wholeness results. It is to connect the dots, so to speak, in all the areas of our lives so that we function from a unified perspective. To disintegrate, however, is to break into pieces that which was connected, to operate in a disconnected manner. In this case, wholeness disintegrates. When music architects set out to create a canon of song, they are attempting to pursue integrity in both ways. They are looking for the songs that keep a community honest, songs that signify all parts of our particular place in God's story, not just the easy or seemingly "relevant" ones. They are also seeking songs that, when combined, reflect a holistic picture of Christian reality, with its triumphs *and* its challenges.

The songs in every canon must represent integrity *within* each song and *among* all songs. First, let's think about the degree of integrity within a given song. (I have written elsewhere of evaluating worship songs theologically, lyrically, and musically, including practical guidelines for use among local church worship leaders.)[12] In general, consider these things:

- *There must be theological integrity*: consistency of thought with regard to the fundamental truths of the Christian faith.

10. David Brooks, "The Segmented Society," *New York Times*, November 20, 2007, http://www.nytimes.com/2007/11/20/opinion/20brooks.html?_r=0.
11. Ibid.
12. Two books may prove helpful in providing practical exercises to help local church leaders discern the quality of specific songs for worship: Constance M. Cherry, Mary M. Brown, and Christopher T. Bounds, *Selecting Worship Songs: A Guide for Leaders* (Marion, IN: Triangle, 2011); and Constance M. Cherry, *The Worship Architect: A Blueprint for Designing Culturally Relevant and Biblically Faithful Services* (Grand Rapids: Baker Academic, 2010), esp. chap. 11.

- *There must be lyrical integrity*: well-formed lyrics, beautiful word patterns, correct use of grammar and punctuation,[13] and coherence of thought from beginning to end. N. T. Wright cautions worship leaders:

> I worry when the words of some of the modern worship songs seem to me just a random selection of Christian slogans, as it were, rather than actually a narrative of the world as claimed by Jesus and as rescued by Jesus in his death and resurrection—songs that recognize that the world is still a suffering place, but looking forward to the new creation. Some worship songs are struggling to say that, but if the narrative is broken then it's not actually helping the people who are singing it in the way that it should.[14]

- *There must be musical integrity*: tuneful melodies, interesting harmonies, and lively rhythm patterns. (Even a slower and less involved rhythm can be considered lively if it helps the song to express its nature. Lively, here, refers to rhythms that breathe a sustaining quality into the text.) Musical integrity is important because it's not just the words that tell the story; music tells a story too. Wright adds:

> The point about a tune is that it's telling a story. It's going somewhere. And I am very anxious about worship songs that have deconstructed the tune—the idea of a tune. That's the radical nature of post-modernity to deconstruct the narrative. That's where our culture is. But we ought to be discerning how to create fresh actual tunes, not simply copying what was done in the 16th or 17th or 19th or whatever century. You can feel the difference in the congregation when they're given a real tune to sing.[15]

John Witvliet emphasizes the integration of lyric and music by calling *both* an "important and terrifying priestly task . . . not only words but also the melodies that interpret those words and give them affective shape."[16]

- *There must be liturgical integrity*: songs that serve every aspect of the worship service (chaps. 3 and 4 address this issue at length). Each song serves a specific role in worship. Songs are not used primarily for inspiration or

13. Worship leaders must use punctuation when projecting lyrics for congregational song. Contemporary practice is to strip punctuation away; however, this does not represent our best offered to God. Nor does it make the lyrics crystal clear in terms of intent. We must not simply throw words up on a screen or wall.
14. Andrea Hunter, "Remembering Not to Forget: An Interview with N. T. Wright," in *Worship Leader*, May 2012, 20.
15. Ibid., 21.
16. Witvliet, *Worship Seeking Understanding*, 232.

to create a mood; they are a means for calling God's people to worship, acknowledging God's presence, sending God's people out to expand the kingdom of God, and so forth.

- *There must be pastoral integrity*: songs that speak to all aspects of the Christian life in such a way that the whole person is addressed. It can be tempting to sing exclusively of the comfortable or triumphant side of Christianity, but there is the dark night of the soul to mention as well. People have always needed soulful songs to both express despair and to receive encouragement.

A canon of song is composed of songs that are valuable, each with its own merit. Integrity of choice depends upon wise music architects who understand that each song is multidimensional and that each single dimension contributes to the song's overall worthiness for use in worship.

Evaluating the Canon of Song for Balance

While each component may be strong, making for a terrific song to be sung in worship, that is not the end of evaluation. Songs must also relate to one another (be integrated with one another) in such a way that the whole is greater than the sum of its parts. We may see the importance of clarifying our rationales for making sound choices and also that of forming a list of appropriate songs, yet leaders must assure balance in their canon of song.

Music architects search out fine songs for their people to sing in worship. Like the woman who had ten silver coins but swept the house to find the one that was lost (Luke 15:8–9), we all have a treasure chest filled with worship songs to sing, yet we scour the vast amount of congregational song possibilities for one more precious item to add to the collection. When we find it we rejoice.

The canon of song for any church will often consist of more songs representing a particular type or style. This is natural. However, in thinking about one's canon of song, style isn't the matter at hand; balance of content is. This section does not argue for a balance of styles but a balance of songs that represent the breadth of Christian understanding and practice. Having a balance of styles can be healthy for most congregations. But ultimately matters of style do not create balance within a community's canon of song; instead, a comprehensiveness of content ensures balance.

To arrive at an overall balance of song we must evaluate how adequate our entire collection is. The English word "evaluate" is from the Latin *evalere*, meaning "to be strong, to be worth."[17] The word "evaluate" is related to "value." To evaluate something means to determine its worth, to discover its value, to appraise it in light of what one values.[18] Therefore, when leaders evaluate a church's canon of song they appraise it in light of what the church values. It's possible that when leaders focus on choosing songs for worship they concentrate on individual songs to such a degree that they lose sight of the big picture. Stepping back and taking the bird's-eye view of the repertoire could be surprising. It will tell us what we seem to value (even if we thought otherwise). It will point out what we value but may have overlooked. Jesus said as much: "where your treasure is, there your heart will be also" (Matt. 6:21).

Music architects often need assistance in expanding their horizons as they take up the exciting challenge of establishing a balanced canon of song for their people. To help, a checklist of suggestions for thinking broadly is offered below. While the list of considerations is substantial, the process is simple. Take these steps:

1. Collect the lyrics for all of the songs you have sung in your church over the past three to six months; keep them handy.
2. Read through the whole list of pairings below to acquaint yourself with the territory.
3. Refer to the chart in appendix A, "Assessing Your Canon of Song," and then read the texts of each song currently sung in your church. Simply put a check mark on the side of the pairing that each song leans toward most. If the song seems to have elements of both items in the pairing (such as praise *and* lament), one item will probably be more prominent; choose the prominent item, even if the text is mixed. Don't make it complicated; just go with the obvious.

When you finish evaluating all the songs, take a look at your overall findings. Are check marks clustered in certain columns? Are the songs dramatically loaded in one direction of a pair of items (suggesting an imbalanced view of Christian perspective), in the middle (balanced), or do songs fail to represent either of the two items in a pair (more work to do!)? When you get to the end, you will have a pretty good idea of what types of songs are needed in order to help worshipers sing the full story of God. Begin to search strategically for songs that will strengthen the weak sides of your repertoire.

17. *Webster's New Universal Unabridged Dictionary*, s.v., "evaluate."
18. Ibid.

As you get started, two very important things must be remembered. First, this exercise has one purpose: to ensure that the songs worshipers are invited to sing over time represent the fullness of Christian understanding and experience. Second, never think of these items as "either/or"; they are intended to be "both/and." In each case, two aspects of worship are listed. The best canons of song will represent *both* dimensions. Each is needed to be partners in a dialogue. Striking a balance of song is not necessarily a matter of equality. For example, it is not that there has to be a comparable number of songs using corporate pronouns as personal pronouns. Nevertheless, there must be an *appropriate proportion* to faithfully represent a biblical understanding of worship.

Here, then, is a list of fifteen considerations for evaluating overall balance of song in worship. It is in no particular order. Neither is this list exhaustive; feel free to expand it. A brief explanation is included for each one.

- *Revelation and Response.* Many songs communicate objective statements of revealed truth based on a scriptural depiction of the triune God and his kingdom. Other songs provide an opportunity for the community to sing its response in light of what has been revealed. Revelation songs tend toward third-person accounts; response songs tend toward first-person accounts. A healthy balance suggests lots of dialogical possibilities where God's character and work are proclaimed (revelation) resulting in celebration and commitment to God's will (response).

- *Vertical and Horizontal.* Some songs are addressed to God (Father, Son, and Holy Spirit) and are therefore directed upward. Other songs are addressed to fellow believers for the purpose of edification; these are directed outward. While a few may even be addressed to self ("Be Still, My Soul") or to unbelievers ("Softly and Tenderly Jesus Is Calling"), the vast majority of songs will consist of psalms, hymns, and spiritual songs through which either we teach and admonish one another or sing with gratitude in our hearts to God (Col. 3:16).

- *Praise and Lament.* Many songs focus on praising God. In fact, there is growing concern that the church has overemphasized jubilant praise while songs of lament are so prominent in Scripture. Lament songs help the community to cry out to God, express sorrow, and even question the presence of God. Praise and lament are deeply linked in Scripture and in life.

- *Declarative and Expressive (Objective and Subjective).* Songs are expressed in different voices. Declarative songs declare who God is apart from any personal opinion; they consist of objective statements about

God's character and nature as seen in Scripture. Other songs are expressive; they tell what God means to the believer personally, or they express what the singer feels and experiences. These songs tend toward the subjective because they are based more on personal experience.

• *Corporate and Personal.* In public Lord's Day worship it is most appropriate to use corporate pronouns in our songs and prayers. That is because we are a *people* assembled to keep covenant with God. "We" and "us" best represent the corporate praises and petitions of the community. At the same time, personal pronouns can be fitting, depending on the circumstance. When personal pronouns are used, the "I" and "me" should be clearly understood to refer to statements to which the whole family of God may assent. For instance, to sing "Blessed assurance, Jesus is mine" in no way indicates that Jesus is only *mine*. Rather, all sing it in good faith that this claim is also the claim of everyone present. A good precedence for this interchange of corporate and personal pronouns is found in the Psalms. Witvliet notes: "The Psalms teach us that even prayers offered in the first person singular are not always soliloquies. 'I-Psalms' often express the sentiments not just of an isolated poet, but rather of the entire nation of Israel. . . . They are expressions of a corporate personality that is a hallmark of the faith of Israel and a challenge to any culture marked by individualism."[19]

• *God's Story and Our Story.* Worship songs should clearly rehearse the story of God—what God has done, is doing, and will do on behalf of his creation. No one song covers the whole territory, of course, except perhaps in a most general way. But together, the songs must unveil each scene from the story in its time. Too often our canon of song tells only isolated chapters of the story; Christmas and Easter come to mind. But what about Jesus's temptation in the wilderness, the ascension, and Christ's return? Look carefully to see what gaps in the story may exist in your canon of song, and then work toward filling the gap with strong songs that beautifully tell the story. Other songs must help us to find our place in God's story ("Were You There When They Crucified My Lord?"). We start with God's story, but it includes us! Each person God has created is a character in the drama of creation, fall, and re-creation. Look for songs that depict the grand story of God and also our connection to it, both corporately and individually.

19. John D. Witvliet, *The Biblical Psalms in Christian Worship: A Brief Introduction and Guide to Resources* (Grand Rapids: Eerdmans, 2007), 26.

- *Shorter and Longer.* When God's people sing the story of God, they use a variety of songs that help carry the dialogue of worship. Some songs excel in providing the details of the dialogue while others excel in weaving the story together—almost like scene changes. Longer songs have the structural capacity for the details; shorter songs are brief connectors that help to create a link between content-driven songs and other acts of worship. A healthy balance of both, and knowing where to place them in the service, will provide an effective sense of dialogical worship. (Shorter and longer songs are explained thoroughly in chaps. 6 and 7.)

- *Names and Titles for God.* Naming the One to whom we sing is critical. There should be no ambiguity when addressing adoration and petitions to the Divine Being. The songs of the church should abound with both personal names and symbolic titles for God. Names for God are the eternal names ("Father," "Son," and "Holy Spirit") and have no point of origination or ending; they have been and always will be names for God without reference to the created order. These very names are revealed by God to identify the three persons of the Trinity in reference to their eternal essence and relationship apart from creation. These names have always been true of God, always are true of God, and will always be true of God. Titles for God depict God's activity that is bound in time (by God's will) and express each person's central work (though not exclusively), such as Creator, Redeemer, Sustainer, Sanctifier, and more. Such titles are not eternal in scope (in that they originated in creation). Every church should examine its songs to assure that (1) God is unapologetically named and (2) a wide variety of titles for God are used, not just our favorites. (The names "Lord" and "King" predominate in popular worship music.) To disciple worshipers in a scriptural view of God will require using many divine names and titles representative of all God's work from eternity to eternity.

- *Universal Tradition and Particular Tradition.* Christianity reflects one orthodox faith. The apostle Paul explains: "There is one body and one Spirit . . . one Lord, one faith, one baptism, one God and Father of all" (Eph. 4:4–6a). Universally affirmed tenets of Christianity are collectively referred to as the Tradition of the church. It is this common faith and Lord that is expressed by the church universal when it sings songs that capture these truths or affirms approved creeds. At the same time, while remaining united, various groups of Christians share distinct viewpoints about certain matters of the faith such as salvation, sanctification, redemption, the return of Christ, and so forth. Denominations and independents have written congregational songs that depict these views. It is appropriate to sing songs that express particularized viewpoints of one's tradition. It is one way to pass along each faith heritage.

- *Older and Newer.* Balanced canons of songs have a healthy mix of older songs and newer songs. Many fine songs have a long history of widespread use in the church. While sometimes songs hang around on the basis of sheer nostalgic attachment, in many cases older songs have lasted for generations because of their timeless and eloquent message. There is a long-standing tradition of singing ancient songs in the Bible and throughout history. Mary's Song (Luke 1:46–55), sometimes referred to by its Latin name, *Magnificat*, is just one example. These words, sung by believers for millennia, continue to be used in contemporary settings precisely because they transcend time and culture. Christians will always sing "Amazing Grace" in worship, although it was written more than two hundred years ago. But new songs are needed too. God continues to speak, calling each generation of authors and composers to create musical renderings of God's truth for the church to sing. The terms "new" and "old" can mean different things in different places. Today songs can be considered old pretty quickly, unfortunately. Newer songs sometimes nudge out older ones, as North American culture seems to demand immediate expressions of song, even in the church. But neither older nor newer is better or worse. Both must be judged by their quality and usefulness and kept or discarded on that basis.

- *Eternal and Temporal.* Worship of the triune God is an eternal activity. There has never been nor will there ever be a moment when the universe is not filled with the praise of God's glory. Eternal worship is carried on in the heavenly realm endlessly. Some of our songs should speak of the unceasing nature of worship—of cherubim and seraphim who day and night call out the holiness and wonder of God (Isa. 6:3; Rev. 4:8). Songs should draw our attention to the cosmic nature of our praise to God, giving worshipers a sense that their adoration merges seamlessly with the uninterrupted praise of eternity. Yet songs of worship occur in the temporal dimension of time and place; they are located among a particular group of worshipers who carry on this worship at this time. As such, they call us to sing here and now! Our songs must urge us to enter in as we are, where we are. Worship songs transcend time and place; at the same time they reside in time and place. At once they are both otherworldly and worldly. A good canon of song accepts and points us to both realities.

- *Comforting and Disturbing.* Music has the capacity to emotionally move worshipers. There is something wonderful about consoling music that assures us and comforts us. Familiar, pleasant melodies and words of solace convince us of God's peaceful presence and that all will be well. However, worship songs must also serve as prophetic acts—texts and music that challenge the status quo and even disturb us to the point of action. Worship music should not serve exclusively to insulate us from the in-breaking that God wants to do in our souls. Some songs can provide a great service to the church in their ability to call us out, dislodging us from complacency, so as to do God's will. Sometimes it takes a disturbing piece to do disturbing work. Beware of a canon of song that fails to recognize this.

- *Personal Holiness and Social Holiness.* God calls Christ-followers to holy living: "without holiness no one will see the Lord" (Heb. 12:14). Scriptural holiness is multidimensional; it involves personal holiness and social holiness. One cannot exist without the other. It takes both to fulfill all righteousness. Believers are called to live lives of daily personal surrender, to be slaves to righteousness leading to holiness (Rom. 6:19). But personal holiness has a goal beyond us; it is for the sake of others: "Spiritual formation is a process of being conformed to the image of Christ for the sake of others."[20] Personal holiness results in social holiness, as godly people follow the prophet's call: "But let justice roll down like waters, and righteousness like an ever-flowing stream (Amos 5:24).

- *Lord's Day and 24/7.* True worship is a lifestyle. We live daily lives of worship. Whatever we do or say, we do all to the glory of God (1 Cor. 10:31). Certain songs are more meaningful for quiet devotional moments—songs that speak of personal intimacy with God. Other songs are specifically directed to the gathered community, clearly addressing the broad themes of faith. There's significant overlap, of course, but it's good to remember that a leader should advise worshipers on songs related to various aspects of Christian living. While we have been considering the canon of song for corporate worship (songs for the Lord's Day), pastoral musicians should also guide worshipers toward other songs that encourage them more personally (songs for 24/7).

- *Adults and Youth.* Intergenerational worship is an ideal that should be pursued. The family of God is composed of persons of every age group,

20. M. Robert Mulholland Jr., *Invitation to a Journey: A Road Map for Spiritual Formation* (Downers Grove, IL: InterVarsity, 1993), 12.

all of whom gain much from offering worship to God together. Worshipers should sing songs for all ages, both in terms of lyrical/theological development and musical styling. Some songs should contain mature expressions of faith, and some should contain simpler, even repetitive lyrics that are purposeful and accessible to young children and youth. Simple doesn't mean trite. Look for songs that say something to all ages. Children will grow into the more developed songs that help to shape their faith, and adults will appreciate the simple strains that inspire their faith as well.

Discerning a balanced canon of song is one of the most important duties of the music architect. As one experienced worship leader says, "One of the signs of maturity in a worship planner is their increased humility in choosing the right words for others to sing in our worship gatherings."[21] Where does the leader begin? It could seem overwhelming at first. Do not undertake a comprehensive overhaul all at once! Just take small steps over time. Change in ministry almost always happens best when done incrementally. Identify the area that needs the most immediate strengthening. Start there. Also, remember that canons should be flexible; change always occurs. It is natural that songs are added and subtracted as needed. However, at any given stage of the church's journey, the church should have the benefit of a thoughtful and secure repertoire that was prayerfully and intentionally created to the glory of God and the welfare of God's people. Imagine the apostle Paul is writing to your congregation, not just the Philippian church, with these words: "Finally, beloved, whatever is true, whatever is honorable, whatever is just, whatever is pure, whatever is pleasing, whatever is commendable, if there is any excellence and if there is anything worthy of praise, think about these things" (Phil. 4:8).

Conclusion

When music architects create a stable canon of song for their people, they are investing in profoundly significant work—that of creating spiritual and cultural cohesion among believers. In a modern world many songs are disposable; they serve their purpose and then become oldies but goodies that are brought back periodically for the sake of nostalgia. This can make it very challenging to create a master list of songs that have staying power and are sung on a regular basis. Canons of song allow communities the opportunity

21. Paul Sunderland, "The Language of Our Songs in Worship" (class paper, The Robert E. Webber Institute for Worship Studies, Jacksonville, FL, May 15, 2014), 3. Used with permission.

to sing not only of their current experiences but also of their past, shared histories. A solid canon provides songs for a full range of historical perspective, past, present, and future. Songs must not only express who we are today as members of our ecclesial group but they must also sing of where we have been and of our aspirations for where we hope to go as God calls us forward.

Key Term

canon of song. A body of song that has been vetted or authorized for use in the worship of a given Christian community.

To Learn More

Cherry, Constance M., Mary M. Brown, and Christopher T. Bounds. *Selecting Worship Songs: A Guide for Leaders*. Marion, IN: Triangle, 2011.

Woods, Robert, and Brian Walrath, eds. *The Message in the Music: Studying Contemporary Praise and Worship*. Nashville: Abingdon, 2007.

Engage

A few centuries have passed. A team of sociologists is doing research on the religious beliefs that influenced your particular congregation long ago. Most of the artifacts were destroyed over time, but they did find a record of the song texts that were sung in worship. Based upon only the lyrics to the songs your church sings now, what conclusions could these researchers reasonably make concerning the following things:

- your view of God
- your view of humanity
- the trinitarian nature of God
- evil
- redemption
- holiness
- eternity
- providence
- the church
- worship
- creation
- love
- mercy
- judgment
- social responsibility
- freedom

Take inventory on the strength of your canon of song. If you did not yet complete the assessment tool in appendix A ("Assessing Your Canon of Song"), do so now. Once you have completed it, take the following steps to consider how best to improve on the core songs of your church.

1. List the top three things that stand out to you as a result of completing the chart.
2. Show the list to someone in your music or worship ministry and explain your findings. Ask them for their thoughts.
3. Write down two ideas for improving your canon of song.
4. Make one change this coming week. (Remember, little is much. Go slow!) Maintain the change for consistency.
5. Select two pairs on the list of fifteen that you may not have thought much about so far. Investigate biblical principles relating to these two pairs.
6. Develop a brief devotional on these two pairs for you to lead at your next two music rehearsals.

Interlude

Introduction to Shorter and Longer Song Forms

In the next two chapters, we will explore many different types of congregational songs that are of great use for the church—any church, anywhere. In chapter 6 we will examine shorter song forms; in chapter 7, we will look at longer song forms. I will use these two broad categories to help us collect our thoughts about what both shorter and longer forms have to offer every worshiping community. Perhaps these questions could be raised: Why even use a variety of songs at all? Why not just stay with one or two types—the ones with which we are familiar and comfortable? There are a number of reasons to sing a great variety of worship songs:

- Because songs connect us to worshipers past, present, and future
- Because worshipers in both the Old and New Testaments sang a variety of songs
- Because various types of songs function in different ways to support the liturgy
- Because no congregation is composed of persons who relate to only one type of song
- Because singing one another's songs deepens the sense of community
- Because variety introduces worshipers to the songs of the church universal being sung today

One frequently used rationale for singing a variety of songs is to appeal to Paul's exhortations found in Ephesians 5:18–20 ("sing psalms and hymns and spiritual songs among yourselves, singing and making melody to the Lord in your hearts") and Colossians 3:16–17 ("with gratitude in your hearts sing psalms, hymns, and spiritual songs to God"). While there are different opinions on the meaning of Paul's exact use of the terms "psalms, hymns, and spiritual songs," most scholars agree that his larger intention was to teach the church that a wide variety of song was expected and valued because (1) one type of song could not possibly portray the richness of the word of Christ,[1] (2) many expressions of song were needed for the pluralistic cultures of Mediterranean cities,[2] and (3) the Old Testament psalms set a biblical precedence for a wide range of song needed for liturgical purposes.[3] Biblical scholar Daniel I. Block writes: "Although it is unclear whether 'psalms, hymns, and spiritual songs' function as synonyms or reflect three kinds of music, it is clear that together these terms signify all kinds of music."[4]

Embracing a breadth of song encourages us to create a multimusical world that encourages "the ability to speak multiple musical languages with fluency."[5] Our world is not unlike the complex, multicultural world of the first century where a "one song fits all" approach was not recommended. Today, more than ever, the worshiping church exists in an ever-widening global culture. Because of this, each community must seek to become musically and liturgically multilingual so as to reflect not only the songs of the community's first musical language (the language of preference) but also types of songs that may represent second and third musical languages, thereby becoming multimusical.[6] When we do this, our chance of being relevant to a wider group of worshipers increases greatly.

In chapter 6, I describe three types of shorter songs: responsorial songs, freestanding songs, and spontaneous songs. In chapter 7, I describe two types of longer songs: "pure stanza" songs and "stanza plus" songs. Within each section in each chapter, I first discuss the features, functions, and forms of

1. Gordon D. Fee, *God's Empowering Presence: The Holy Spirit in the Letters of Paul* (Peabody, MA: Hendrickson, 1994), 650.
2. Barry Leisch, *The New Worship: Straight Talk on Music and the Church*, expanded ed. (Grand Rapids: Baker Books, 2001), 41–42.
3. Ibid., 42.
4. Daniel I. Block, *For the Glory of God: Recovering a Biblical Theology of Worship* (Grand Rapids: Baker Academic, 2014), 234. For an insightful comparison of Eph. 5:18–20 and Col. 3:15–17, see 231–34.
5. C. Randall Bradley, *From Memory to Imagination: Reforming the Church's Music* (Grand Rapids: Eerdmans, 2012), 184.
6. Ibid.

each song type, then I detail specific genres within that song type and provide examples. We cover a lot of ground in the next two chapters, so I've provided an outline below. The outline for each chapter is repeated within chapters 6 and 7.

Chapter 6: Shorter Songs

Responsorial Songs (which include call and response songs and verse and refrain songs)

Negro Spirituals (call and response)

Black Gospel Songs (call and response)

Antiphons (verse and refrain)

Freestanding Songs (which include cyclical songs and through-composed songs)

Global Songs (cyclical)

Taizé Songs (cyclical; can also be call and response)

Choruses (through-composed)

Service Music (through-composed)

Spontaneous Songs

Familiar Songs

Improvised Songs

Singing in Tongues

Chapter 7: Longer Songs

Pure Stanza Songs

Classic Hymns

Metrical Psalms

Stanza Plus Songs

Gospel Songs

Modern Hymns

Modern Worship Songs

6

Maximizing
Shorter Song Forms

Explore

Every church, from long-established ones to newer church plants, has a song history. Try to discover yours. Before reading this chapter, think about the types of songs you tend to use in your worshiping community and why this might be so. As always, reflecting on these topics with others is more advantageous than working solely with your own assumptions. To stimulate your thinking, initiate an informal discussion with people from your church who have a long tenure there. Invite a mix of people who may have different perspectives from your own. Once gathered, use the following questions to get started:

1. Without referring to musical style, how would you describe the lyrics of the songs currently sung in your church (simple, wordy, poetic, objective, subjective, dense, light, newer, older, repetitious, etc.)? Write down as many descriptors as you can.
2. Does one descriptor seem to describe the majority of songs sung in your church? If so, why?
3. Have the kinds of songs used in your church shifted over time? Be sure to ask persons who have been there the longest, or go back in your files and do some real investigative work. Don't just assume you know the answer to this question based on hearsay.
4. We sing our kind of songs because _____ (lead pastor's view).

5. We sing our kind of songs because _____ (worship leader's view).
6. We sing our kind of songs because _____ (average congregant's view).

Now that you have begun to reflect on the types of songs currently used in your worshiping community, read this chapter in order to think critically and practically about broadening your repertoire of congregational song.

Expand

In the Interlude above, we discovered that multiple song types are to be valued in Christian worship. Two common approaches used to compare or categorize types of congregational songs include historical surveys and stylistic studies.[1] We depart from such approaches and focus instead on how various types of songs are well suited for the worship service. While historical perspective and style of presentation inform our ministry greatly, the choices of song for congregations do not orbit around these spheres alone. There is merit in lifting the discussion of song choices out of the confines in which we commonly place them in order to look at them more functionally. While I will refer to the historical roots and stylings of songs used as examples, I intend it only as a very basic introduction—enough orientation to provide the music architect with a good understanding of how to employ a song to its highest potential in the liturgy. The reader is encouraged to examine many different song genres much more thoroughly in the future. Our purpose here is to see how worship stands to benefit from capturing the unique strength of each genre.

To achieve this goal, chapters 6 and 7 present a simple taxonomy[2] of song types, consisting broadly of two categories: shorter song forms and longer song forms. By discussing songs as shorter or longer, we can look closely at how each uniquely and practically serves the greater purposes of worship. In doing so, I do not intend to create a dichotomy of shorter *versus* longer. Instead, I hope to present the two categories of song as interdependent, working together to give the church complementary approaches.

1. Excellent examples include Harry Eskew and Hugh T. McElrath, *Sing with Understanding: Introduction to Christian Hymnology*, 2nd ed. (Nashville: Church Street Press, 1995) for a historical survey; and C. Michael Hawn, ed., *New Songs of Celebration Render: Congregational Song in the Twenty-First Century* (Chicago: GIA, 2013) for a stylistic study.
2. A taxonomy is a system created for classifying information into logical groupings for the purpose of comparison.

This chapter looks at three types of shorter songs—responsorial songs, freestanding songs, and spontaneous songs—and ten specific genres within those types—Negro spirituals, Black gospel songs, antiphons, global songs, Taizé songs, choruses, service music, spontaneous familiar songs, improvised songs, and singing in tongues (see outline below). Bear in mind that the types of shorter songs presented here are representative of still others, all of which hold huge potential for the corporate worship of any congregation.

Shorter Songs

Responsorial Songs (which include call and response songs and verse and refrain songs)

Negro Spirituals

Black Gospel Songs

Antiphons

Freestanding Songs (which include cyclical songs and through-composed songs)

Global Songs

Taizé Songs

Choruses

Service Music

Spontaneous Songs

Familiar Songs

Improvised Songs

Singing in Tongues

Also, it is important to note the way in which certain terms will be used throughout chapters 6 and 7.

- *Type* refers to classifying songs according to some of their common features, functions, and forms.
- *Feature* refers to defining characteristics that help to identify signature aspects of a type of song.
- *Function* refers to how certain types of song are uniquely prepared to aid in carrying out the dialogical nature of worship.
- *Form* refers to the actual compositional structure of a song.

- *Genre* refers to a unique expression of song that has its own distinctive history, idioms, performance practices, and stylings, which, altogether, give it an unmistakable character and sound. For instance, Negro spirituals appeared on Southern plantations before the Civil War (distinctive history); are characterized by references to deliverance, freedom, and lament (idioms); are primarily sung a cappella (performance practice); and make use of improvised harmonies (styling).

The big idea is to grasp the widely diverse number of song types available for today's church and to consider their real potential for enlivening the congregational singing in any worshiping community. These shorter songs are transcultural in nature—useful within any worship style when used for just the right purpose. The goal is not to replace the congregational songs presently used but to widen the repertoire. We are about to embark on an adventurous expedition through a sampling of shorter songs. Let's begin!

Introduction

One umbrella under which we can place a large number of worship songs will be referred to simply as "shorter song forms."[3] Shorter songs have a relatively brief amount of text and tune material. That is not necessarily to say that they are sung a brief amount of time, for as you will see, many types of shorter songs are repeated; therefore, even the time given to a short song can be far from brief, depending on its function and use in worship. Nor is it to say that shorter songs are musically elementary or theologically "soft." Many shorter songs hold profound spiritual depth and are musically sophisticated. So perhaps the first idea we must overcome is to presume that "shorter" means inferior. This is not the case. If a shorter song is found to be weak, it is not because of the form itself; it is because of the unimaginative work of the lyricist and composer. (The same is also true of longer song forms.) Quality of song does not have to do with length.

We will discuss three types of shorter songs: responsorial songs, freestanding songs, and spontaneous songs. Within each type, I will (1) explain special *features* that help to give it its identity; (2) suggest some unique *functions* it

3. Referring to songs as either "short/shorter" or "long/longer" is not original with me. C. Randall Bradley uses the terms in *From Memory to Imagination: Reforming the Church's Music* (Grand Rapids: Eerdmans, 2012), 177–79. Others have mentioned these designations as well. I add the word "form" because there are distinguishing compositional structures to the shorter and longer forms that are explained in chaps. 6 and 7.

contributes to worship; and (3) note some particular representative *forms*. Then I will give examples of various genres of congregational song. There are many different genres of shorter songs ranging from Euro-American praise choruses to global songs, from Negro spirituals to Taizé songs from France. Genres of song tend to be culturally based expressions of the various types. While some of the shorter song types discussed in this chapter overlap, I will deal with the primary aspects of each one and not get weighed down with detailed comparisons. Again, capturing the big idea is the most beneficial thing for our purposes.

Any and all of these shorter song types hold real potential for enlivening the congregational singing in any worshiping community. If leaders will capture the essence of each one, great adventure awaits congregations! Together shorter songs provide a wide palette of choices and opportunities for the music architect.

Responsorial Songs

One of the earliest and most dominant shorter song types is the **responsorial song**. It predates the Christian era (see Ps. 136 for one example) and has been in continuous use throughout Judeo-Christian history.[4] Generally, a responsorial song is a brief sung response interwoven with related liturgical material—sometimes Scripture, the words of a prayer, or stanzas of a hymn, to name a few. It can be creatively used in any number of circumstances. I have experienced responsorial singing done beautifully between extemporaneous testimonies, for example.

Features. The primary feature of responsorial singing is alternation. The entire group does not sing the whole song together at once; in most instances a song leader alternates with the congregation. The use of vocal alternation appears in various forms. For example, it is often used with black gospel music where the soloist plays a significant role, alternating with repetitive refrains by the congregation. It can also happen in the more formal cantor/congregation format (explained below). Shorter songs are frequently seen in cultures that depend on oral communication, a mode of communication that encourages responsorial singing. The simple and often repetitive nature of responsorial songs makes them accessible to anyone, regardless of age or musical experience. Engagement is possible without the need for written materials. It happens through entering into a dynamic dialogue of

4. Responsorial singing occurs in many cultures and is not limited to Christianity. Religions of all kinds, as well as secular venues, have used responsorial singing for millennia.

song—listening to the voices that surround you, carrying your part of the conversation, relishing the fellowship so central to the experience, and offering a communal song to the triune God.

Functions. The function of responsorial songs is not to add creativity to worship or to provide interesting variety or to divide up the responsibilities of singing. Rather, *its primary purpose is to portray the innate dialogical nature of worship.* Responsorial singing can capture well the vertical and horizontal dialogue that is native to Christian worship. Responsorial songs also provide great opportunity for involvement. They lend themselves to full participation of the community. A few representative genres to explore can be found below.

Forms. Responsorial singing draws on very basic musical forms in keeping with its rather simple nature. Much responsorial singing is found in two-part forms such as *call and response* or *verse and refrain.* (Cyclical forms are also popular in responsorial singing such as *theme and variations,* so common in much global song. Global songs will be discussed later under "Freestanding Songs.") The form itself tends not to be complex, though the expression of it may indeed be quite involved.

Negro Spirituals

Negro spirituals (as well as black gospel songs discussed next) are a genre of responsorial songs that use call and response extensively. (Other genres employ call and response as well.) Call and response is perhaps the truest expression of dialogical singing. It consists of a solo voice initiating a conversation (the "call") and a group replying directly (the "response"). The call can be an invitation, a statement, a question—any number of possibilities that the leader uses to engage others in conversational song; the response is the collective reply. Call and response resembles verse and refrain in that it engages two parties; it is different in that it is truly much more of a conversation. Call and response has many different manifestations, such as echoes, completing the sentence of the caller, story form, and many more.[5] The structure is amazing in its flexibility. "It can be adapted, augmented, shortened, and expanded. It all depends on the needs and goals of the song at the time that it is sung."[6] Improvisation is an important dimension of call and response, especially for the caller who may take full advantage of extemporaneous expressions; in fact, this is one of its most delightful aspects.

5. See Roberta R. King, *A Time to Sing: A Manual for the African Church* (Nairobi, Kenya: Evangel, 1999), 57–77.
6. Ibid., 60.

Negro spirituals[7] emerged during the late eighteenth century[8] among the West African captives imported to North America as they worked on the plantations in the South.[9] Spirituals were birthed in lament. Slaves on board the ships sang about their fears, their longing for the familiar cultural conditions of their home country, their despair of separation from family, and their torturous physical abuse. As with the laments in the Bible, spirituals intermingled despair with hope. Many spirituals display a remarkable interplay between articulating deep sorrow while also expressing the expectation of deliverance.

Slaves were not permitted to form churches prior to the 1770s; therefore, two alternative centers of worship emerged for them: (1) segregated areas of seating in white churches where limited participation could occur, and (2) "praise houses" or brush arbors of a secret location where slaves could worship in their own way.[10] "The 'spirituals' sung in these meetings drew variously on hymns, the Scriptures, and African styles of singing, their language using rich imagery, often from Old Testament narratives, to express secret yearnings for freedom and veiled critiques of slavery."[11] An amazing synthesis of musical and textual material was the result—a combination of rhythmic and melodic inflections from Africa as well as the folk songs of colonial America.[12] Integrated camp meetings during the period of the Second Great Awakening (a revival movement from about 1790 to 1850) also played a role in the expansion of and exposure to Negro spirituals.[13] (Blacks living in the North were free to participate in camp meetings; blacks in the South could do so after emancipation.) The camp meetings provided a venue where the music of the slaves was welcomed: "The style and performance of camp-meeting music encouraged improvisation—shouted responses, riffs on favourite phrases, stretching and bending the sounds—all features that African-Americans used in spirituals, as they did later in gospel, blues, and jazz."[14]

Musical features of spirituals included complex rhythms, ornamentation of the melodic lines, improvised harmonies, and flatted thirds, fifths, and

---

7. White spirituals are a separate category not discussed here. The term "spirituals" will refer to Negro spirituals throughout this chapter.

8. Angela M. S. Nelson, "The Spiritual," *Christian History* 31 (1991): 31. While the first slaves were brought to America in the sixteenth century, the spiritual developed later.

9. The spiritual was one of three primary musical forms produced by the slaves during the eighteenth and nineteenth centuries, the other two being field hollers and work songs. Ibid., 30.

10. Tim Dowley, *Christian Music: A Global History* (Minneapolis: Fortress, 2011), 191.

11. Ibid.

12. Ibid.

13. Horace Clarence Boyer, *The Golden Age of Gospel* (Chicago: University of Illinois Press, 2000), 8–9.

14. Dowley, *Christian Music*, 191.

sevenths.[15] They often took advantage of **pentatonic** (five-note) scales more representative of West African influence, rather than the seven-note diatonic scale heard in the Western culture around them.

Call and response is easily seen in the Negro spiritual "It's Alright."

Call	When it gets dark and I can't see my way,
Response	Jesus said He'll fix it and it's alright.
Call	I know He's gonna send me a brighter day.
Response	Jesus said He'll fix it and it's alright.
Refrain (All)	It's alright, it's alright. My Jesus said He'll fix it and it's alright. It's alright, it's alright. My Jesus said He'll fix it and it's alright.*

* "It's Alright," author and composer unknown, public domain, http://www.hymnary.org/text /when_it_gets_dark_and_i_cant_see_my_way.

In addition to the call and response structure, spirituals frequently used two other forms: aaab and aaba.

> (Example: aaab form)
> In the morning when I rise,
> In the morning when I rise,
> In the morning when I rise,
> Give me Jesus.
> (refrain: aaba)
> Give me Jesus.
> Give me Jesus.
> You may have all this world,
> Give me Jesus.[16]

> (Example: aaba form)
> Were you there when they crucified my Lord?
> Were you there when they crucified my Lord?
> Oh! Sometimes it causes me to tremble, tremble, tremble.
> Were you there when they crucified my Lord?[17]

If you have not sung spirituals in your church, it is quite easy to do so. Listen to some recordings of spirituals performed **a cappella**. Identify the structure

15. Edward Foley, ed., *Worship Music: A Concise Dictionary* (Collegeville, MN: Liturgical Press, 2000), 288.

16. "Give Me Jesus," author and composer unknown, public domain, http://www.hymnary .org/text/in_the_morning_when_i_rise_in_the_morn.

17. "Were You There?," author and composer unknown, public domain, http://www.hymnary .org/text/were_you_there_when_they_crucified_my_lo.

of the song and note its tone (gleeful, mournful, etc.). Introduce a spiritual to your music leaders; get comfortable with the sounds and the words. Experiment with possible ways to sing it. When it is time to sing it in church, be daring—try it unaccompanied. Let your people hear the pure sound of human voices. Small percussion instruments may be added depending on the song, but the sound of the singing must predominate. Don't cover it up with guitars or keyboards or organs. Also, be sure to place each spiritual where it belongs in the service; this will help to ensure its success. For example, the spiritual "Steal Away to Jesus" is perfectly suited to lead into intercessory prayer; "Go Tell It on the Mountain" would make a great sending song at certain times of the Christian year. The composers of most spirituals are unknown; therefore, the songs are in the public domain and no copyright permission is needed unless you are using a recent arrangement.

Negro spirituals, while rooted in the pre–Civil War era of the United States, belong to the worldwide church. They provide singing congregations with profound texts and melodies full of pathos, both celebrative and mournful. Their universal appeal is a testimony to their infinite worth. They are timeless and transcultural.

Black Gospel Songs

Spirituals were birthed in the pre-emancipation era of American history; black gospel songs developed in the post-emancipation era.[18] The latter took shape by combining certain American musical forces of the late nineteenth and early twentieth centuries—primarily ragtime, blues, and jazz. Early in the twentieth century, Thomas A. Dorsey, considered to be the father of gospel music, named this genre of song "gospel music" as a way to distinguish it from the gospel hymns used in the crusades of Dwight L. Moody and Ira D. Sankey.[19] *Gospel hymns* reflected features of standard Protestant hymnody, whereas *gospel music* leaned heavily on improvisation, altered scale degrees, and intricate rhythms.[20] Gospel music shares many musical expressions common to the spirituals (e.g., both use call and response singing), but it developed in urban areas of the United States. It became deeply tied to the struggles of the African American community. Its roots in the songs of slavery, along with its development in turn-of-the-century American musical stylings popular in urban America earned it its name: black gospel.

18. James Abbington, "If It Had Not Been for the Lord on My Side: Hymnody in African-American Churches," in *New Songs of Celebration Render: Congregational Song in the Twenty-First Century*, ed. C. Michael Hawn (Chicago: GIA, 2013), 73.
19. Ibid., 74.
20. Ibid., 75.

Black gospel has spanned the twentieth century and beyond. It has articulated, interpreted, and expressed the pathos of the various movements of African American cultures including the Civil Rights Movement. James Abbington affirms "the direct transference of the Negro Spiritual form to the . . . developing 'freedom song.'"[21] Freedom songs were sung in marches and rallies but also regularly in church.[22] Abbington concludes, "Simply put, what black people are singing religiously will provide a clue to what is happening to them sociologically."[23]

Black gospel is alive and well today in many parts of the world and popular among persons of all racial backgrounds. It belongs in the shorter forms of congregational song because of its limited texts with repetitions. It is interactive, employs much call and response, and engages the body with dancing, swaying, clapping, and so on. It is lively and full of pathos. Black gospel uses a significant amount of electronic instrumentation, especially keyboards with piano and organ sounds, guitars, bass, drums, and myriad smaller percussion instruments.

To begin to explore the black gospel genre, investigate a few of the noteworthy artists of the latter half of the twentieth century, such as James Cleveland, Edwin Hawkins, and Andraé Crouch. Crouch's "Soon and Very Soon"[24] is a fine place to start, given its easy lyrics and tune and its overall infectious sound. Listen to some of the current leaders such as Israel Houghton, Dorothy Norwood, and William McDowell. Visit local black congregations; invite local musicians to your church to educate your leaders. Once you capture the ethos of black gospel, you will revel in the inspiration it provides.

Antiphons

In Christian practice, the most common responsorial singing has involved the biblical psalms. In the case of the responsorial psalm, a group, typically the whole congregation, sings a **response**, also called a "refrain," that is based on the psalm. The intervening material is called a "**versicle**" (referring to the verses of the psalm) and is usually sung by a solo voice (sometimes referred to as a **cantor**)[25] or a subgroup of voices such as a choir or praise team. In

21. Ibid., 73.
22. Ibid., 74.
23. Ibid., 79.
24. Andraé Crouch (words and music), "Soon and Very Soon," 1976, Bud John Songs/Crouch Music (administered by EMI Christian Music Publishing).
25. The term "cantor" (Latin for "singer") has been used in Judeo-Christian worship for millennia. A similar term in Hebrew, *sh'liach tzibur*, refers to "prayer messenger," a representative voice of the congregation that leads in the sung prayer.

less liturgical settings the leader speaks the verses, and the response is sung or spoken by the group. Historically, there have been many different ways to sing the verse and refrain. (A different type of verse and refrain related to gospel hymnody will be discussed in chapter 7.)

One genre of verse and refrain singing is antiphonal psalm singing, a mode of singing with ancient roots. As it originally developed, antiphonal psalm singing referred primarily to a method of singing wherein two ensembles sang a psalm in alternation, verse by verse. Monks and nuns have chanted the 150 psalms of the daily office in this manner for many centuries. In this case the **antiphon** consisted of a verse from the psalm that was sung at the beginning and again at the conclusion of the entire psalm (which was sung antiphonally throughout). Today, antiphons are used in various ways: at the beginning and end of an entire psalm, interspersed throughout groups of verses, or at the beginning of the psalm and after every verse.[26] A primary phrase or verse from the psalm is chosen for the antiphon that captures the main theme of the psalm. It is sung by the congregation at various designated points throughout the psalm verses, which are spoken or sung by the leader(s). It is easy to see how the back-and-forth sung participation of the antiphon suggests a dialogue, so fitting for the conversational nature of worship. In addition, because the antiphon is repeated at various points throughout the psalm, it takes root deep in the soil of worshipers' hearts and minds. Appendix B contains an example of a contemporary antiphon that you may try with your congregation with permission of the composer.

Antiphons are easy to sing and delightful to experience. Here are two practical suggestions for introducing antiphons to your congregation, even if they have never attempted this genre of short song before. First, choose one phrase of a familiar song and use that as the antiphon alternating with verses from a psalm. (The antiphon does not have to be from the psalm itself, though historically that was the case.) For example, the opening line of Isaac Watts's hymn, "Joy to the world, the Lord is come," would serve as a fine antiphon interspersed with Psalm 98:4–9. Both the hymn and the psalm allude to the Lord's coming in final judgment. (Surprise! It's really not a Christmas hymn, though it works fine at Christmas too.) Invite the congregation to sing the well-known words, "Joy to the world! The Lord is come; let earth receive her King," prior to someone reading or singing Psalm 98:4. Then sing the same line of the hymn again after verses 5, 7, and 9. Virtually every psalm

26. Raymond F. Glover, "Liturgical Music: Its Forms and Functions," in *Liturgy and Music: Lifetime Learning*, ed. Robin A. Leaver and Joyce Ann Zimmerman (Collegeville, MN: Liturgical Press, 1998), 234.

will suggest a song already known to your congregation, a phrase of which you can use as an antiphon.

Second, antiphons are very easy to compose. Simply choose one of the salient phrases or verses from a psalm and give it a good melody. Score the melody for your congregation or teach it by rote. Ask a singer or reader to offer the psalm while you lead the congregation in singing your created melody at junctures in the psalm. Keep it simple. You don't really need to give pitches or introductions to the congregation's antiphon each time they sing it. Just start in by gesturing, smiling, and singing. They'll follow just fine. It's a wonderful way to *experience* the psalm instead of just *hearing* the psalm.

Many good collections of published antiphons are available. A good place to start is with hymnals, as some include sections with antiphons. However, I have found that the best way to begin is with what is familiar, to give people security.

There are many more genres of responsorial songs to be explored. Take full advantage of dialogical singing and enjoy the new sense of participation you will discover in worship.

Freestanding Songs

A second type of shorter songs is what I call "freestanding songs." They are brief songs that stand by themselves—without stanzas or refrains. Unlike responsorial songs, freestanding songs are sung entirely by all worshipers at once.

Features. The primary feature of the freestanding song is that it consists of a very limited amount of text and tune. Ethnomusicologist Roberta R. King refers to these as "low text load" songs—there are "few words or phrases that are different. Only a few words change throughout the song."[27] Economy of text and tune allow for immediate participation as well as freedom to dance, clap, and move around while singing, thereby entering into the liturgy in multiple levels at once (vertical) as well as directly engaging other worshipers (horizontal). Due to their brevity, freestanding songs tend to make one point with little verbal elaboration. Precisely because they are brief, repetition is also a feature. Freestanding songs depend on the full repetition of the song in order to internalize its message. Singing once through, without repeating, would not afford worshipers enough time to meditate on the words, whereas several repetitions allow for a deeper experience of the song.

27. King, *A Time to Sing*, 61.

Functions. Freestanding songs can be very useful for worship. First is their ability to join elements of worship together, creating a sense of continuum and flow as the service progresses. They are uniquely capable to serve as invitations or responses to surrounding liturgical actions (e.g., after a spoken call to worship, leading into prayer, in response to the sermon, while receiving Holy Communion.). Precisely because of their thinner texts and memorable melodies, they flow in and out of other elements of worship with ease. This also frees worshipers from focusing on printed texts, enabling them to participate in liturgical actions as they sing. Also, many freestanding songs serve well as the very texts for certain worship actions: as prayers of confession, calls to worship, petitions for healing, testimonies, and more. Because freestanding songs are simple and often repeated, they are highly accessible, allowing everyone to join in immediately and with confidence.

Forms. The compositional forms of freestanding songs also tend toward simple structures. In this section, I highlight especially the cyclical structure expressed in theme and variations and through-composed chorus structures. In discussing global songs and Taizé songs as cyclical genres (see below) either one could have been discussed under "Responsorial Songs" because they each often use responsorial singing. However, since both genres also consist of numerous pieces in freestanding forms, I have chosen to place them here. Again, there is much overlap among various shorter song forms.

Global Songs

One of the greatest blessings of the worldwide church today is the growing awareness of and participation in Christian songs of many nations. Worshipers of Jesus Christ have sung God's praises in many parts of the globe for centuries, but their songs have largely gone unheard beyond their locale until fairly recently when the floodgates have opened wide due to increased travel, accelerated communication (especially the internet), and a shift in missiological emphases that has encouraged worshipers around the world to create and expand their own body of indigenous sacred songs that reflects their own culture and time. These factors, along with emerging organizations that are dedicated to advancing global song, have greatly added to Western exposure of the heart songs of our sisters and brothers from every continent.[28] The result is an outpouring of Christian worship music to be celebrated and sung by all believers internationally. We live in an exciting time!

---

28. I highly recommend that the reader investigate the work of the International Council of Ethnodoxologists, http://www.worldofworship.org.

Global songs are, of course, vastly different from one another in every way—language, tonalities, rhythmic patterns, harmonic structures, and compositional forms—and are played using very different musical instruments. Yet many non-Western songs share one thing in common: they fit the shorter responsorial types of song forms discussed above, especially call and response songs and verse and refrain songs. This is largely due to the majority of global songs originating from oral traditions and being sung in cultures with a very high view of community; hence, the conversational and highly participatory nature of singing is organic. Many global songs provide us with excellent examples of the cyclical structure.

In **cyclical songs**, a brief song is sung by the entire community and then repeated a number of times for the purpose of internalizing its meaning. How many repetitions are sung depends on several factors, including the culture from where it originates, its purpose in the liturgy, the leader's sensitivities to group dynamics, and so forth. Cyclical structures depend on repetition, but not vain repetition. Typically each repetition is not the same; the song is not repeated simply to stretch the experience. Rather, each recurrence is an opportunity for the community to embellish, improvise, personalize, and "own" the song. In that sense, while a song is repeated, it is not duplicated. The repetition *is* the story—the story of God at work in the community.

Michael Hawn considers cyclical songs to be a type of **theme and variations**.[29] In theme and variations, a melodic theme is established in the first sung statement, which is then followed by successive presentations of the same theme, each of which is varied in a different way as it alternates with the original melodic theme. When Western instrumental composers employ theme and variations as a compositional plan, they create musical scores for rehearsal and performance sake; this tends to yield highly similar interpretations from concert to concert. In contrast, *sung* theme and variations, in the case of much global song, are typically not committed to written scores. This tends to yield an infinite number of interpretations from place to place. In fact, that is the point. Cyclical songs live and breathe and change with each cycle. It is not intended that they be reproduced identically for each occasion; rather, they are simply to be experienced for the moment as each member of the community brings her or his contribution to the song. When the initial sung statement is strong, it is able to sustain many improvisatory elaborations with each repetition and not lose its vitality. Each time the song recurs, the message and experience of the song weave their way into the worshiper's communion

29. C. Michael Hawn, *Gather Into One: Praying and Singing Globally* (Grand Rapids: Eerdmans, 2003), 231.

with God. This forges a path whereby singers meet God in the simplicity of song, unencumbered by performance expectations and techniques. Precisely because it is brief, worshipers are able to devote their full attention to the salient words being voiced and enter in as full participants at the same time.

Sometimes church folks resist the very idea of singing something they perceive is "not our song." While strides forward have been made, many North American congregations have been slow to include global songs in worship. Their sense of suitable songs tends toward the parochial. This is understandable but not acceptable. Pastoral musicians have a great opportunity to gently lead others to see the church as a big church! Assist them in expanding their vision of the world offering unceasing worship, and then encourage them to add their voice to those of their sisters and brothers whom they will never meet. Three approaches will help. First, take seriously the public prayers of intercession for the needs of the world.[30] Work to embrace the whole world in prayer, and then slowly let your songs partner with the prayers of the world. Second, define the community of the faithful as worldwide. It is true that each church represents a local assembly at worship; still, each one is only a small voice of a much, much larger entity—the worldwide church of Jesus Christ, past, present, and future. Sermons, small group studies, Sunday school classes, and so forth can intentionally create an expansive view of the composition of the Christian community. Third, hold before your people the ultimate community of the eternal kingdom. When Christ returns, it is to reconcile all people, all creation, into the one body for worship that was God's purpose all along. On that day, there will be "a great multitude that no one [can] count, from every nation, from all tribes and peoples and languages, standing before the throne and before the Lamb . . . saying, 'Salvation belongs to our God who is seated on the throne, and to the Lamb'" (Rev. 7:9–10)! Hawn says it well: "The church needs to sing itself into a new reality."[31] We might as well sing on earth as it will be in heaven.

To get started on your journey of embracing global songs, here are a few easy steps you can take: (1) visit ethnic congregations or multicultural churches in your region; (2) make friends with Christian sisters and brothers for which English is not their first language; (3) listen to global songs on the internet; (4) purchase some CDs or iTunes titles that represent samples of global song; (5) visit the website of the International Council of Ethnodoxologists to acquaint yourself and other worship leaders with the sights and sounds of global

30. C. Michael Hawn, "Worshiping with the Global Church," in *Worship and Mission for the Global Church: An Ethnodoxology Handbook*, ed. James R. Krabill (Pasadena, CA: William Carey Library, 2013), 431.

31. Ibid., 429.

song;[32] (6) explore some hymnals that include global songs (most mainline denominational hymnals are a great place to start); and (7) purchase some songbooks with a breadth of songs from many countries that include English translations formatted for congregational use.[33]

Don't be timid. Sometimes just doing it without a major explanation is a good thing. Simply invite worshipers to *pray with* sisters and brothers from Zimbabwe, Mexico, or Brazil. Or ask them to *lend their praise* with believers from Singapore, India, or Greece. Don't hesitate to teach the new songs to the congregation before asking them to join in. Let them hear a new song first by the leader(s). Unfortunately, song leaders have often neglected this very important dimension. Be prepared, invite warmly, frame the surrounding worship elements intentionally for good flow and purpose, lead confidently, and enjoy the results! Also, throughout the ensuing weeks continue to use the new songs; revisiting them helps to secure them in the minds and hearts of the people. If it's worth singing once, it's worth singing again.

Taizé Songs

Taizé, a unique style of worship, consists of short, cyclical songs that draw worshipers into an experience of God with each repetition. One could think of Taizé as sung Christian meditation. Silence is also an important feature of Taizé worship and is interwoven with the singing to aid in contemplation and prayer.

Much of the music of Taizé originated with Brother Robert, a member of the Taizé community in France, and an extraordinary French musician from nearby Paris, Jacques Berthier. Together they collaborated in composing much of the Taizé repertoire[34] and were especially devoted to writing songs that were easily sung by the many young people visiting from around the world. Taizé is a small village located in southeastern France from where an ecumenical group of Christian brothers have taken their community's name. Brother Roger Louis Schutz-Marsauche moved to Taizé from Switzerland in 1940, feeling called to minister to Jews, orphans, and others needing refuge from destruction in Nazi Germany. In 1944 Brother Roger founded an ecumenical community of brothers who agreed to live in poverty, celibacy, and obedience to Christ. Since World War II, the Taizé community has evolved into an

32. International Council of Ethnodoxologists, http://www.worldofworship.org.

33. I recommend C. Michael Hawn, *Halle, Halle: We Sing the World Round; Songs from the World Church for Children, Youth, and Congregation* (Garland, TX: Choristers Guild, 1999).

34. C. Michael Hawn, "Through Every Land, by Every Tongue," in *New Songs of Celebration Render: Congregational Song in the Twenty-First Century*, ed. C. Michael Hawn (Chicago: GIA, 2013), 306.

interdenominational, international community that draws many thousands of worshipers yearly, especially young adults on pilgrimage from all over the world. There are official Taizé communities now formed on every continent.

Taizé music is characterized by simple and repetitive melodies; it often uses refrains, **canons** (rounds), and **ostinatos** (repeated phrases)—various devices that make it easy for diverse worshipers to join in singing easily without printed music before them. Taizé makes use of acoustic instrumentation, primarily winds and strings. It tends to use cyclical structures or call and response with a cantor alternating with the congregation. One notable feature is the creation of layers of sounds by the addition (and eventual subtraction) of both instrumentalists and vocalists as each repetition ensues. Each song builds to a natural arc and then slowly declines in volume and intensity with each repetition.

Taizé songs now appear in many hymnals and song collections produced in the late twentieth and early twenty-first centuries. Two of the most popular songs to make their way into North American hymnals include, "Jesus, Remember Me When You Come into Your Kingdom" (the entire text is nine words), enabling singers to join the prayer of one of the thieves crucified with Jesus, and "O Lord, Hear My Prayer" based on Psalm 102. Taizé uses a wide variety of texts from psalms, **canticles**, other biblical passages, and traditional prayers. Because reconciliation is a prominent theme of the Taizé community, musicians attempt to produce songs that are intentionally ecumenical in nature—using texts and phrases familiar across denominations.[35] Taizé songs are a beautiful addition to any worship service. Their natural beauty and accessibility make them easily accepted and appreciated. In an unusual sort of way, the songs of Taizé could be described as a combination of praise chorus meets chant. The members of the Taizé community have given to the world a body of song that is universally accessible and aesthetically lovely.

A great place to begin exploring Taizé is by listening to songs from the Taizé community through their website[36] or on CDs or iTunes. Visit a Taizé service in your area (many churches have Taizé services regularly). Begin by singing one of these short songs *as* prayer during worship. A leader could sing it once with an instrument playing the melody only, and then gently invite the congregation to join in, singing it several times while adding instrumentation, if available. A very large collection of Taizé arrangements is available through GIA Publications.[37] It's a good idea to let folks *experience* a new song before

35. Some Taizé songs are written in Latin for this very reason, Latin having a long-standing tradition of use in the church and therefore being a type of cross-cultural language for Christians.
36. Taizé, http://www.taize.fr/en.
37. GIA Publications, www.giamusic.com.

they are inundated with information. If the connection between the song and the liturgical action is clear, and if the leaders are fully prepared to lead the song, worshipers will be able to enter in with ease.

Cyclical songs are growing in popularity. Hawn observes: "Although strophic hymnody remains vital, even a cursory look at the most recent hymnals reveals that refrain and cyclic structures are on the rise."[38] Our modern culture is very welcoming to songs that feel easily accessible and that engage people in multiple ways. Western society is also becoming increasingly multicultural in many places. Global song and Taizé are everyone's song. Surely it is a foretaste of the eternal kingdom when "people will come from east and west, from north and south, and will eat in the kingdom of God" (Luke 13:29).

Choruses

One genre of freestanding shorter songs is the chorus that uses a short, **through-composed** form. Compositions that do not have repeated sections are considered to be through-composed; all material, phrase by phrase, is new material. Technically, a **chorus** is a brief Christian song with one central theme. Choruses characteristically display praise or devotion of a more personal nature. This is largely due to the venues where some of the choruses have originated and thrived: the inspirational children's choruses of Sunday schools, the personal experience songs of camps and retreats, and the witness songs of gospel choruses. While Sunday school and camp songs may not be that appropriate for most corporate worship settings today, the gospel chorus has some potential, depending on the context. Coming to prominence in the 1940s and 1950s, the gospel chorus "might be described as a gospel hymn refrain without the stanzas."[39] They were used in many large evangelistic crusades and parachurch settings such as Youth for Christ.[40] Examples of freestanding gospel choruses include "Spirit of the Living God"[41] and "Turn Your Eyes upon Jesus."[42]

A more recent development of the chorus is the shorter songs that emerged out of the early years of the contemporary worship movement. During the Jesus Movement of the 1960s and 1970s, this first wave of new Christian music used idioms and instrumentation from rock 'n' roll and early rock music.

38. C. Michael Hawn, introduction to *New Songs of Celebration Render: Congregational Song in the Twenty-First Century*, ed. C. Michael Hawn (Chicago: GIA, 2013), xli.

39. David W. Music, "I Sing for I Cannot Be Silent: Gospel and Revival Hymnody in the Twentieth Century," in *New Songs of Celebration Render: Congregational Song in the Twenty-First Century*, ed. C. Michael Hawn (Chicago: GIA, 2013), 110.

40. Ibid.

41. Daniel Iverson (words and music), "Spirit of the Living God," 1926.

42. Helen H. Lemmel (words and music), "Turn Your Eyes upon Jesus," 1922.

These choruses were often referred to as "praise choruses" (praise predominated as the theme) or "Scripture choruses" (much of the content had direct quotes from Scripture or had strong scriptural allusions). The contemporary choruses were used evangelistically early on as revival fires spread first among disenfranchised youth of the cultural revolution in America beginning in the 1960s. The use of choruses in the church was very controversial in the beginning, but reinforced by the charismatic renewal movement (from the early 1960s to mid-1980s) and the reforms of Vatican II (1962–1965) that were occurring at approximately the same time, they eventually became very popular in many churches. Today these simple, freestanding songs enjoy widespread use in a broad variety of churches. Even though the contemporary worship movement has moved on from its simple beginnings, experiencing further waves of development, these choruses still serve useful purposes in worship today and should not be overlooked.

Choruses use the simplest of musical forms. All that is required are a few measures to communicate one central idea presented in a brief set of phrases. They could be described as "song bytes." Many people confuse the words "chorus" and "refrain." Gospel hymns have refrains that are mistakenly referred to as a chorus. What's more, most modern worship songs today have "choruses" that are really functioning as refrains! A refrain can't be a true refrain *without* the stanza; a chorus can't be a chorus *with* verses. Some freestanding choruses might appear to be a longer song form because they seem to have several stanzas. However, look closely, and you will see that it is the *same text* with only one or two words that are changed. In this case, it's a chorus that repeats itself with minimal word change(s). There are not enough word changes to qualify as an entirely new stanza. "He's Got the Whole World in His Hands" is a good example. Every repetition is the same text with simple word substitutions each time:[43]

> He's got the whole world in his hands . . .
> He's got you and me brother . . .
> He's got you and me sister . . .
> He's got the little bitty baby . . .[44]

Because choruses are short songs, they are typically repeated several times in order to sustain the song. One significant difference between the freestanding

43. Word changes such as "father," "mother," "brother," "sister," etc. are referred to as "family words."

44. "He's Got the Whole World in His Hands," author and composer unknown, public domain, http://www.hymnary.org/text/hes_got_the_whole_world_in_his_hands.

chorus and the cyclical or theme and variations songs is that when the contemporary chorus is repeated, it is not varied or embellished, whereas both
global songs and Taizé songs strategically vary each repetition of the cycle.
There is little to no intentional variation when choruses are repeated. This
may very well be why some congregants have critiqued the early choruses as
boring and redundant.

Like cyclical songs, choruses are beneficial in that they lend themselves
to intergenerational worship. People of all ages and backgrounds can grab
onto choruses with ease due to their low text load. When intermingled with
songs that carry a high text load, they provide musical landing places where
everyone can get on board easily. Whether your church has never used praise
choruses or has not used them recently, why not discover or rediscover them?

To get started with introducing choruses, here are two suggestions. First,
investigate some of the earlier praise chorus collections of the 1970s and
1980s. No doubt you will recall ones you knew but have forgotten. Second,
ask around in your church; there will be persons who have appreciation for
a chorus that meant something to them at an earlier time. When you find an
oldie but goodie, use it strategically in the service for two or three weeks. Come
back to it every now and then. Used properly, choruses can be comfortable
and meaningful worship expressions for all ages.

Service Music

A fourth genre of freestanding songs is what I'll call service music.
This term refers to the "musical setting[s] of the parts of the liturgy that
are to be sung."[45] Some churches invite worshipers to sing only the congregational songs while the rest of the service is entirely spoken. Other
churches have a rich heritage of singing many of the various small parts
of the worship service. Whether sung or spoken, every service, regardless
of style, makes use of brief invitations, acclamations of praise, petitions,
and so forth. Service music is an opportunity for worshipers to sing many
of the connecting parts of the liturgy as these short songs weave their way
around and through the whole service unifying the conversation between
God and people.

Service music, then, consists of brief congregational songs woven throughout the service as functional acts of the liturgy. While it is by no means inciden-
tal, service music is largely intended to carry the transitions of the liturgical
action, resulting in a "sung liturgy." It's a matter of perspective. For some

45. Foley, *Worship Music*, 279.

churches, songs constitute a distinct portion of an otherwise spoken service; for other churches, the service feels much more like a sung service with fewer portions that are spoken. Portions of the worship service that are commonly sung include doxologies and the *Kyrie*.

A **doxology** is any short song of direct praise to God, often using Trinitarian affirmations. Translated from the Greek as "words of glory,"[46] doxologies appear frequently in the Old and New Testaments[47] and have been an integral part of Christian worship from the very beginning. Presumably used at the conclusion of teaching, exhortation, and sermons, doxologies likely "gave the congregation the opportunity to make the message its own."[48] Thomas Ken's doxology, set to the tune "OLD 100th," is the most well known of the doxologies today. Because of this, it has earned the popular title, "The Doxology." It is only one part of a long hymn, but the brief, Trinitarian song of praise has been sung as service music for centuries.

> Praise God from whom all blessings flow;
> Praise him, all creatures here below;
> Praise him above, ye heavenly host;
> Praise Father, Son and Holy Ghost.[49]

Another example of a doxology is known as the ***Gloria Patri***. The title comes from its Latin origin: "Glory to the Father." It is another example of Trinitarian praise:

> Glory be to the Father, and to the Son, and to the Holy Ghost;
> as it was in the beginning, is now, and ever shall be,
> world without end. Amen.[50]

The text of the *Gloria Patri* dates from the second century. It has been used by Christians to conclude the psalter lesson since the fourth century.[51] Today it is available in myriad musical settings from chant to contemporary, and

---

46. Ibid., 94.

47. For instance, there are many spontaneous doxologies throughout Paul's letters. See Rom. 11:33–36.

48. Gerhard Delling, *Worship in the New Testament*, trans. Percy Scott (Philadelphia: Westminster, 1962), 64, quoted in Edward Foley, *Foundations of Christian Music: The Music of Pre-Constantinian Christianity* (Collegeville, MN: Liturgical Press, 1996), 77.

49. Thomas Ken, "Praise God from Whom All Blessings Flow," 1674, public domain, http://www.hymnary.org/text/praise_god_from_whom_all_blessings_ken.

50. "Glory Be to the Father," author and composer unknown, public domain, http://www.hymnary.org/text/glory_be_to_the_father_and_to_the_son.

51. Foley, *Worship Music*, 126.

it is still appropriate for the conclusion of Scripture readings, though it is fitting in other places as well. (Wouldn't it make for a great affirmation at the
conclusion of the service?)

Another part of the worship service that is often sung is the *Kyrie* (also
called the ***Kyrie eleison***, meaning "Lord, have mercy"). A corporate petition
sung by the community, the *Kyrie* calls on the favor of God. It is an appeal
for divine help in time of need. The *Kyrie* is a Greek addition to Christian
worship since at least the eighth century,[52] and its text is composed of three
main parts: *Kyrie eleison* ("Lord, have mercy"), *Christe eleison* ("Christ, have
mercy"), concluding again with *Kyrie eleison*. It was originally sung at the time
of the primary intercessory prayers;[53] later it appeared near the beginning of
the service. It is also appropriate to pray "Lord, have mercy" in conjunction
with prayers of confession or in preparation for Holy Communion. Though
the *Kyrie* has ancient roots, it has received recent attention as evidenced by
settings from contemporary artists such as David Crowder, Keith and Krysten
Getty, and Michael Gungor.

To get started with including service music in worship, here are a few
tips: (1) Start small. Don't get bogged down with liturgical intricacies, and
don't do too much at once. Just try one piece for a while, until it becomes
comfortable. (2) Examine your service and find places where spoken words
could be sung. Find a well-known chorus or fragment of a song that could
be used as a call to prayer, a benediction, and so on. Don't change the order
of service; simply translate something that would ordinarily be spoken into
a song. (3) Stay within your style. It's true that more traditional or liturgical
churches have historically used service music, but that doesn't mean a different kind of congregation has to sing in that style. Any of the types of songs
presented in this chapter supply options for service music.

Service music, though forgotten about in many settings, is one more
great way to involve people. It helps them to understand that the liturgy
is not static but is on the move, and they are participating in its dynamic
forward motion.

Spontaneous Songs

One final type of shorter songs to consider is spontaneous songs. It may
seem odd to think of spontaneous songs as a type at all, but believe it or not,

---

52. Ibid., 173.

53. Dennis C. Smolarski, SJ, *Liturgical Literacy: From Anamnesis to Worship* (New York:
Paulist Press, 1989), 134.

spontaneous singing has a long history in the church and is something that might just be a breath of fresh air for today's worshipers.

Features. What is meant by spontaneous congregational song? It has one primary feature: it is singing that is not anticipated or premeditated but occurs "in the moment" through the Holy Spirit's leading. It is unplanned singing that happens often because a response is felt to be urgent. A song allows for the needed release. Spontaneous songs are shorter songs sung from memory or created in "real time." They are part of what was likely meant when Paul encouraged the churches to sing "spiritual songs."

Functions. The purpose for spontaneous singing is the same as that of all congregational song: to glorify God and to edify believers. However, one aspect is unique: greater shared leadership. Spontaneous singing opens up the possibility for song leading *from within the congregation* rather than *from the front.* While the pastoral musician continues to perform her or his duties, he or she does so while watching for whomever God will use to accomplish his purposes for the assembly. Does *anyone* have a song? They should sing it if the setting seems right for the purpose of edification. It is not done to perform a solo or for self-gratification; it is done with the hope of everyone joining in. This is horizontal leadership. The song leader does not need to initiate or lead every song; other worshipers can contribute spontaneous leadership when appropriate. Pastoral musicians will learn to work *with* the community and discerningly guide spontaneous singing wisely.

Forms. The structure used for some of the genres explained below tend to be **free form** or through-composed. Free form suggests independence from the constraints of conventional composition.[54] However, no form is completely free, for there is arguably always some measure of coherence that occurs in order for it to be viable.[55] Since some spontaneous song is created on the spot, no previously conceived compositional form drives it. It may take shape with a noticeable structure, but that becomes recognizable only as it occurs. The use of free form often results in through-composed music because the song tends to be *received* rather than *composed.* Inspired by the Holy Spirit, a message is delivered through the singer, who is more concerned with the word to be delivered than with the musical organization of the song. Spontaneous songs could refer to a number of things, but I will identify three in particular: (1) singing familiar songs as the Spirit leads, (2) improvised songs, and (3) singing in tongues.

54. Wallace Berry, *Form in Music: An Examination of Traditional Techniques of Musical Structure and Their Application in Historical and Contemporary Styles* (Englewood Cliffs, NJ: Prentice-Hall, 1966), 436.
55. Ibid.

Familiar Songs

Occasionally in worship someone may feel inspired to lead a familiar song. Have you ever been in such a setting? Perhaps there was an especially moving time of prayer or testimony or sermon that occurred. Unexpectedly, a voice just began singing—someone from the congregation—and suddenly other worshipers joined in, seizing the moment. In this case nothing was programmed or prepared; someone just naturally voiced the song that was in his or her heart, and it became the heartfelt song, for that moment, of the whole community. If you've experienced this, it can feel like the most natural thing in the world. No rehearsal, no introduction, no explanation, no instrumentation—just a simple, lovely song that rises from someone's heart and is taken up by other worshipers and then fades into the heavens.

Naturally, familiar songs are in the memory bank of the community; therefore, folks are able to sing without needing printed words. Shorter songs suit spontaneous singing well, not only because they are more likely memorized but also because songs that carry a low text load often serve as response-type songs rather than revelation-type songs. Lengthy songs that carry a high text load would detract from the situation.

Improvised Songs

Improvised songs are songs that have not been previously composed and are not intended to be written down for future use. They are sung ad lib by someone who is urged by the Spirit to sing what is on his or her heart on behalf of the community. The apostle Paul alludes to such a practice when he writes to the Corinthian church, "When you come together, each one has a hymn" (1 Cor. 14:26). More definitive is Tertullian's description of singing at the agape meal: "After the washing of hands and the lighting of lamps (*lumina*), each is urged to come into the middle and sing to God, either from the sacred scriptures or from his own invention (*de proprio ingenio*)."[56]

With improvised songs the community cannot sing along, for no one knows the song; it is created on the spot. Perhaps it is a Scripture verse that is given a melody, or a prophetic message that is intoned. Whatever the case, it is a song that can be understood by everyone and is edifying in character. It should be brief, serve its purpose of glorifying God and encouraging others, and then conclude. For the Quakers, who wait silently for the Spirit to move

56. James McKinnon, *Music in Early Christian Literature* (Cambridge: Cambridge University Press, 1993), 43.

a worshiper to speak, pray, or sing impromptu, music is *only* spontaneous.[57] Some worshiping communities will be more conducive than others for improvised singing. If this is something that fits your church's ethos, learn to welcome it but also to establish its proper parameters.

Singing in Tongues

Singing in tongues is spontaneous singing inspired by the Holy Spirit that transcends known language. This practice has a long history in the church, though it is perceived and explained in various ways. It can consist of nondistinct syllables that flood worshipers' speech when mortals are at a loss for words in praise of God. St. Augustine referred positively to "jubilation"—singing ecstatically when mere words were inadequate. He wrote of the great tension one experiences when "you cannot speak of [God] because he transcends our speech; and if you cannot speak of him, yet may not remain silent, what else can you do but cry out in jubilation, so that your heart may tell its joy without words, and the unbounded rush of gladness not be cramped by syllables?"[58] Singing in tongues can also refer to singing in an unknown language, similar to speaking in tongues. Paul refers to this as "speaking mysteries in the Spirit" (1 Cor. 14:2).

Obviously this type of spontaneous singing is most fitting for those congregations of the Pentecostal or charismatic traditions—communities that

57. James F. White, *Protestant Worship: Traditions in Transition* (Louisville: Westminster John Knox, 1989), 143.

58. Augustine, "Exposition on the Psalms," in *Expositions on the Psalms 1–32*, trans. Maria Boulding (Hyde Park, NY: New City, 2000), 401. A question arises regarding Augustine's reference to singing in a way that cannot be "articulated in words" and "abandons distinct syllables." Is this a reference to guttural jubilant singing or possibly singing in tongues? While there is debate on the spiritual gift of "known" and "unknown" tongues in the ante-Nicene, Nicene, and post-Nicene fathers, Augustine clearly believed that the gifts of "known" tongues had ceased to exist in the church. He states,

> In the earliest times, "the Holy Ghost fell upon them that believed: and they spake with tongues," which they had not learned, "as the Spirit gave them utterance." These were signs adapted to the time. For there behooved to be that betokening of the Holy Spirit in all tongues, to shew that the Gospel of God was to run through all tongues over the whole earth. That thing was done for a betokening, *and it passed away.* (Augustine, "Homilies on the First Epistle of John," trans. H. Browne, *The Nicene and Post-Nicene Fathers*, First Series, ed. Philip Schaff [Grand Rapids: Eerdmans, 1956], 7:497–98 [emphasis in original])

While Augustine's statement does not rule out the possibility of "unknown" tongues in this passage, there is no corroborating evidence that Augustine believed in this type of tongues as a spiritual gift. For further discussion and debate on the gift of "known" and "unknown" tongues and the early church fathers including Augustine, see Nathan Busenitz, "The Gift of Tongues: Comparing the Church Fathers with Contemporary Pentecostalism," *The Master's Seminary Journal* 17, no. 1 (Spring 2006): 61–78; Richard Hogue, *Tongues: A Theological History of Christian Glossolalia* (Mustang, OK: Tate Publishing, 2010); and Ronald A. N. Kydd, *Charismatic Gifts in the Early Church* (Peabody, MA: Hendrickson, 1984).

welcome manifestations of the gifts of the Spirit during worship. For those who encourage speaking or singing in tongues in public worship, such spontaneous singing can be inspirational. Occasionally an individual will sing in tongues during worship, but it is more common for many or all of the worshipers present to do so at once. Generally, the same admonition of the apostle Paul applies to *singing* in tongues that does to *speaking* in tongues. Specifically, if an individual is singing in tongues, interpretation is necessary (1 Cor. 14:27b). The case of the whole congregation singing in tongues at once should be viewed as a corporate prayer to God and thus not needing interpretation. In all cases, it must be done strictly for building up believers (1 Cor. 14:26b), and all things are to be done decently and in order (1 Cor. 14:40). This is likely what Paul had in mind when he wrote to the Corinthian church: "What should be done then, my friends? When you come together, each one has a hymn, a lesson, a revelation, a tongue, or an interpretation. Let all things be done for building up" (1 Cor. 14:26).

Conclusion

This chapter has introduced the music architect to the incredible value of using shorter song forms in worship. They have much to offer any and all congregations. Their many benefits include their easy engagement, their inclusive nature, their lending of themselves so naturally as response in the revelation/response dialogue, their accompaniment to and content for all kinds of liturgical actions, and their ability to provide commentary on the primary words and actions of worship. In the next chapter we will discuss longer songs. Together they provide a fully orbed expression of song for today's singing church.

Key Terms

a cappella. "In the chapel style," referring to unaccompanied singing.

antiphon. The congregational singing of a repeated phrase from a psalm alternating with the leader singing the verses.

canons. A melody begun by one party is also sung in its entirety by another party in exact imitation while entering slightly after the first; canons may include multiple voices entering similarly, resulting in a layering of one melodic line; called a "round" in popular use.

canticles. Song texts taken from parts of the Bible other than the book of Psalms.

cantor. In present usage, a leader of congregational song; also, one who sings the verses in responsorial singing.

chorus. A short Christian song with one central theme, often of personal praise or devotion.

cyclical songs. Brief songs repeated a number of times, usually with variation.

doxology. Any short song of direct praise to God, often using Trinitarian affirmations.

free form. Improvisatory singing.

Gloria Patri. A Trinitarian doxology beginning, "Glory be to the Father."

Kyrie eleison. Greek for "Lord, have mercy"; part of a three-part sung prayer of the ancient Christian church: "*Kyrie eleison, Christe eleison, Kyrie eleison.*"

ostinatos. A musical phrase that is repeated in one part (vocal or instrumental) persistently throughout the piece.

pentatonic. A composition based on a five-note scale; in Western music, gaps appear in two places within the stepwise movement of notes in the seven-note diatonic scale, creating a somewhat open, ambiguous tonal effect.

response. A brief refrain sung in alternation to verses or stanzas sung by the cantor.

responsorial song. Song that is sung in alternation with a leader or other singers.

service music. Brief congregational songs woven throughout the service as functional acts of the liturgy.

theme and variations. A melodic theme is established in the first sung statement, which is then followed by successive, varied presentations of the same theme and that alternate with the original melody.

through-composed. Compositions that do not have repeated sections; all material, section by section, is new material.

versicle. A short statement sung from Scripture followed by a response; e.g., Ps. 51:15: "O Lord, open my lips" (versicle) "and my mouth will declare your praise" (response).

To Learn More

Books

Abbington, James, ed. *Readings in African American Church Music and Worship.* Chicago: GIA, 2001.

Boyer, Horace Clarence. *The Golden Age of Gospel*. Chicago: University of Illinois Press, 2000.

Hawn, C. Michael. *Gather Into One: Praying and Singing Globally*. Grand Rapids: Eerdmans, 2003.

King, Roberta R. *A Time to Sing: A Manual for the African Church*. Nairobi, Kenya: Evangel, 1999.

Krabill, James R., ed. *Worship and Mission for the Global Church: An Ethnodoxology Handbook*. Pasadena, CA: William Carey Library, 2013.

Witvliet, John D. *The Biblical Psalms in Christian Worship: A Brief Introduction and Guide to Resources*. Grand Rapids: Eerdmans, 2007.

Songbooks

Bell, John L. *We Walk His Way: Shorter Songs for Worship*. Glasgow, UK: Wild Goose Resource Group, 2008.

Damon, Dan, ed. *At Your Altars: Chants, Refrains, and Short Songs*. Carol Stream, IL: Hope, 2014.

Hawn, C. Michael. *Halle, Halle: We Sing the World Round; Songs from the World Church for Children, Youth, and Congregation*. Garland, TX: Choristers Guild, 1999.

Websites

The International Council of Ethnodoxologists, www.worldofworship.org.

Engage

Reading about shorter songs is one thing; incorporating them in worship is another. The most important result of this chapter must be that music architects will expand their repertoire of shorter songs to enrich worship. To get started, follow these suggestions:

1. Out of the ten genres discussed in this chapter (Negro spirituals, black gospel songs, antiphons, global songs, Taizé songs, choruses, service music, spontaneous familiar songs, improvised songs, and singing in tongues), choose two that are new to you and your congregation and that you could envision being helpful in your worship service.
2. Research more about the two genres' history and features. Then write a brief, interesting article for a church newsletter to introduce this type of song to the congregation. Include an engaging graphic to go with the article.

3. Find one actual song for each of your two choices. Experiment with ways to sing it. Teach it to your praise team or choir. Consider which instruments, if any, would help to capture the original feel of the song. (Little is much for shorter songs.)

4. Ask yourself what function each song could play in the service. Is it a prayer or an invitation to a specific worship element or an affirmation of faith?

5. After you are at ease with a new shorter song, give it a try in worship. Don't overexplain it; just do it well and with enthusiasm.

6. Repeat the song in the next few weeks to allow the congregation to become comfortable with it.

7. Now move on to the next new song. The possibilities are endless!

7

Maximizing
Longer Song Forms

In this chapter, various genres of longer songs will be explored. These include classic hymns, metrical psalms, gospel songs, modern hymns, and modern worship songs. Before reading about them (don't look ahead!), simply begin to think about the longer songs you may or may not presently use in your context and why. Though you may not be familiar with some of these genres yet, just begin where you are at the moment. Here are some questions to get you started:

1. What genres of longer songs does your church sing now?
2. Why are these included in your repertoire of congregational song?
3. Do they tend to be of one stylistic type or several different types?
4. Do you use longer and shorter songs in the same service? If not, why not? If so, how do they relate to each other?
5. What format is used to give singers the words of longer songs (projected electronically, songbooks, inserts in printed orders of service, etc.)? What are the advantages and/or disadvantages of various formats?

Now, read the rest of this chapter to expand your thinking about the use of longer songs in worship today.

Expand

As we are discovering, each structural form has certain things in which it excels. Remember, both shorter and longer songs working interdependently offer the fullest and richest experience that a pastoral musician can provide. Each one complementing the other throughout a service of worship is ideal. A taxonomy for categorizing types of songs was begun in chapter 6 where shorter songs were examined. This chapter will complete the two-part taxonomy by explaining the unique characteristics of longer songs, identifying various types, offering examples, and giving practical guidance for the music architect in taking full advantage of longer forms.

Because much material is presented, please review this outline of the chapter to get your bearings before reading further.

Longer Songs
Pure Stanza Songs
    Classic Hymns
    Metrical Psalms
Stanza Plus Songs
    Gospel Songs
    Modern Hymns
    Modern Worship Songs

Introduction

A second broad category of worship song is longer song forms. Longer songs refer to songs that are more substantial in length and developed in content than those discussed in the previous chapter. How long is long? This question can't be answered by counting the number of words or measures of music. Perhaps the best answer is long enough to fully develop an idea, long enough to narrate a story, long enough to paraphrase a psalm, long enough to give a detailed personal witness of salvation or an experience of God's faithfulness, or long enough to offer a thoughtful prayer. Longer songs offer songwriters the time and space needed to go into poetic and musical detail. Remember, long doesn't necessarily mean better; nevertheless, well-developed statements related to Christian faith are needed for public worship. Longer song forms are vehicles to meet that need.

Longer songs have a different goal than shorter songs: they exist for elaboration. Have you ever asked a child a question and received a one-word response? The answer may have told you *what* you needed to know, but not *why* or *how*. Perhaps you followed up with, "Please explain." Longer songs give the songwriter opportunity to explain—to say more about the subject so that worshipers have the chance to elaborate their thoughts and feelings about or to God and others. Longer songs accommodate lyrics that are more word-dense. Songs that carry a "high text load" are songs that include much content.[1] They are not "wordy" in the negative sense, but they do allow for lyricists to use many words economically in order to make concepts of a divine nature both clear and beautiful. Because more room is afforded for explanation and elaboration than short songs can supply, longer songs most often make use of the structural device of the stanza (explained below). Shorter songs often repeat a brief amount of text and tune; the meaning of the words is assumed. Longer songs, however, stretch the structure to allow for the meaning to be made clear as the stanzas unfold; the meaning of the words is not assumed but made explicit. Long songs have the capacity to narrate God's story in greater detail, provide educational instruction in the Christian faith, give us a means to sing creedal statements corporately, and call the church to holy living for the sake of the world. They will "instruct, educate, nurture, cultivate, rebuke, exhort, discipline, warn, delight, enlighten, edify, develop."[2]

Longer song structures enable things that shorter song structures are simply not designed to do. First, longer forms can provide for reasoned theological statements. While longer structures do have their limits, a rational presentation of developed theological thought can be artfully written for the congregation to sing. (Charles Wesley's hymn "Love Divine, All Loves Excelling" is a fine example.) Second, they can assist with reasoned praise. In this case, praise is associated with specific works of God; praise does not just circle around overhead but comes in for a landing. God's praise is connected with God's actions (the gospel song "How Great Thou Art" by Stuart Hine is a good illustration). Third, longer songs can accommodate extended testimony. A testimony is a personal story of God's intervention and deliverance (e.g., John Newton's gospel hymn "Amazing Grace"). Fourth, they can supply an expansive framework for paraphrasing whole portions of Scripture (e.g., "The Lord's My Shepherd, I'll Not Want," a paraphrase of Psalm 23 from the *Scottish Psalter*).

Because the longer worship songs typically include stanzas, we will look at two types of stanza songs. I call them "pure stanza" songs and "stanza plus"

1. Roberta R. King, *A Time to Sing: A Manual for the African Church* (Nairobi, Kenya: Evangel, 1999), 61.
2. Marva J. Dawn, *A Royal "Waste" of Time: The Splendor of Worshiping God and Being Church for the World* (Grand Rapids: Eerdmans, 1999), 15–16.

songs (stanzas with developed refrains and other additional components). Each one's features, functions, and form will be explored briefly. We will then examine a few primary genres of song that fall under these two types: classic hymns, metrical psalms, gospel songs, modern hymns, and modern worship songs.

Pure Stanza Songs

Pure stanza songs are composed exclusively of a series of stanzas, all working together to carry a primary idea or narrative from beginning to end.

Features. In pure stanza songs, the stanza is the primary organizational unit of the song. A **stanza** is a set of poetic lines that is unified around one aspect of the overall theme of the song. Stanzas are like paragraphs of a poem; in fact, most longer songs are exactly that—poems to be sung corporately. Each stanza carries one subtheme to completion while all of the stanzas work together to support the main idea of the song. Consequently, pure stanza songs use a linear lyrical approach to the text. Stanzas help to unwrap a scriptural idea or make a theological argument, to spin a story line or to deepen a prayer. They depend on continuity of thought as the whole song unfolds coherently, taking the singers from point A to point B, often with a sense of building toward a climax of some sort (ending with the big point summarized, or with praise, or with petitions for ourselves or the world, etc.).

The number of stanzas varies widely according to what is needed to accomplish a song's purpose. A pure stanza song may have as few as two stanzas or up to dozens of stanzas. Oftentimes hymnals include only a portion of the stanzas of the original hymn. Charles Wesley's "O for a Thousand Tongues to Sing" will typically appear in hymnals with four to seven stanzas, yet the full hymn consists of eighteen stanzas.[3]

Functions. The primary function of pure stanza songs is to perpetuate the Christian faith more expansively through song—faith *affirmed* in doctrinal propositions, and faith *expressed* in praise and prayer. The body of Christ singing its faith is a primary means for the transmission of truth, both in terms of objective reality and in how believers experience that truth in their lives. Pure stanza songs are the most spacious liturgical song structure to do this. This type of song functions in worship then as a means for Christian education, transmission of dogma, creedal statements, elaborate praise, profound prayers, exhortation of believers, calls for action, and witnessing of personal transformation.

3. Robin Knowles Wallace, "O for a Thousand Tongues to Sing," *The Hymn*, no. 2 (April 1998): 9, 46.

Form. As mentioned, pure stanza songs depend entirely upon stanzas to communicate a developed message. They may be aptly described as a sequential structure.[4] Typically none of the text is repeated; however, there may be an occasional brief phrase that recurs as a device for emphasis (e.g., each stanza in the hymn "Holy, Holy, Holy! Lord God, Almighty," by Reginald Heber, begins with the threefold acclamation, "Holy, Holy, Holy!" in praise of the Trinity).

The tune from stanza to stanza is the same for each strophe (another word for stanza, used especially in poetry). When the identical melody is used for each stanza, the music is said to be **strophic**. This musical repetition makes the song easier to sing by lending a sense of security and familiarity. The tunes for pure stanza songs must be composed well in order to (1) serve each individual stanza well, and (2) bear repetition. Let's now explore two prominent genres of congregational song that consistently use pure stanza form: classic hymns and metrical psalms.

Classic Hymns

The most obvious genre that uses pure stanza form is classic hymns (modern hymns, defined differently, are addressed below). Hymns have been a part of Christian worship since the New Testament era. Each generation since then has sung hymns, though the hymnic forms have varied widely over the centuries and from place to place. New Testament hymns to Christ, early Christian hymns written to combat specific heresies, Greek and Latin hymns, medieval office hymns, Reformation hymns, and more—each has its distinctive characteristics and place in worship history. For our purposes we will consider classic hymns to refer to the poetically conceived Western hymnody of Protestantism, written over a wide range of time (approximately the past six hundred years), and originating largely in Europe and North America. Described this way, classic hymns would include hymns from Martin Luther's German Reformation to current hymns of the twenty-first century. This is admittedly a wide swath of territory, but it is necessarily broad because many fine examples of hymns with staying power have been produced in these centuries and locales. Hymns rooted in the British hymn tradition of the seventeenth through nineteenth centuries are especially noteworthy for their well-written poems in stanza form and their use of classical poetic devices, meters, rhyme schemes, and so on.

What is a hymn? A **hymn** is a well-constructed poem that conveys developed statements of Christian faith, to or about the triune God, expressed in metered

4. C. Michael Hawn, *One Bread, One Body: Exploring Cultural Diversity in Worship* (Herndon, VA: Alban Institute, 2003), 127.

stanzas, and written to be sung devotionally by the Christian community.[5] Because classic hymns are poems, the stanzas are most often rhymed and have a metrical pattern of strong/weak accents to the syllables in each line. The text's rhyme and meter greatly enhance the ability to sing corporately and also to memorize easily. Technically speaking, the term "hymn" refers strictly to the text of the song; "hymn tune" refers to the melody assigned to the text. Most hymn tunes are available to be paired with a number of different hymn texts; this variable can add a refreshing perspective if matched wisely. (The practice of interchanging song texts with various tunes is even noted in the book of Psalms when assigned tunes are designated at the beginning of some of the psalms [see Pss. 56, 57, 58].) Hymns are distinguished, then, from shorter songs because they have more developed thought, are highly influenced by Western poetic practices, and include virtually no repetition.

In some respects a hymn offers unlimited possibilities for creative renderings with regard to length, styling, topic, and various musical choices (meter, key, rhythmic patterns, etc.). At the same time, it is one of the more difficult art forms to master for there are several established boundaries that must be observed all at once: a hymn must be understandable, singable, theologically accurate, tight in poetic form, self-restrained in musical expression, convincing in text/tune relationship, corporate in voice, and so forth.

Some great hymn writers were master poets of their era, including George Herbert, John Milton, and John Bunyan. Charles Wesley and Isaac Watts are two exceptional examples from the British hymn tradition. At the same time, most hymns have been written by common folk who made their significant contributions. Tunes for hymns come from a variety of places: commissioned, local folk tunes, and classical composers of the day.[6]

Perhaps you noted that I included the twenty-first century in the period of classic hymn writing. That is because hymn writing has never died out. Not only does it continue today but it is also gathering steam! Many people have the mistaken impression that the era of hymn writing is over and that hymnals are closed collections, representing only the songs of the past. Nothing could be farther from reality. Many major new **hymnals** have been published in the twenty-first century, each of which contains the profound work of noted new hymnists. (They also contain a very wide variety of congregational songs that are not exclusively hymns.) Numerous contemporary authors and composers are producing masterful hymns for the church today. Of special note is the

5. Constance M. Cherry, *The Worship Architect: A Blueprint for Designing Culturally Relevant and Biblically Faithful Services* (Grand Rapids: Baker Academic, 2010), 161 (adapted).
6. Harry Eskew and Hugh T. McElrath, *Sing with Understanding: An Introduction to Christian Hymnology*, 2nd ed., rev. and expanded (Nashville: Church Street Press, 1995), 139–40.

work of Brian Wren, Thomas Troeger, Carl Daw, Richard Leach, Ruth Duck, Shirley Murray, Daniel Damon, Timothy Dudley-Smith, Sylvia Dunstan, Fred Kaan, Gracia Grindal, Bryan Leach, John Bell, Jane Marshall, Susan Cherwien, and Adam Tice, to name only some.[7] Their hymns are faithful to the expectations of classic hymns—they are in stanza form,[8] they use poetic devices, they are written for corporate expression, and so on—yet they are also fresh and creative in lyrical expression and much broader in subject. While they write new, vibrant, and refreshing hymns, they still choose to accept the constraints necessary to make the meaning understandable to many singers at once. Hymn writers do not have the same kind of freedom of expression permitted by poets who write primarily for self-expression. Instead, they sacrifice freedom for service to the community.

Many churches that have neglected hymns in recent years are rediscovering the profound value of hymns. If you are a music architect who wants to become acquainted (or reacquainted) with hymns, here are some practical suggestions. First, borrow some hymnals, both older and newer. Look at how the hymnal is organized by section. Sing several hymns from each section—don't just read them. Find a pianist and some friends and begin to enjoy the musical sounds and lovely phrases. Second, become friends with someone who knows and loves hymn singing. Ask them to share their passion for singing hymns and to suggest a few of their favorites. Third, listen to CDs or watch YouTube examples of great hymns. Pay attention to the distinctly different ways hymns are presented according to their original styling. By no means should every hymn be sung with piano and/or organ accompaniment. Start to think about how you can help your people capture the essence of each hymn as it might have sounded when originally sung.[9]

Hymns in pure stanza form have a great deal to offer every worshiping community. Many young people today welcome the chance to explore this rich heritage of song that not only connects them to the past but also gives them an opportunity to reaffirm and express a spirituality that is timeless.

Metrical Psalms

A second genre of pure stanza songs is known as the **metrical psalm**, a biblical psalm that is paraphrased and refashioned into poetic verse for the purpose

---

7. Most of these modern-day hymnists are presented as significant hymn writers of the latter half of the twentieth century by Paul Westermeyer in *With Tongues of Fire: Profiles in 20th-Century Hymn Writing* (St. Louis: Concordia, 1995).

8. Some noted hymnists also use refrain form.

9. The videos and books by Alice Parker are of great assistance.

of corporate song in worship. Altering the text as needed, the words of the psalm are arranged in metrical patterns of strong/weak stresses; rhyme and other poetic devices are also employed. The end result is a clear resemblance to one of the psalms for the sake of believers singing it together. It would be too difficult to pick up a Bible and sing a psalm corporately without someone arranging the text and composing a tune. Paraphrases range in degree of literal restatement; however, metrical psalms follow along with the actual lines of the psalms in an obvious way. There are many different themes of metrical psalms including praise, petition, and lament.

Most metrical psalms are written in pure stanza form. They very much resemble hymns: they have well-crafted, lengthier texts that appear in stanzas; they use metered phrases; they have traditional rhyme schemes; and they employ other poetic devices liberally. Also like the hymn, the music is strophic (the same melody accompanies each stanza). The main difference is that metrical psalms restate Scripture directly, whereas hymns are free to address any Christian devotional topic. A hymn may be *based on* a psalm through use of allusion rather than directly incorporating the psalm's phrases (e.g., "A Mighty Fortress Is Our God" [Martin Luther/Psalm 46], "O God Our Help in Ages Past" [Isaac Watts/Psalm 90], and "O Worship the King" [Robert Grant/Psalm 104]).[10] But metrical psalms make a more intentional, obvious attempt to restate psalms fairly strictly from verse to verse. Of course, some connections are clearer than others.

Metrical psalms developed in the early sixteenth century as a direct result of the influence of several Reformers, especially John Calvin. With congregations liberated to sing in worship once again (something previously not encouraged—or worse, forbidden in late medieval liturgical practice), it became necessary to create congregational songs for the people to sing. In Germany, Luther encouraged the writing of hymns and tunes in addition to the singing of psalms. He took a broader view of congregational song than that of his French counterpart, John Calvin, who did not support the singing of hymns because their texts were not directly from Scripture and therefore did not enable the people to sing only the pure word of God. Calvin did not invent metrical psalmody; he "first heard psalm singing during his first visit to Strasbourg."[11] However, shortly thereafter he produced his first **psalter** (a book of songs with text directly from the psalms) consisting of twenty-two

10. Examples are from John D. Witvliet, *The Biblical Psalms in Christian Worship: A Brief Introduction and Guide to Resources* (Grand Rapids: Eerdmans, 2007), 108.

11. John D. Witvliet, *Worship Seeking Understanding: Windows into Christian Practice* (Grand Rapids: Baker Academic, 2003), 205.

texts authored by Clement Marot and himself.[12] They "were set to tunes drawn primarily from the earlier German psalters."[13] After several evolving editions, the complete *Genevan Psalter* was published in 1562 and included all 150 psalms plus a setting of the Ten Commandments and the Song of Simeon from the Gospel of Luke. These texts were versified by Marot, with Theodore de Béze completing the task on Marot's death, and were set to 125 different tunes, primarily written by Louis Bourgeois, a distinguished composer whom Calvin enlisted for the task.

Calvin's commitment to psalm singing was nothing short of remarkable. Detailed tables, indicating which psalms were to be sung at each Sunday morning, Sunday afternoon, and Wednesday service "were framed and hung in the three Genevan churches."[14] This allowed for the entire psalter to be sung in seventeen to twenty-five weeks, depending on which psalter edition was in use.[15] The metrical psalms of Calvin's reformation work in France and Switzerland are a distinct contribution to Protestant hymnody.

Virtually every denomination sings psalms in some form, but churches in the Reformed tradition with direct historical and spiritual ties to Calvin have faithfully maintained and further developed the singing of psalms in worship. Their current hymnals and/or psalters continue to testify to this emphasis. A great source, therefore, for exploring metrical psalms are the hymnals and songbooks from within various Reformed denominations. However, virtually every significant hymnal contains fine metrical psalms. Some of the more common psalms to cross denominational boundaries include "All People That on Earth Do Dwell" (Ps. 100), "I'll Praise My Maker While I've Breath" (Ps. 146), and "My Shepherd Will Supply My Need" (Ps. 23), to name just a few.

If you'd like to explore the beauty and power of metrical psalm singing, here are a few tips for getting started. First, research your church's hymnal or database to discover if you are already singing metrical psalms and just didn't know it. Bringing awareness to psalm singing will help your church to know when they are quite literally singing Scripture. Second, borrow some hymnals from churches in the Reformed tradition (the Christian Reformed Church, the Reformed Church in America, various Presbyterian denominations, etc.). Using the index, try to find some gems. Third, introduce metrical psalm singing to other worship leaders in your church. Acquaint them with the beauty of singing versified psalms. Fourth, do a group Bible study on a psalm passage while also studying the corresponding metrical psalm. For example,

12. Ibid., 205–6.
13. Ibid., 206.
14. Ibid., 210.
15. Ibid.

study Psalm 103 in conjunction with the lovely "O Bless the Lord, My Soul"
by James Montgomery.[16] Fifth, try writing your own metrical psalm; it is a
wonderful devotional and artistic experience. You just may arrive at a very
useful psalm setting for your congregation.

In this section, we have explored one type of longer song, the pure stanza
song, and two representative genres: classic hymns and metrical psalms. Their
value is summarized well by Paul Jones:

> Hymns and psalms are not simply an optional part of worship; they are central
> to it. . . . They represent the corporate voice of God's people, over the span of
> many generations, responding to his Word, to creation, to teaching, to creeds,
> and to truth. Good Christian hymns help protect us from a theology-of-the-
> moment, and they bolster our knowledge of God. This is no dead form or
> antiquated art. It is a living, organic, energizing force that often calls us to ser-
> vice and reminds us of why we should serve. Hymns and psalms communicate
> cardinal Christian doctrines and biblical teaching.[17]

Hymns and psalms are vital for the church to sing—any and all churches.
What they contribute to the body of Christ in terms of theological understanding, spiritual formation, and internalization of the word of God is beyond
measure. Leaders in recent decades have made the unfortunate assumption
that certain age groups prefer hymns while others do not. This kind of dichotomy needs to be challenged. To make these types of age-specific claims
demonstrates a lack of relevancy in relating to postmodern worshipers who
generally defy such dichotomies.

Stanza Plus Songs

A second type of longer song may be called stanza plus—stanzas that conclude
with an additional well-developed refrain. The refrain is sometimes referred
to as a "chorus," but as we have seen a chorus is really a freestanding form
in its own right (see chap. 6).

Features. The primary feature of stanza plus songs is the use of the refrain.
A **refrain** is the portion of a song that recurs at the conclusion of each stanza,
using the same music and text as it returns each time. The term is used in the
same manner in poetry where the refrain is "a phrase or verse that recurs at

16. James Montgomery, "O Bless the Lord, My Soul," public domain, http://www.hymnary
.org/text/o_bless_the_lord_my_soul_his_grace_to_th.

17. Paul S. Jones, *Singing and Making Music: Issues in Church Music Today* (Phillipsburg,
NJ: P&R, 2006), 69–70.

intervals, especially at the end of a stanza."[18] The refrain's use in poetry is relevant since the tradition of hymn singing is that of sung poems.

Refrains come in a variety of types and sizes. They have been used throughout the ages in many different sacred settings with songs of a religious nature. Ancient Hebrew chant involved the congregation in short, simple refrains, perhaps as brief as intoning a singular word such as "alleluia" or "amen" after each verse of a psalm.[19] Some classic hymns include a very brief, minimally developed litany-type response at the end of each stanza that is considered a short refrain. For example, the hymn "For the Beauty of the Earth" concludes each stanza with this simple acclamation of praise, "Lord of all, to thee we raise this our song of grateful praise."[20] Interlinear refrains are repeated phrases that appear *between* the lines of the stanzas:

> O for a thousand tongues to sing,
>   blessed be the name of the Lord!
> The glories of my God and King,
>   blessed be the name of the Lord![21]

Lengthier refrains have appeared in particular song forms that have developed relatively recently: they are used extensively in the gospel hymns from nineteenth-century American frontier revivalism; they are a primary feature of much Roman Catholic worship music of the twentieth century; and they are very common in modern worship songs of the twenty-first century. Refrains have been around a long time and are popular with a wide variety of worshipers.

Refrains are characterized by their simplicity (use of fewer words), their repetition (their recurrence at the end of stanzas), and their ability to capture the more emotionally expressive side of the song (in counterpart to the stanzas). While refrains vary in substance and use, we will limit our discussion of refrains to developed refrains that are attached to hymnlike stanzas.

Functions. Developed refrains provide a way for the singers to respond to the overall message found in the stanzas. As noted above (in the section on pure stanza songs), the stanza's lengthier, linear approach is used to proclaim

18. Suzannah Clark, "Refrain," in *The New Grove Dictionary of Music and Musicians*, ed. Stanley Sadie, 2nd ed. (London: Macmillan, 2001), 21:87.

19. Ibid.

20. Folliott Sandford Pierpoint (words), "For the Beauty of the Earth," 1864, http://www .hymnary.org/text/for_the_beauty_of_the_earth.

21. The lines of Charles Wesley's text, "O for a thousand tongues to sing" (1739) are interspersed with lines from the refrain of a gospel song by Ralph E. Hudson (1887). See J. Thomas McAfee et al., eds., *Celebrating Grace Hymnal* (Macon, GA: Celebrating Grace, 2010), hymn #350.

truths of the Christian faith or as a means for articulating various acts of
worship such as praise or intercession. Stanza plus songs offer an immediate
opportunity for singers to engage with the meaning of the song for themselves.
Refrains essentially highlight the message of the whole song with simple,
succinct phrases that help to conclude the thoughts expressed in the stanzas.
Sometimes refrains summarize the stanzas in crisp, positive statements, or
they may offer commentary or give acclamations of praise or express personal
testimony or intentions of commitment—all as a direct result of the themes
presented in the stanzas. *The interaction between the statements of the stanzas
and the response expressed in the refrains creates its own dialogue of revelation and response.* The singers are provided with a means for instantaneously
replying to the song's message, thereby personally engaging all the more.

Forms. Stanza plus songs essentially have one basic structure: alternating
stanzas and refrains. Each stanza contains *different* words as the message of
the song unfolds; each refrain contains the *same* words in direct response to
the stanzas. The same tune is repeated for each complete cycle of stanza plus
refrain. Stanza plus form emerges from the union of two other forms. Pure
stanza form is sequential in nature (using many words) while many other song
forms are cyclical in nature (using few words).[22] Stanza plus songs link the
sequential with the cyclical by combining stanza and refrain. The result is a
hybrid form that is delightfully conversational. These songs may be considered
medium text load—for refrains do not add much to the word weightiness of
the song because they are repeated.[23] This combination effectively results in
a distinctive form all its own.

Three genres of stanza plus songs are especially relevant today and are
explored below: gospel songs, modern hymns, and modern worship songs.

Gospel Songs

Revival hymnody was born in America in the earliest days of the nineteenth
century, during the Second Great Awakening.[24] The songs sung in camp meetings on the frontier came to be known later as "gospel songs" (also known as
gospel hymns; the terms are essentially interchangeable). Most scholars fix the

22. C. Michael Hawn, "Introduction: Streams of Song," in *New Songs of Celebration Render:
Congregational Song in the Twenty-First Century*, ed. C. Michael Hawn (Chicago: GIA, 2013), xl.
23. King, *A Time to Sing*, 63. King does not apply the term "medium text load" to Western
songs with stanzas but rather to global songs. However, I find her terminology helpful in
discussing stanza plus songs.
24. David W. Music, "I Sing for I Cannot Be Silent: Gospel and Revival Hymnody in the
Twentieth Century," in *New Songs of Celebration Render: Congregational Song in the Twenty-
First Century*, ed. C. Michael Hawn (Chicago: GIA, 2013), 105.

beginning of frontier revivalism at 1800, the year of the first major open-air revival among Kentucky settlers in Logan County, led by Presbyterian minister James McGready.[25] Together with the second (and much larger) major revival of 1801 at Cane Ridge, Kentucky (one in which another Presbyterian minister, Barton W. Stone, was a primary leader),[26] a unique American phenomenon was launched—the so-called frontier tradition[27]—one that would persist in some form throughout the century. Its characteristics would be identifiable for generations to come as camp meeting practices became urbanized by such notable figures as Charles G. Finney, Dwight L. Moody, Billy Sunday, and Billy Graham. The influence of the frontier tradition in North American worshiping communities is still felt to this day in many churches.

Outdoor camp meetings followed the pioneers as the Western territories were settled. They drew large crowds and took place over many days, even weeks. Because people traveled significant distances, the length of stay had to be worth their while. Camp meetings were ecumenical, interracial, intergenerational, and characterized by enthusiastic preaching and singing. They also provided a social outlet for folks who were relatively isolated by great geographical distances.

As the camp meeting tradition took shape, so did some unique expressions of worship. Among these were certain features of corporate singing. New types of congregational song arose that were more informal and improvisatory in nature.[28] Hymnals were not a viable resource for worship on the frontier. Illiteracy was a very real factor even if hymnbooks could be afforded. Revivalist hymnody was accomplished through the use of oral transmission.

The stanza plus form organically emerged in the camp meeting culture largely in one of two ways: (1) improvised call and response, and (2) refrains attached to classic hymns. In the early days of the camp meetings, the preacher would lead the singing (designated song leaders were not prominent until later).[29] It was common for the preacher to initiate a "call" by singing out a phrase, and the people would respond with energetic shouts of "Amen!," "Glory!," "Hallelujah!," and so on, which bore musical tones and became extended in length.[30] Many of these responses were remembered and came to be repeated, thus securing them as simple refrains that took on a life of their own.

25. James F. White, *Protestant Worship: Traditions in Transition* (Louisville: Westminster John Knox, 1989), 173.
26. Ibid.
27. Ibid., 171.
28. Music, "I Sing for I Cannot Be Silent," 105.
29. James Sallee, *A History of Evangelistic Hymnody* (Grand Rapids: Baker, 1978), 36.
30. Ellen Jane Lorenz, "Chorus, Refrain, Burden," *The Hymn* 45, no. 1 (January 1994): 19.

In other cases, the leader would sing the stanzas of well-known hymns from the classic British hymn tradition to which the people attached independent refrains of their own creation. After each stanza, often sung as a solo by the leader who knew the words of the hymn, the refrain would be sung with great enthusiasm by the crowd. Early refrains could appear rather random in thought. They seldom rhymed and often lacked direct connection to the stanzas due to their improvisational origin.[31] Consequently, refrains were free to be sung to any number of different hymns—and they were. This phenomenon came to be known as a "wandering refrain" or "traveling refrain."[32] For example, the Isaac Watts text, "Alas! And did my savior bleed," has been the recipient of numerous wandering refrains spanning decades. A number of present-day hymnals include Watts's text both in pure stanza form and in stanza plus form using a popular refrain that was composed much later:

> Alas! and did my Savior bleed,
> and did my Sovereign die?
> Would he devote that sacred head
> for sinners such as I?

> *Refrain*:

> At the cross, at the cross where I first saw the light,
> and the burden of my heart rolled away,
> it was there by faith I received my sight,
> and now I am happy all the day![33]

Frontier revivalism eventually faded but its style of singing did not, though it became more refined and standardized over time. The enthusiasm of camp meeting songs transitioned to songs in support of the Sunday School Movement, a mid-nineteenth-century system of Christian education for children held on Sunday mornings.[34] Gospel hymnody for children was written for use

---

31. Ibid.

32. David W. Music and Paul A. Richardson, *I Will Sing the Wondrous Story: A History of Baptist Hymnody in North America* (Macon, GA: Mercer University Press, 2008), 308.

33. Ralph E. Hudson, "At the Cross," in *Worship and Rejoice* (Carol Stream, IL: Hope, 2001), #258.

34. The Sunday School Movement began in England as a means to help poor children learn to read. When it began in the 1780s, children were working six days a week in factories as a result of the Industrial Revolution. Christian workers held literacy classes on Sundays, the only non-workday, to fill the gap created by their inability to attend school. The Bible and other Christian literature served as the primary curriculum. These events were called Sunday schools. As the movement spread to the United States, Sunday schools became the primary means of Christian education in North America. See Timothy Larsen, "When Did Sunday

in Sunday schools. The most notable composer of tunes for Sunday school songs was William B. Bradbury, who wrote the music for such well-loved songs as "Jesus Loves Me," "He Leadeth Me," "Sweet Hour of Prayer," and "Savior, Like a Shepherd Lead Me." Today these songs are often thought of as adult hymns, largely due to their inclusion in hymnals; nevertheless, they were born out of ministry to children. The movement created its own distinctive repertoire.

A later nineteenth-century movement produced yet another round of gospel hymnody—the urban revivals of well-known evangelists and their song-leading counterparts. It was during this period that the terms "gospel song" and "gospel hymn" came into common use.[35] The urban revival efforts of Charles G. Finney took full advantage of gospel hymnody. So did the evangelistic crusades of Dwight L. Moody and Ira D. Sankey, and Billy Sunday and Homer A. Rodeheaver (in the early twentieth century). The queen of gospel hymn texts during this period is the renowned Fanny Crosby, who contributed a significant body of songs in her lifetime—approximately eight thousand song texts,[36] many of which were disseminated widely through her association with Moody. Among her most well-known songs are "I Am Thine, O Lord," "To God Be the Glory," "Pass Me Not, O Gentle Savior," "Blessed Assurance," and "Rescue the Perishing." Each of these and many others emphasize the need for personal conversion, making them very well suited to the new urban revivals. The mass evangelism efforts of Billy Graham with song leader Cliff Barrows continued the singing of gospel hymns well into the twenty-first century, including the compositions of key figures of the period such as John W. Peterson and Bill and Gloria Gaither.

The nineteenth century was the era of gospel hymnody in North America. The first third of the century saw the origination of the gospel song in frontier camp meetings; the midcentury produced a new wave in conjunction with the Sunday School Movement, and the latter third added to the collection through urban revivals. David W. Music sums up the situation: "The classic form of revival hymnody was achieved during the last thirty years of the nineteenth century when earlier revival hymnody, the Sunday School song, and popular secular musical styles coalesced into the gospel hymn."[37]

The words of gospel hymnody were plain and largely expressive of personal experience—that of salvation, sanctification, devotion, and so on. Its music was equally simple and direct, characterized by the predominant use of

Schools Start?," *Christianity Today*, August 28, 2008, http://www.christianitytoday.com/ch/asktheexpert/whendidsundayschoolstart.html.

35. Eskew and McElrath, *Sing with Understanding*, 196.

36. Ibid., 198.

37. Music, "I Sing for I Cannot Be Silent," 106.

major keys, basic harmonic progressions, and a memorable melody.[38] It was reflective of popular parlor songs of the day, a criticism that song evangelist Rodeheaver defended:

> It was never intended for a Sunday morning service, not for a devotional meeting—its purpose was to bridge the gap between the popular song of the day and great hymns and gospel songs, and to give men a simple, easy lilting melody which they could learn the first time they heard it, and which they could whistle and sing wherever they might be.[39]

A number of Protestant denominations birthed in the United States with revivalist roots have a strong heritage of gospel hymnody to this day, including the Assemblies of God, the Churches of Christ, the Church of the Nazarene, the Southern Baptists, the Seventh-day Adventists, the Wesleyan Church, and numerous Pentecostal groups.

Gospel songs are classic examples of the stanza plus form. The alternation of stanzas and refrain are well defined, and the dialogical nature of the form is evident. They can be quite effective when used as response songs—songs that aid singers in expressing their love and devotion to God while surrounded by others of like-minded faith singing together. They are best used, therefore, following an act of worship that has proclaimed objective truth such as that found in Scripture readings, sermons, songs with texts that contain propositional statements, and so forth. Many gospel hymns make wonderful responses to the word in the Gospel Model for the order of worship (see chap. 4).

Modern Hymns

A second genre of stanza plus songs is the modern hymn. The classic hymn was explained above as an example of pure stanza songs. There we discovered that hymns continue to be written today. In that sense, the word "modern" can be a little confusing. Essentially, modern hymns are considered "hymns" because they employ stanzas; they are considered "modern" because they are situated within the contemporary worship movement. Modern hymns refer to a slightly different genre than that of the classic hymn. They share a form yet vary in style because the two genres have a different point of origination. On the one hand, classic hymns written today originate with roots deep in traditional hymnody; those poets currently writing classic hymns are highly influenced by the traditional hymnic stream. Modern hymns, on the other

38. Ibid., 107.
39. Homer A. Rodeheaver, *Twenty Years with Billy Sunday* (Nashville: Cokesbury, 1936), 78, quoted in Eskew and McElrath, *Sing with Understanding*, 202.

hand, originate from within the praise and worship culture and are consequently highly influenced by that stream.

The praise and worship movement may be characterized by three traits: "it is a product of American Evangelicalism, its aesthetic is drawn from pop culture, and it has a personal and ecstatic spiritual orientation."[40] Modern hymns distinctly fit these traits. Because it is fairly common for modern hymns to include a refrain, I place them here under the longer song type of stanza plus. Precisely because modern hymns have arisen within the more contemporary worship music venues, they bear contemporary stylings but retain the stanza form. Modern hymns reflect the popular music of Western culture in their rhythmic patterns, chord progressions, and lyrical idioms. They also consistently use instrumentation associated with pop culture: guitars, drum kits, keyboards, hand drums, winds, strings, and so on. Modern hymns are band-driven yet committed to the stanza form.

The modern hymn came into its own in the late twentieth century. It may be thought of as a contemporary hybrid of the classic hymn and the gospel song. It resembles the classic hymn in its use of stanzas, regular meter, rhyming patterns, and common poetic devices. At the same time, modern hymn writers tend to be freer with such features, allowing for their more irregular use, or abandoning the normal poetic constraints of traditional hymnody altogether. Nevertheless, standard hymnic influence is evident. The modern hymn is also similar to the gospel song in that it often includes a more personal expression of faith and frequently includes a refrain (though certainly not always).

Some exemplary artists who have consistently written modern hymns in recent decades are Graham Kendrick as well as the writing team of Keith Getty, Kristyn Getty, and Stuart Townend. Kendrick, internationally recognized worship leader and songwriter whose ministry has spanned four decades, was among the first to develop the verse and chorus (stanza and refrain) form[41] in the early 1980s in the United Kingdom—an extension of the early praise or Scripture chorus. Some of his best-known songs demonstrate the stanza plus structure of verse and chorus very well, including "Shine, Jesus Shine," "Knowing You, Jesus," "The Servant King," and "Amazing Love." His modern hymn "God of the Poor" (a pure stanza song) is a lovely example of this genre (notice the regularity of meter and rhyme):

40. Greg Scheer, "Shout to the Lord: Praise and Worship from Jesus People to Gen X," in *New Songs of Celebration Render: Congregational Song in the Twenty-First Century*, ed. C. Michael Hawn (Chicago: GIA, 2013), 175.

41. The terms "verse" and "chorus" are appropriately used in conjunction with contemporary forms, whereas "stanza" and "refrain," which function similarly, are appropriate terms for the classic hymn and gospel song.

Beauty for brokenness
Hope for despair
Lord, in your suffering world
This is our prayer
Bread for the children
Justice, joy, peace
Sunrise to sunset
Your kingdom increase!

God of the poor
Friend of the weak
Give us compassion we pray
Melt our cold hearts
Let tears fall like rain
Come, change our love
From a spark to a flame

Lighten our darkness
Breathe on this flame
Until your justice burns
Brightly again
Until the nations
Learn of your ways
Seek your salvation
And bring you their praise

God of the poor
Friend of the weak
Give us compassion we pray
Melt our cold hearts
Let tears fall like rain
Come, change our love
From a spark to a flame[42]

Irish-born singers and songwriters Keith and Kristyn Getty are also well known for their modern hymn writing. They view their writing of modern hymns to be a calling.[43] While committed to the stanza structure, they have a desire to combine understandable lyrics in the vernacular with highly me-

42. Graham Kendrick, "God of the Poor (Beauty for Brokenness)," © 1993 Make Way Music (administered in the Western Hemisphere by Music Services). All rights reserved. Used by permission. http://www.grahamkendrick.co.uk.

43. Emily R. Brink, "Teaching the Faith, Expanding the Song: An Interview with Irish Hymn writer Keith Getty," *Reformed Worship*, September 2006, http://www.reformedworship .org/article/september-2006/teaching-faith-expanding-song.

lodic tunes that persons in all generations can easily sing.[44] The Gettys have often partnered with songwriter Stuart Townend to produce such gems as "In Christ Alone," "The Power of the Cross," "Come, People of the Risen King," and "Speak, O Lord."

Modern Worship Songs

A third genre that exemplifies stanza plus songs is modern worship songs. One can see that the terminology has begun to overlap a bit, but modern worship songs constitutes its own significant genre and is a major force in worship music today. They, like the modern hymn, are firmly rooted in the contemporary worship movement, but they are not characterized by pure stanzas. The structure of modern worship songs is not nearly as fixed as that of the modern or classic hymn; it definitely continues to evolve (and at a very fast rate).

What began in the early days of the movement as simple praise or Scripture choruses (see chap. 6) gave way to songs that were more extended in length to include a verse with the chorus. This was an immediate way to add more of a substantive narrative to the song. In the beginning, the verse and chorus pattern may have seemed to resemble the stanza and refrain of gospel hymnody in its simple, two-part form. But modern worship music has no direct, historical lineage to revivalist hymnody. It is largely the Christian counterpart to popular music of the day in its structure. There are no strict rules or unified practice as to the number of verses that occur before the first chorus, how often the chorus may be repeated, and so forth. There is an abundance of variables as to how the verse and the chorus relate to each other in any given song.

Kendrick notes that the verse and chorus structure was evident in the United Kingdom by the late 1970s and quickly rose in popularity.[45] He attributes the structure directly to the verse and chorus form that had already become somewhat standardized in commercial popular music of the rock 'n' roll era. Kendrick states, "Worship songwriters since the 70s have grown up listening to commercial popular music which mostly has had a verse/chorus structure, making it very natural to compose worship songs in that way."[46] Without question, the chorus became, and remains, the emotional high point of the song, as was the case for popular song as well. It constitutes the "hook"—the catchy, memorable, repetitive part that recurs in alternation with the verses. Kendrick explains: "The phenomenon of the chorus providing emotional release (often

44. Ibid.
45. Graham Kendrick, email message to author, September 4, 2014.
46. Ibid.

simultaneous with the highest note and a lyrical 'hook line' that sums up the message of the song), is so embedded into popular culture that a song may be perceived as incomplete or unsatisfying without it."[47]

The verse and chorus served as a standard structure for modern worship songs for years. However, relatively recently it has unfolded in ever-increasing levels of complexity and is maturing in form before our eyes. Various structural dimensions to songs have been added and continue to be added. Contemporary worship historian Lester Ruth calls the newer compound forms of modern worship music "VC+": verse and chorus plus some other features—such as bridge, prechorus, or ending, and so on.[48] "The result has been a demonstrable shift in the musical forms of congregational song in contemporary services."[49] He pinpoints the rise of the complexity of modern worship music as coming into its own in the late 1990s.[50] In his analysis of songs appearing on the top twenty-five list of Christian Copyright Licensing International (CCLI) he finds a significant increase in songs using VC+ forms.[51] (The list, which is compiled every six months, contains songs that are played most often in churches, as reported by churches.) Ruth concludes that recent decades have witnessed "an evolution in the most used forms of contemporary worship songs: the earlier simple forms have been supplanted by more complex compound forms involving combinations of verses, choruses, bridges and other miscellaneous pieces."[52] Ruth concludes: "The VC or VC+ form now dominates. . . . Even with the growing interest in hymns—whether classic or newly written—the tendency is to make a simple verse form more complex. . . . The structural complexity of the most popular songs today means contemporary worship has entered a new phase."[53] Today, structural features of modern worship music go far beyond verse and chorus plus bridge. They include prechorus, bridge, channel, intro, outro, tag, ending, and so on, in many different configurations. Numerous modern worship songwriters and artists push the boundaries of complexity and style in a genre that seems to accommodate innovation.

Other twists and turns in modern worship music are noteworthy but can be only mentioned. These include adding new, modern choruses to older hymns, popularized by the musicians of the Passion Movement. Chris Tomlin's "The

47. Ibid.
48. Lester Ruth, "How 'Pop' Are the New Worship Songs: Investigating the Levels of Popular Cultural Influence on Contemporary Worship Music," in Global Forum on Arts and Christian Faith, 2015, www.artsandchristianfaith.org, vol. 3, no. 1, page 4.
49. Ibid.
50. Ibid., 5.
51. Ibid., 4–5.
52. Ibid., 3.
53. Ibid., 5.

Wonderful Cross" is a prime example.[54] The stanzas belong to eighteenth-century Isaac Watts ("When I survey the wondrous cross on which the Prince of glory died").[55] The chorus is an addition by Tomlin ("O the wonderful cross").[56] The chorus serves the same function as that of all modern worship songs—it provides the emotional climax of the song; it also tends to provide more personal commentary on the statements found in the older hymn to which it is attached.

Another very popular approach is that of "retuning" hymns. In this case musicians provide entirely new tunes for older hymn texts; hence, they are retuned. This movement was made popular by Kevin Twit, campus minister for the Reformed University Fellowship (Presbyterian Church of America), ministering to students at Belmont University. He formed the group Indelible Grace, which has produced an impressive body of work related to the retuning movement. Twit's work has spread to dozens of similar campus ministries, resulting in many hymn recordings by numerous artists and labels.[57] The retuning movement is broad in scope, so much so that it goes by many names: updated hymns movement, revamped hymns movement, new old hymns movement, and more.[58]

Conclusion

In many respects, longer songs have formed the core of congregational singing from the Protestant Reformation to the present day. They offer substantive ways to sing the story of God in community. The music architect who wishes to provide a rich body of song will draw on the longer song forms in connection with the shorter song forms. This dialogue of song will place holy words on the lips of God's people, magnificently carrying the conversation of worship that will glorify God and edify the fellowship of believers.

In chapters 6 and 7 we explored two large categories of song for the music architect to consider for leading a robust experience of song in worship. Shorter and longer songs are not to be thought of as "either/or" but "both/and." Each one plays a special role in Christian worship. Each needs the

---

54. Chris Tomlin, J. D. Walt, and Jesse Reeves, "The Wonderful Cross," 2000, Six Steps Music (administered by Capital CMG Publishing).

55. Isaac Watts, "When I Survey the Wondrous Cross," 1707, public domain, http://www.hymnary.org/text/when_i_survey_the_wondrous_cross.

56. Tomlin, Walt, and Reeves, "Wonderful Cross."

57. "List of Retuned Hymn Projects," *Cardiphonia*, July 29, 2013, http://cardiphonia.org/2013/07/29/list-of-retuned-hymn-projects.

58. Zac Hicks, "The Rehymn Movement," http://www.zachicks.com/the-hymns-movement.

other in complementary fashion. Any conversation among friends consists of both sustained dialogue and shorter interjections woven throughout. Together they partner to provide a more complete encounter that benefits the relationship.

Providing a mix of shorter and longer songs is greatly encouraged. Place a few of these songs in conversation with each other within every service and you will find that the worship dialogue carries itself along in meaningful and dynamic ways as engagement takes place on many levels.

Key Terms

hymn. A well-constructed poem that conveys developed statements of Christian faith, to or about the triune God, expressed in metered stanzas, and written to be sung devotionally by the Christian community.

hymnals. Published collections of hymns (and other genres of song) to be sung in corporate worship.

metrical psalm. A biblical psalm that is paraphrased and refashioned into poetic verse for the purpose of corporate song in worship.

psalter. A songbook consisting of settings from the book of Psalms.

refrain. The portion of a song that recurs at the conclusion of each stanza and uses the same music and text as it returns each time.

stanza. A set of lines that is unified around one aspect of the overall theme of the song; a "paragraph" of an extended song.

strophic. When the same melody accompanies each stanza of a song; very common in hymns and folk songs.

To Learn More

Books

Hawn, C. Michael, ed. *New Songs of Celebration Render: Congregational Song in the Twenty-First Century.* Chicago: GIA, 2013.

Lovelace, Austin C. *The Anatomy of Hymnody.* Chicago: GIA, 1965.

Wren, Brian. *Praying Twice: The Music and Words of Congregational Song.* Louisville: Westminster John Knox, 2000.

Wright, N. T. *The Case for the Psalms: Why They Are Essential.* New York: HarperCollins, 2013.

Hymnals

African American Heritage Hymnal. Chicago: GIA, 2001.

Lift Up Your Hearts: Psalms, Hymns, and Spiritual Songs. Grand Rapids: Faith Alive Christian Resources, 2013.

Psalms for All Seasons: A Complete Psalter for Worship. Grand Rapids: Calvin Institute of Christian Worship/Faith Alive Christian Resources/Brazos, 2012.

Websites

Hymnary.org, www.hymnary.org.

The Hymn Society, http://www.thehymnsociety.org.

Engage

Most music architects have a stronger background in some song genres than others. That's natural. With which of the genres discussed in this chapter do you have the least experience (classic hymns, metrical psalms, gospel songs, modern hymns, or modern worship songs)? Begin to explore your less developed genres by following these suggestions:

1. Find someone in your community who is well informed about a genre you wish to explore. Ask to interview them to learn more about them and the genre of song they enjoy. Explore why they appreciate and relate to this particular genre. Before you meet, prepare a series of questions to ask. Journal about their responses, noting areas of growth for you.
2. Locate song collections of the genre you wish to explore (a hymnal, a gospel songbook, a database collection, etc.). Spend some time acquainting yourself with representative songs. Ask the person you interviewed to suggest some collections.
3. Try preparing a song from this collection with your worship leaders. Think about how you could introduce it to your congregation, given the resources available for vocal leadership, instrumentation, and so on.
4. Think about where you could place the new song in your service so that it functions well liturgically.
5. Think of a shorter song that could partner with the longer song either as a lead-in or a response to it. What worship act would it help to interpret or embellish? Try to package a spoken worship element or action with a shorter and longer song, weaving them together seamlessly. Think of them as a minivignette in the service. Then give it a try in worship!

8

Discovering the Congregation's Worship Voice

An Alternative Vision for Musical Style

Explore

Musical style in worship has been a huge topic of discussion in recent decades among church leaders. While the music of worship has periodically been a significant factor in various movements in church history, perhaps never has it been on center stage to the degree that it has been in the last half century. Churches of many kinds on every continent have experienced massive changes in corporate worship, largely centered in musical styles.

Before reading this chapter, give some thought to the impact that musical style plays or does not play in the worship service(s) of your local church. Here are a few questions to help you get started:

1. Does your church describe its primary worship service(s) by a term related to music style (traditional, alternative, contemplative, etc.)?
2. Does your church have multiple services identified by musical style?
3. Has your local congregation experienced significant stylistic changes in the recent past? If so, how did things change? When? Why?

4. If musical style changes have taken place, what were the short-term and long-term effects?

Now that you have reflected briefly on the musical style(s) used in worship in your context, read the rest of this chapter to consider further ways of approaching musical style as a worship music architect.

Expand

A church musician approached me during a break at a worship conference in Canada and said with a smile, "You were right. People are counting." Curious, I asked what she meant. "We have a blended worship style at our church. I'm on a team that plans the music for the services. Our pastor has given us a quota; every service must have a blend of 60 percent praise choruses and 40 percent hymns. If we adjust the percentages in either direction, it is unacceptable, and it's back to the drawing board until we get the balance just right!" She went on to explain that various congregants had complained about their musical preferences not being met, so her pastor was taking a mathematical approach to the solution!

Conversations about musical styles have predominated the North American worship scene for a long time, spreading to many places around the globe. The past fifty years have witnessed waves of dramatic stylistic changes, affecting the worship landscape like a tsunami. The churches of today, both Protestant and Catholic, are for the most part not your parents' churches anymore (regardless of how old you are). In many places, worship is unrecognizable from a mere five years ago. The pace of change is accelerating, due largely to internet communication. Change is in the forecast almost everywhere.

Often these changes produce conflict; hence the colloquial term "worship wars"—arguments about which musical styles should or shouldn't be included in corporate worship—became part of the common vocabulary of church life. At one point in the drama it seemed that conflict was all but inevitable and that every congregation would eventually become the site of either a skirmish or an epic battle. Now, while there are still some uprisings here and there, after decades of discord a truce has been called in most places.

One of the common conditions for the truce has been to go separate ways, to agree to disagree. This has taken various forms. In some cases, it was taken literally with worshipers leaving after being told by their church, "If our musical style doesn't connect with you, go find a church with music that does." Many worshipers went church shopping; music was a commodity that was bought and sold, so to speak, on the open worship market. In other cases, churches that were large enough to have multiple services already in place simply dedicated each service to a particular musical style. What were formerly two or three identical services held at different times (to accommodate attendance or convenience) became flagship services for a particular style (traditional, contemporary, gospel, etc.). The remarkable thing was that the only difference among the services was the music, along with perhaps a few cosmetic changes in staging and attire to create a perception of informality versus formality. The Scripture readings, prayers, sermons, offerings, and so on were untouched; music was supposed to carry the weight of renewal. Yet another approach to truce making was simply to take the niche approach: "Our church will carve out a niche based on one musical style. That's what we do. We'll let other congregations cover other niches for other people. God bless them."

The result of these various approaches has been a plethora of services that are focused on one particular musical style. As musical tastes have become increasingly broad and sophisticated within the general population due to the rapid expansion of musical styles worldwide (each identified by its own stylistic label), so worship services are emerging to reflect that interest. Witness the variety of categories on iTunes specifically for worship music: jazz, alternative, hip-hop, country, classical, rock, world, and more. Individuals create playlists of their favorite songs; worship services follow suit to satisfy the North American cultural infatuation with whatever is new.

The past fifty years has left us with dichotomies: traditional versus contemporary, formal versus informal, relevant versus irrelevant, old versus new, young versus old, change versus status quo. The problem with dichotomies is that the two positions are assumed to be extreme opposites and adversaries, sharing little common ground. They are set up to be either/or. Dichotomies may be practical in helping to define what things are, but the problem is they often define things against what they are not. In other words, it's often easier to promote one's product by comparing it to what one perceives as an inferior alternative. The goal is *not* to share views (and act in deference to others) but to attract like-minded persons. The past five decades have shown us that it is much easier to stake our claim than to make consensus our aim. Then at least we wouldn't have to try to be all things to all people.

Pastors and other leaders have been persuaded to help their churches find a worship style. But perhaps it's not so much a matter of finding one's worship *style* as it is finding one's worship *voice*.[1] This chapter seeks to

1. Constance M. Cherry, "Merging Tradition and Innovation in the Life of the Church: Moving from Style to Encountering God in Worship," in *The Conviction of Things Not*

help the music architect distinguish between musical style and worship voice. Style tends to focus on connecting worshipers with persons of like-minded musical preferences; voice focuses on the broader local context. This chapter will briefly discuss some assumptions about musical style, note its purpose, explain what is meant by finding and using one's "worship voice," and offer a way forward by helping church members become "bilingual" worshipers.

Musical Style in Worship

Musical style is the way that basic musical elements (form, melody, harmony, rhythm, etc.) are similarly treated so as to produce a recognizable overall sound as distinguishable from other styles. It is what makes someone able to say, "That's ragtime," or "That's early Elvis." There are several different musical styles prominently used in worship today. It is not the point of this chapter to identify and compare each one.[2] Instead, music architects *must examine the role* of musical style in worship today. Musical style has been given a very big job. It has been appointed to bring new levels of energy, life, and vitality to worship services. In some cases it is expected to make worship more exciting, to raise a dead church to new life, or to draw in the unchurched so as to evangelize through worship. In all cases, hopes are resting in the power of musical styles to do the miraculous. Musical style is assumed to have a specific purpose: to attract people to church. It really doesn't matter so much which style is called on to achieve renewal. Both traditional and contemporary styles have had much weight placed on them by leaders making very high demands; both the inspiring classical choir director and the rock-star bandleader are counted on to make an impression.

This has happened because leaders make assumptions about the effects of musical styles in worship. They assume the following:

- Certain musical styles grow larger churches.
- People in North America primarily appreciate contemporary music.
- Unchurched people are looking for a church that imitates the musical styles of popular culture.
- Certain age groups relate more to certain styles than others.

Seen: Worship and Ministry in the 21st Century, ed. Todd E. Johnson (Grand Rapids: Brazos, 2002), 32.

2. For a thorough explanation of specific worship styles in standard use today, see Paul Basden, ed., *Exploring the Worship Spectrum: Six Views* (Grand Rapids: Zondervan, 2004).

- Certain styles represent certain denominations. ("Contemporary" music doesn't represent Episcopal worship; "liturgical" music isn't relevant to Baptists, etc.)
- Churches can compete with the level of excellence produced by popular culture.
- People want their kind of music more than they want to be together.

However, these assumptions should not go unchallenged. For instance, there are many factors that contribute to church growth (or decline) other than the music, such as the effectiveness of preaching, friendliness of people, location, and more. And if someone claims that North Americans appreciate one style of music the most, what would that style be, given the myriad styles they listen to on a daily basis? Consider the possibility that lost people are not seeking yet another venue to hear their music, but they are seeking a true experience of God. Also, the lines defining which age groups like which type of music are blurring. It has been far too easy to claim that older people like hymns and young people like pop-based worship music. That just may be an unsubstantiated myth given the large number of young people involved in retuning[3] these days. There are too many exceptions for that to be the rule anymore. Is it really true that certain styles cannot cross borders into any Christian worship tradition? Would "contemporary" come off as "liturgical" just because it's in a neo-Gothic setting? Do most churches have the financial means and human resources to produce the level of excellence expected by a population that consistently hears expertly mixed music by sound engineers sitting in studios? Perhaps most of all, are we absolutely sure that people want music more than authentic community? Some voices would have us believe it, yet many folks, especially the millennial generation, prize personal relationships in church over all other aspects.[4]

Lest I give the wrong impression, let me say that musical style is not unimportant; style does matter. But it may not matter in the ways we have assumed. Musical style simply needs to be kept in perspective. Perhaps it's time to challenge the assumptions that have been circulating widely concerning music styles in worship. To depend on one dimension of worship to carry the weight of renewal is not only unreasonable it is impossible. Incredible power

3. Retuning is the art of arranging old tunes or composing new tunes for older hymn texts for corporate singing; see the section "Modern Worship Songs" in chap. 7.

4. David McAllister-Wilson, "Think Bigger: The Challenge of Reaching Millennials," *Leading Ideas*, e-newsletter of the Lewis Center for Church Leadership, Wesley Theological Seminary, January 14, 2015, http://www.churchleadership.com/leadingideas/leaddocs/2015/150114_article.html.

has been vested in musical styles to accomplish goals for which they were never intended. Harold Best summarizes the concern well:

> As much as I love music . . . we have placed far too much faith in it and not nearly enough in the power of the Word, the authority and sweep of fearless prophecy and earnest, yet hope-filled, intercessory prayer. I have often wondered what would happen if we got music out of the way, especially in its upfront dress, and spent abundant time in interceding prayer, reading and searching the Scriptures, sitting in silence, prophesying and perhaps only then singing and making music.[5]

The Purpose of Musical Style

What is the purpose of musical style in reference to Christian worship? Is it to attract or to express? One's answer will likely depend on one's view of church. The evangelistic, "attractional" church spends its energies trying to get unchurched people to church.[6] Musical style is a big piece of the attraction, and the church embodies the mentality of "If you build it, they will come." A word of caution is in order: "We must ask ourselves if our intense desire to have our worship relate to the culture around us is motivated by the hope that if our worship does relate corporately to the unredeemed culture, we, as individuals, won't have to."[7]

Typically the term "missional church" is viewed as the counterpart to the attractional church. Missional folks focus on ministry outside the church and are therefore less concerned with getting people into a building.[8] In a sense, they take church *to* others. Musical style for them may emphasize expression instead of attraction.

Should musical style attract or express? Here we have yet another stark dichotomy. The truth is that the answer is "yes." Musical style will probably attract like-minded worshipers, *and* it will also express a community's worship.

To summarize, musical style in worship plays an important role, just not necessarily the role we automatically presumed. It is certainly not neutral, for music, apart from any lyrics, communicates a message too. Nevertheless,

---

5. Harold M. Best, *Unceasing Worship: Biblical Perspectives on Worship and the Arts* (Downers Grove, IL: InterVarsity, 2003), 140.

6. Paul S. Williams, "Missional or Attractional—Who Cares?," *Christian Standard*, March 31, 2012, http://christianstandard.com/2012/03/missional-or-attractional%E2%80%94who-cares.

7. Terry W. York and C. David Bolin, *The Voice of Our Congregation: Seeking and Celebrating God's Song for Us* (Nashville: Abingdon, 2005), 38.

8. Williams, "Missional or Attractional."

it is simply "perplexing to think of the burden we have placed on music, this fleeting human construct. . . . The church desperately needs an artistic reformation that . . . takes music out of the limelight and puts Christ and his Word back into prominence."[9] Neither worship music nor its style should be the primary defining mark of any church. Its real engagement with the living Lord should be that defining mark in both attractional and missional ways. While leaders must give loving guidance to and development of the musical style of their community, there is something more profound to discover: its worship voice.

Finding Your Worship Voice

"I'd know your voice anywhere." Has anyone ever said that to you? Perhaps you phoned a friend you hadn't spoken with in a while, and they recognized your voice from just your "Hello"—even without caller ID! Human voices have a distinct quality about them that include pitch, timbre, accent, and so on. Voice recognition alone has been enough for a witness to testify in court as to a defendant's guilt or innocence.

Jesus spoke to his disciples about voice recognition:

> Very truly, I tell you, anyone who does not enter the sheepfold by the gate but climbs in by another way is a thief and a bandit. The one who enters by the gate is the shepherd of the sheep. The gatekeeper opens the gate for him, and the sheep hear his voice. He calls his own sheep by name and leads them out. When he has brought out all his own, he goes ahead of them, and the sheep follow him because they know his voice. They will not follow a stranger, but they will run from him because they do not know the voice of strangers. (John 10:1–5)

Jesus used this figure of speech to emphasize the power of relationship. In explaining the meaning of his words to his disciples who did not understand, Jesus said, "I am the good shepherd. I know my own and my own know me" (John 10:14). In this case, recognizing the shepherd's voice was a matter of life and death for the sheep.

Every congregation has a **worship voice**—an indigenous way to relate to God in corporate worship, the natural way that it expresses its relationship with God. A congregation's worship voice is the result of several things, the most influential of which is its context. Consequently, the worship voice is discovered precisely there—within one's local community of Christian believers,

9. Best, *Unceasing Worship*, 75.

as opposed to imposing a voice on it from an outside source. Jesus warned in his teaching of the danger of following the voice of a stranger.

Writers often speak of writing in one's "voice."[10] It is a good thing for authors to find their voice. It suggests that they have achieved voice recognition, that their audience of readers is able to differentiate this author's writing from another's. Most of all, it suggests that a writer has acquired a degree of authenticity, for he or she is writing out of both an inherited and an acquired collection of dynamics that contribute to his or her voice. A writer's voice includes style, but it's more than that. Writing style includes such things as sentence lengths, sentence structures, one's personal lexicon (the vocabulary of a writer), and also tone (sarcasm, humor, melancholy, reflective, etc.). What's more, the writer's voice is also informed by point of view or convictions held on matters. There is an underlying belief system that is discernible in subtle, if not obvious, ways in the pieces they compose. Their worldview becomes recognizable. One's personality is very much a part of the writer's voice too. There is an unavoidable vulnerability that naturally emerges, not unlike the personality of musical composers as they put pen to staff paper. For example, the childlike playfulness of Wolfgang Amadeus Mozart and the tempestuous seasons of Ludwig van Beethoven's life each left an impression on their stunning music.

Yet there is still more to the writer's voice. It includes his or her selection of topics—what they choose to write about is a part of finding the writer's voice. So also is what an author would never write about. This dimension of voice can't be addressed through style alone, for it reflects the author's individual core values. When writers determine what kinds of things they will or will not choose as a topic, they have discovered one dimension of their voice. When we speak of "the voice of reason," "the voice of the voiceless," or "the voice of the people," we are speaking about much more than style, for these can be addressed in any number of stylistic approaches. We are speaking, rather, about what foci or themes are significant for the author to communicate to others using the written word as a platform, the issues they are impassioned about for which they desire to affect others. Authors Terry York and David Bolin summarize it well:

> What does it mean when we say that a writer or a performer has finally "found their voice"? It means that there has finally emerged from within them an

10. I am indebted to Mary M. Brown, emeritus professor of English at Indiana Wesleyan University (Marion, Indiana), for sharing her thoughts with me concerning the development of the writer's voice. I have found her insights on this topic, as well as on many other professional and life topics, to be invaluable.

authenticity that makes their performance, their work, their contribution something new and of value, indeed, a *contribution*, no longer simply imitation. Who they are begins to shine through their technical skill. We cannot borrow music or art of any form from someone else and claim it is ours or expect it to speak of our soul unless it connects with who we are and can authentically be expressed by our voice.[11]

Identifying one's worship voice is likewise multidimensional. A community's worship voice includes style, but it's more than that. It encompasses characteristic ways of speaking, vocabulary, and service tone. It also comprises its convictions and point of view that speak to its underlying belief system. Every church has an identifiable personality—a predominant collective persona that reflects the unique combination of subgroups within it. Each worshiping community includes particular foci or themes of faith and ministry that the community is passionate about. Even if the community has never taken the time to articulate what these are, they will emerge regardless.

Where does musical style fit into all of this? We are dealing with two distinct but highly interrelated things: worship voice and musical style. The latter is a subset of the former. Each congregation's musical style is *one dimension* of *several factors* that compose its worship voice. While it is only one dimension, it is a substantial one nonetheless for expressing the overall worship voice of the congregation. A church's predominant musical style will speak volumes as to its identity, but it is never its sole identity. The really important thing to know is that musical style (along with other dimensions of worship voice) has to do with one's context. For it to be authentic, musical style must arise from within the community as a true expression of its culture, not borrowed from another culture and employed for the purpose of trying to be like someone else. Such an approach says more about what a church is told to *wish it were* than what *it is*. "The congregation's [worship] voice is often, if not *most* often, expressed in song. Finding the songs that 'fit' the congregation's voice is very closely associated with finding the voice itself. Their song must express their heart and soul[;] . . . it must be authentic."[12] In short, each congregation has its "heart song." Blessed are the ones who discern it, embrace it, and are set free to sing it.

Both worship voice and musical style have everything to do with context. All societal entities have a **context**—a set of circumstances that surround and define its character. A church's context consists of numerous factors, including its people's educational levels, racial makeup, financial stability, age

11. York and Bolin, *Voice of Our Congregation*, 26.
12. Ibid., 8 (emphasis in original).

levels, previous denominational backgrounds, political views, length of time associated with the church, loyalty to the denomination or movement, and the male/female ratio of the church population. Its context is also affected by societal factors such as the region of the country and breadth of cultural resources available. To be authentic, a church must both *know* its context and *own* its context. Leaders will need to help a church discover things about itself that it never knew. They may also have to help create a sense of ownership for their context if the congregation is not enthused about the circumstances in which they find themselves.

Recalling some of the characteristics of the pastoral musician from chapter 1, leaders must seek to help their people discover their unique worship voice, their meaningful way of communicating with God that is expressive of their cultural context. As a part of that effort, leaders are able to strengthen and bring balance to the musical style that is normative for their community.

While it is critical that congregations discover their worship voice and develop its related musical style, I am not advocating for the status quo or, even worse, for drawing inward. We are not called to recycle our own preferences in order to fortify our context and avoid change. After all,

> the poets and prophets in our midst do not always call us *back* to our authentic voice. Sometimes they call us *forward* to our authentic voice. Either way, it is a call to a continuing deepening of our Christ-following and discipleship. Too often, congregations would rather try to be like another congregation than explore the depths of their own giftedness and mission.[13]

Contexts constantly change, even if at a slow rate. Our worship voice must deepen and widen with every significant change that occurs, if we will recognize the context and embrace it. When we welcome the strangers that appear in our midst to stay, we must also welcome the way they expand our worship voice. This may require us to add songs to our musical repertoire so that the songs of the community are truly reflective of the people God has gathered. There is good news: "The voice of the congregation is not limited to one genre or style. Its one message, one voice, and several emotions may well find expression in more than one type of song. The congregation will accept several styles as long as they are the songs of the one voice."[14] The pastoral musician will discern the worship voice of their congregation through relationships and listening. There is no other way for leaders to help a congregation find its worship voice than to give themselves to the people in servant leadership as

13. Ibid., 32 (emphasis in original).
14. Ibid., 10.

an act of submission to God. It may very well require that leaders lay down their desires and expectations for satisfying their own preferences of musical style, or for their desire to appear that they are "relevant" in the eyes of those who sell worship products to create an image. "Finding the voice of the congregation is submitting our will to God's will, our way to the Shepherd's way. The song possesses us; we do not possess the song."[15]

The question is often asked: What if we have several subcultures within the church? If our musical style in worship is derived from our context, what do we do when there seems to be multiple contexts? Actually, most churches do have multiple subcultures that together constitute its overall context. The subgroups are actually part of what characterizes your context. In this case, your context is multicultural (not necessarily racially or ethnically speaking). One's context is composed of *all* the relevant circumstances that surround and define the character of your community. The best thing to do is: (1) make sure that each true subgroup is represented in the song repertoire, not by filling quotas but by loving acts of the community expressing the desire to sing one another's song; and (2) emphasize that there are several components that help to form the church's worship voice, not just music. Make sure that each group is well represented in governance, is invited to pray and/or read Scripture publicly, is included in planning services of worship, is involved in outreach, and so forth. "It is a breakthrough moment when a congregation decides to look within rather than 'go shopping' when the time comes to consider what their music and worship style should be. The answer to what music and worship style a congregation should employ is to be found within its own giftedness."[16]

Using Your Worship Voice

All of this may be an interesting conversation to have around the water cooler at church, but where does the music architect actually begin? Is there a concrete way to get our minds around musical style in light of the cultural implications of our congregation's worship voice?

One way is to consider exactly how well our song repertoire actually reflects *all* the local, regional, and world cultures of which we are a part. At face value it may seem like our musical style choices are merely between traditional or gospel, contemporary or country—options found in CD categories at the music store. But one's congregational context is not only that which is seen

15. Ibid., 30.
16. Ibid., 31.

but also that which is unseen. There will be a core musical style that best fits your church's worship voice. This will naturally serve as its primary point of reference. But what if we ceased to worry about the stylistic categories for a moment and looked at the larger picture? If we did so we would discover more significant categories that might just give us direction for moving past any remaining worship war dichotomies.

One possible source for helping us to think about music categories differently is to let the Nairobi Statement on Worship and Culture[17] be our guide. This statement, arising out of a meeting in Nairobi, Kenya, in 1996 is a product of several consultations on worship and culture undertaken by the Lutheran World Federation over a period of years. The Nairobi Statement makes four central points regarding Christian worship: (1) it is transcultural (transcends all cultures); (2) it is contextual (takes place in local culture); (3) it is countercultural (worship critiques and corrects culture); and (4) it is cross-cultural (worship demonstrates the unity of the church).[18]

Let's take these same four points and apply them to music in worship.[19] We could say that worship music has a transcultural voice, a local voice, a counter-cultural voice, and a cross-cultural voice. First, music has a transcultural voice. The story of God is transcultural in that it goes beyond any one culture to affect all people. The life, death, resurrection, ascension, and coming again of Jesus Christ is the song of the ages, sung among all Christ-followers past, present, and future. Consequently, the gifts given by God to proclaim and celebrate God's story (the Holy Scriptures, baptism, Holy Communion, the spiritual gifts, etc.) transcend any local culture. They are shared among all believers joyously.

Application: Do we faithfully sing of those things that all believers share? Here we are concerned primarily with content and secondarily with musical style.

Second, music has a local voice. We must seek to honor and develop "a given culture's values and patterns, insofar as they are consonant with the values of the Gospel,"[20] so that worship music is deeply tied to a particular people in a particular place at a particular time.

Application: Are we aware of the musical heritage, expressions, styles, and so forth that help to give meaning to the songs sung by this local group of worshipers? Does it form the core of musical song from which we expand?

17. Lutheran World Federation, "Nairobi Statement on Worship and Culture," 1996, http://download.elca.org/ELCA%20Resource%20Repository/LWF_Nairobi_Statement_1994.pdf.
18. Ibid.
19. In interpreting and applying the principles of the Nairobi Statement on Worship and Culture, I am not attempting to strictly restate the principles. Rather, I am loosely paraphrasing them for the sake of applying the main points of the statement to musical style.
20. Lutheran World Federation, "Nairobi Statement."

Here we are concerned with music that is an authentic expression of a particular worshiping community.

Third, music has a countercultural voice. Worship music has a prophetic side—a responsibility to critique those aspects of every culture that "are sinful, dehumanizing, and contradictory to the values of the Gospel."[21] Transformation of culture is the goal. Some of the community's songs must challenge "all types of oppression and social injustice wherever they exist in earthly cultures."[22]

Application: What songs do we sing that challenge the self-centered patterns of society and call believers to live transformed lives of holiness, leading to purer, healthier, safer communities? Here we are calling one another to not imitate culture's narcissistic ways but rather to call them into question when necessary.

Fourth, music has a cross-cultural voice. Because God's people share God's story in common, worshiping communities greatly benefit from "the sharing of hymns and art and other elements of worship across cultural barriers."[23] Christian worship on any continent is deepened when it includes songs sung by people we will never meet, who live in lands we may never visit. They are the songs of fellowship we sing now in anticipation of the songs we will sing with these same sisters and brothers in the eternal kingdom.

Application: Consider pastorally introducing simple songs from other nations in worship services, not for novelty but for unity. In time, worshipers' sense of context will expand from local to global. Singing one another's song is a great witness that "there is one body and one Spirit . . . one Lord, one faith, one baptism, one God and Father of all" (Eph. 4:4–6a).

The Nairobi Statement does not offer the church a menu from which to choose the dimensions of worship it wishes to actively engage. All the dimensions are critical to the authentic worshiping church. Similarly, music architects are called to employ music that advances the vision for transcultural, contextual, countercultural, and cross-cultural worship. In this way, the church becomes the church on earth as it is in heaven.

Where Do We Go from Here? Becoming "Bilingual" in Our Worship Voice

Music is a type of language that worshipers use to communicate with God and one another. It helps us to sing the great themes of our faith as we tell the wondrous story of God in song. All believers share the language of music. It

21. Ibid.
22. Ibid.
23. Ibid.

allows us to sing transculturally, contextually, counterculturally, and cross-culturally. Music helps us to "sing globally."

Musical *style* functions like a dialect within the language;[24] it consists of the indigenous and natural musical idioms and expressions with which a particular subculture identifies. It allows us to sing contextually. Musical dialects (styles) are determined by who we are sociologically[25] and spiritually. We discover them rather than choose them, for the most part. Musical style helps us to "sing locally."

So which is it? Do we sing the dialect of our local context and contentedly sing that which is comfortable and familiar to us? Or should we enlarge our song base to reflect a sense of the whole family of God? How can we avoid another either/or dichotomy?

Churches need to become bilingual in their worship voice.[26] People who are bilingual have the vocabulary, the syntax, and the inflection to communicate in two languages effectively and can flow back and forth between the languages with ease in any given conversation. Both languages have become native tongues for them; they do not have to stop to analyze the grammar before speaking; they simply speak and listen. Musical style can be thought of as our first language—the language of origin, the language in which we feel most at home. It is the language sung in the dialect of our local church family. At the same time, we are bilingual; we have learned a second language—one that allows us to communicate beyond our familiar circles and our comfort zones, one that acknowledges the music of the whole family of God in order to affirm, critique, and unite. Style-driven worship usually attempts to relate to one certain constituency. Bilingual worship attempts to communicate to multiple constituencies. The end result is to think globally and sing locally. In doing so, our song becomes large enough to represent the cosmic church, yet small enough to represent one's local church, not focused exclusively on musical styles but recognizing the unique worship voice that speaks to much more. It becomes bilingual.

Conclusion

We began this chapter by admitting that musical styles have captivated the attention of leaders, and leaders have made a number of assumptions about

24. David B. Pass, *Music and the Church: A Theology of Church Music* (Nashville: Broadman, 1989), 91–92.

25. Ibid., 92–93.

26. This paragraph is adapted from Cherry, "Merging Tradition and Innovation in the Life of the Church," 31–32.

the benefits and power of certain styles. On occasion, musical style has become a tool for ulterior motives. I have proposed that there is a larger venue to consider: a community's "worship voice" that is rooted in a congregation's context, not in marketing strategies. Style dichotomies have too often led to divisions not only *among* churches but also *within* churches. Instead, a clear understanding of one's worship voice is necessary if we truly believe that worship is the occasion for a corporate conversation with God. We must not use others' voices; all we have is our own voice, given by God to use for God's glory.

Key Terms

context. The circumstances that surround and define the character of a person, group, movement, etc.

musical style. The way that basic musical elements (form, melody, harmony, rhythm, etc.) are similarly treated so as to produce a recognizable overall sound as distinguishable from other styles.

worship voice. The result of many contextual factors; the indigenous way a church relates to God in corporate worship; the natural way that it expresses its relationship with God in light of its overall circumstances.

To Learn More

Basden, Paul, ed. *Exploring the Worship Spectrum: Six Views*. Grand Rapids: Zondervan, 2004.

Best, Harold M. *Unceasing Worship: Biblical Perspectives on Worship and the Arts*. Downers Grove, IL: InterVarsity, 2003.

York, Terry W., and C. David Bolin. *The Voice of Our Congregation: Seeking and Celebrating God's Song for Us*. Nashville: Abingdon, 2005.

Engage

To take the first steps in discovering your community's worship voice, investigate your context.

  1. Make a list of every contextual dimension you can think of that affects any worshiping community (educational levels, ages, urban or rural locations, ethnic backgrounds, denominations represented, etc.).

2. How would you describe your context? Write a one-page description as you see it today.
3. Ask a long-term parishioner to edit your description for the sake of clarity.
4. Reflect on the ways in which your musical style in worship relates to people in your context. Are all persons represented?
5. Try to discover if musical styles have changed because of or in spite of contextual changes.
6. What would bilingual worship look like in your church?

9

Leading
Congregational Song

Practical Guidance from the Trenches

Explore

Before reading this chapter, think about what makes for effective or ineffective song leadership in worship. Begin by reflecting on these questions:

1. Have you observed a very effective song leader recently? What made his or her leadership effective?
2. Think of an occasion when you observed an ineffective song leader in worship. What did he or she do (or not do) that seemed to hinder effectiveness?
3. If you have responsibilities for leading congregational songs in worship, what do you consider to be your strengths? What would you specifically like to improve on? Why?

Now that you have begun to think about skills and qualities helpful for song leading, read the rest of this chapter for practical guidance in improving this most important role of the worship music architect.

Expand

Congregational song is the heart of music ministry in worship. Music in its many manifestations is glorious to experience—excellent choirs, vibrant praise bands, instruments of all kinds, specialized vocal ensembles, soloists, and dynamic accompaniments. However, nothing can replace the beauty of enthusiastic congregational singing in corporate worship. If for some reason, one and only one aspect of musical worship could be retained, it must be congregational song. The people of God joining in song are the prime element of all musical offerings in worship.

St. Augustine, early church theologian and philosopher, affirmed the importance of congregational song in worship:

> But is not any time appropriate for singing sacred hymns when the brethren gather in the church, except when there is reading or discussion or praying aloud by the bishop, or praying in common, led by the voice of the deacon? In the intervals of time, I do not know of anything better or more profitable or more holy for Christians to do when they are gathered together.[1]

As Augustine suggests, and as we have seen, corporate song is indispensable to Christian worship. Singing songs of adoration is the holy calling of each and every worshiper who is intent on serving God wholeheartedly. As with all central aspects of worship, leaders are key to facilitating and enhancing them. They help the people to pray, to hear the Scriptures, to engage with the sermon, to dedicate the offering, and to receive the sacraments. Leaders also help people to sing the songs of faith. They guide, coach, exhort, and demonstrate the songs of the church so that many voices are collected and fashioned into one voice to the glory of God. Primarily, music leadership is a ministry of encouragement.

Pastoral musician Virgil Funk contends that three musical challenges face every worshiping community: "How to get our assembly to sing, how to sustain our singing, and how to improve our singing."[2] These are the duties of the song leader. As mentioned in chapter 1, various titles are used for song leaders in the church. "Worship leader" is common in more contemporary venues, while "cantor" tends to be used in more liturgical settings. Remember that the term "pastoral musician" covers a broad spectrum of musical

---

1. Augustine, "Letter 55: Augustine to Januarious, Regarding the Celebration of Easter," trans. Wilfrid Parsons, *The Fathers of the Church*, ed. Roy Joseph Deferrari (New York: Fathers of the Church, 1951), 12:290.

2. Virgil C. Funk, "Do It with Style," in *The Singing Assembly*, vol. 6 of *Pastoral Music in Practice*, ed. Virgil C. Funk (Washington, DC: Pastoral Press, 1991), 35.

leadership that may not involve actual music leading at all. This chapter will deal exclusively with "song leaders"—persons who are charged with directing and enlivening the congregation's song. "Song leaders" specifically refers to vocalists who help the people to sing, sustain their singing, and improve the singing of the congregation. The phrase is narrow enough to refer explicitly to leading the church's song (only one of the duties of the pastoral musician), yet broad enough to be inclusive of any type of song regardless of style (since the terms "worship leader" and "cantor" are used rather exclusively according to certain styles).

To put it simply, this chapter is dedicated to helping the song leader lead others in song. Two primary aspects are addressed: directing the song and enlivening the song. Since instrumental accompaniment is also usually a major aspect of song leadership, a third section deals with the use of instruments in worship. (Many song leaders also play instruments, of course, but instrumentation will be handled separately.) At various junctures throughout the chapter, I will offer practical tips for becoming a more secure song leader.

Leading congregational singing is a multidimensional ministry to be developed over time. Simply having a good natural singing voice does not necessarily make for an effective song leader. A complement of assets and skills are needed. Therefore, basic information and technique will be introduced as a starting place for beginning the exciting ministry of song leading in the church.

Directing the Church's Song

Being an effective song leader involves giving direction to singers. This does not necessarily mean directing in the sense of using arm gestures to conduct the music. Some traditions do have a strong history of using standard conducting practices to lead congregational song. Certain styles of song lend themselves to the gestures of the conductor more than others, especially classic hymns and gospel songs. Yet while some churches, especially those rooted in the American revivalist tradition, still expect the song leader to conduct the songs, this practice is presently in decline. There are some possible reasons for it. The Liturgical Renewal Movement of the early twentieth century re-emphasized classic hymnody, led by the organist and choir, over gospel songs that were typically led by a solo song leader. Also, the growing influence of contemporary worship in the latter part of the century played a role in the marginalization of the conductor because praise teams and bands became the leaders. Praise team members often hold microphones or play instruments, so their hands are not free to conduct. Also, song lyrics are often projected on screens, drawing the eyes of the congregation over the heads of the praise team, making it difficult to follow arm gestures of the leader. Today, directing the song doesn't necessarily mean conducting the song.

Directing song has to do with guiding multiple singers in the corporate act of singing. Much of it is accomplished through features other than conducting. Two characteristics in particular are critical to good song leading. First, leaders need to possess a secure singing voice, which means

1. They are able to consistently sing in tune. Having good **intonation**—the ability to sing with accuracy of musical pitch—is critical to good song leading. Singers need to be able to hear and produce pitches accurately and clearly.
2. They have a solid voice—a voice that can appeal to the average singer. A loud voice is not of particular benefit nor is a soloist's voice. Either of these stands to overpower or draw attention to the leader. Instead, a sturdy "congregational" voice[3] can be more helpful.

Tip for better intonation: Refine your ability to hear and match pitches by practicing. Ask a secure singer to sing pitches (or play notes on a piano) while you sing them. Listen carefully for accurate intonation.

A second desirable characteristic for the good song leader is that of a lively and delightful spirit. Good direction will have more to do with the spirit of the song leader than almost anything else, second only to singing in tune. The leader's passion for congregational song will be natural and evident. There will be a sparkle in his or her eyes, warmth to his or her demeanor, an inviting facial expression, and a hospitable approach to inviting people into the song. I will never forget being led by a Malaysian song leader at a worship conference in Singapore. I have experienced a multitude of song services in my lifetime but have rarely, if ever, witnessed such a delightful and engaging persona in a song leader. He led us in singing with a spirit that seemed completely genuine, energetic, and compelling. His smiling face, dancing eyes, and perfect gesturing drew us all in immediately. After the service I learned that he had no formal training for music leadership, but his giftedness and spirit were more than enough to make him a dynamic song leader.

Leading with a lively spirit begins with a warm and inviting facial expression that comes from a genuine joy of song from deep within the leader. Leaders should have a genuine passion for the sound of the church singing its song.

3. Alice Parker, gifted leader of corporate song, often refers to her voice as a "congregational" voice (as opposed to a trained soloist voice).

This passion will naturally show itself, not through hyped-up actions but through an inner love for Christ, his church, and the music itself. One's facial expression is an outward demonstration of the life within.

A lively spirit is also communicated through a person's eyes. Song leaders should not stand in front of worshipers with their eyes closed. It can easily appear that the leaders are in their own worship zone, involved in their private moment with God, unconcerned for those around them. It is vital that leaders look into the eyes of the people they are serving. An immense amount of communication takes place in relationships through the eyes. "I can see it in your eyes" is not just a euphemism; it's a reality. Eye-to-eye contact is the primary means through which the leader connects with the people to establish relationship. It is very appropriate to look at various persons throughout the worship space while leading. Connect through the eyes. Worshipers who truly believe that the leader is invested in their experience of song will raise their level of participation. The enthusiasm of the leader will be contagious.

Tip for improving personal presence: Videotape your leadership in worship. Review it carefully with someone who will be honest. Note areas where you appear to be uninvolved with the worshipers. Identify three ways to improve on your engagement with the people.

Becoming an effective song leader involves both *natural* abilities and *acquired* skills. One's voice and personality are considered to be natural abilities for the most part. However, be careful never to write off someone who doesn't demonstrate these capabilities at first. Someone could have these natural gifts but may have never been shown how to discover and nurture them. Through coaching, encouragement, and mentoring, untapped resources can be found and placed in service.

Song leaders also need a number of acquired skills, which are addressed below.

Leading Strong Entrances

Congregational singers need to know when to begin singing and also when to enter at other subsequent places throughout the song. Make sure it is absolutely clear from the first syllable when to sing. Eye contact with the people and a confident arm gesture are the best ways to lead people into the song. Make sure you are looking directly at them rather than at a monitor screen or songbook or guitar pedal. An upbeat or downbeat of the right arm will prepare them for a secure entrance into the song. No extra beats are needed since there will most often be an instrumental introduction that sets the tempo. Just look directly at the people and give them an arm gesture along with a smile. If the leader's hands are preoccupied with playing an instrument, a slight uplift of the head as a lead-in and/or a very definitive starting note helps immensely. The leader's own security of presence and gesture will go a long way to give the people confidence in starting the song together.

Unfortunately, many leaders just start singing without motioning to the people. The congregation is left to wander in as they catch on that the song has begun. Never forget that congregational song is a group activity. Starting together is a big part of creating energy and confidence among singers. Congregational song is not the leader's song that the people get to join; it is the people's song that the leader is facilitating with thoughtful intention.

Setting Tempos

Establishing the best **tempo** (the speed) for each song is a very important part of song leadership. Songs can live or die by the tempo chosen. Instrumentalists should be well rehearsed prior to the service so that they are familiar with the speed desired by the leader. Tempos are communicated to the congregation in various ways, from a well-rehearsed instrumental introduction or the drummer clicking his or her sticks. However it occurs, the song leader ultimately sets the pace for the song.

Here are some guidelines for deciding on an appropriate tempo. First and most important, let each song speak for itself. The lyrics will lean toward an appropriate tempo; so will the tune. (Remember, technically speaking, a song is a combination of both text and tune.) Some songs suggest bright, vibrant, snappy tempos; others suggest slower, more reflective ones. Consider, for example, two songs, each of which includes the lyrics "Holy! Holy! Holy!," referring to heaven's eternal song. The popular "Revelation Song"[4] reflects a mystical foreshadowing of heaven's song, and the lyrics succeed in creating "awestruck wonder" through the use of biblical descriptions of all creation's praise to God and to the Lamb. Its reflective nature calls for a moderately slower pace that allows singers to bask in anticipation of the coming cosmic event even while singing their praise now. The classic hymn "Holy, Holy, Holy! Lord God Almighty!"[5] depicts the same scene but in a different way. It expresses more of a celebration of the ongoing praise to the triune God to which the church is invited to join in now. Both text and

4. Jennie Lee Riddle, "Revelation Song," 2004, Gateway Create Publishing (administered by Capitol CMG Publishing, IMI). This song has been recorded by multiple artists, including Kari Jobe, Jesus Culture, and Sandi Patty.
5. Reginald Heber (words) and John B. Dykes (music), "Holy, Holy, Holy! Lord God Almighty!," public domain, http://www.hymnary.org/text/holy_holy_holy_lord_god_almighty_early.

tune are sturdier—almost marchlike—as opposed to the more fluid feel of "Revelation Song." The hymn lends itself well to a bright, vibrant tempo. To reverse tempos on either song would not only misrepresent the spirit of the song but also kill its energy.

A second guideline for deciding on an appropriate tempo is the song's place in the service. As demonstrated in chapter 4, songs are best placed in the service according to their liturgical function. Look carefully at the meaning of the song and its consequent purpose in the service. This too will help you to determine an appropriate tempo. A lament will likely suggest a slower pace for sorrow. A doxology will probably indicate a faster pace. (These interpretations vary according to cultures.) However, feel free to mildly adjust the tempo of a song to help it fit in the service without removing it from its natural feel.

Third, tempos are affected by wordiness. If the lyrics contain many non-repeated words (that is, the song carries a high text load), a slightly slower tempo can be helpful; it enables singers to pronounce each word. If there are fewer words with text that is repeated (a low text load), an adjustment is not needed.

Fourth, consider the familiarity factor. Are you attempting a new song? If so, select a moderated tempo for ease of learning, without slowing it down too much. Then, as the congregation becomes friends with each new song, singing at its more natural tempo is much easier. Build in every possibility for singers to get on board.

Tip for setting tempos: Purchase a **metronome** *at a music store or download a free metronome app. Experiment with a variety of tempos for each song.*

Determining Vocal Range

Groups of untrained singers have a general **range** of notes that they are comfortable in producing. Much like musical instruments, human voices have a limit to the lowest and highest notes they can physically produce. Trained voices can expand the range with proper conditioning; however, the average worshiper has had no such training. It is common practice for hymnal committees to establish a certain range of notes for all the tunes included in the collection. Interestingly, this range has become both narrower and lower in recent publications. While some folks lament the lower range, it is, nevertheless, a reality. Being aware of the low or high notes you expect the congregation to sing is important to their success in singing.

Song leaders of contemporary worship music in particular have expressed concern for a long time about the range of high notes of contemporary music. Many contemporary songs are originally written for performance venues (worship bands on tour) and then make their way into the church. (This is not a new practice at all. Consider the songs of Andraé Crouch, Amy Grant, etc.) The problem is that songs are often written for professional singers who can produce higher notes, not the average singer in church. Song leaders will sometimes need to **transpose** songs into a more manageable musical key based on the capabilities of their congregation. One seasoned worship leader remarks,

> I really wrestle with how to address our worship bands' consistent choice to sing too high for congregations. It's such a common problem. . . . I believe that our leaders who choose songs in keys only fit for skilled singers are creating obstacles for the people's worship. We are making our approach to singing reserved for only the privileged. We are simply losing sight of being a pastoral musician.[6]

He's right. Without transposing out-of-range keys to workable ones, we frustrate and ultimately eliminate people from full participation.

Limiting songs to a manageable vocal range applies not only to the music but also to the song leader. Recently I was worshiping in a congregation where the leader had a beautiful tenor voice. The first verse and chorus of the opening song went just fine. However, on leading into the second verse, the leader, in an apparent moment of personal inspiration, jumped an octave higher resulting in confusion as to how the congregation was to proceed. Eventually they figured it out. (Note to self: Just because you *can* doesn't mean you *should*!) Again, this would be fine if it were a concert. Self-control is needed when fulfilling the role of song leader.

Tip for determining vocal range: Write down the lowest and highest note of every single song in your worship repertoire. Be aware of what you are asking folks to sing. Identify a few good but untrained singers from your congregation. Test what would be a realistic range. Then transpose songs if necessary.

Noting Levels of Difficulty

A similar challenge exists regarding the song's level of difficulty. Again, some songs are written for concert settings. More sophisticated vocal gymnastics are possible for the professional musician than the average singer. A difficult song is even more challenging when dozens or hundreds of people are asked to sing as one voice. Some songs are just too complicated for corporate worship. One leader offers these reflections: "Many worship leaders are blindly asking the gathered people to sing a song that's *way* too difficult for them.

6. Paul Sunderland, email message to author, February 24, 2014.

I believe lack of sing-ability is a major contributing factor in the decline of corporate singing in the contemporary church."[7]

Again, this is not a new challenge. When hymnals began to include contemporary songs decades ago, the transcriptions tended to emulate the way the songs were recorded without adapting them for congregational use. They were difficult to sing as a group. Tricky rhythmic patterns were especially problematic.

Tip for using more complicated songs: Perhaps the worship band could periodically offer a more difficult contemporary song as a presentational song, much like a choir would do an anthem. In this case the congregation is not expected to sing along. The leader will want to avoid a "show" mentality at all costs. (The same risk exists for a choir anthem too.) But the occasional song could feasibly serve well as a musical offering on behalf of the congregation at just the right place.[8]

Creating Effective Instrumental Introductions

Instrumental introductions are key to a song leader's success. Most songs in worship today are accompanied (though a few traditions disallow instruments in corporate worship). The purpose of an introduction is to assist singers by establishing the tempo, style, and volume of the song in advance of the singers' entrance. Good introductions get the song under way on solid footing. It is highly recommended that the introduction incorporate a portion of the song's melody so that singers can immediately hear and recognize what they will be singing. Practically speaking, it does very little good for accompanists to play music that may be beautifully orchestrated but unrecognizable to the congregation. It can be exciting to hear accomplished musicians offer an impressive display of musical skillfulness prior to the singers' entrance (e.g., an organist's improvisatory free harmonization or a brass choir's fanfare); however, the melody must be obviously woven throughout the introduction or be clearly established as the introduction concludes. The point is that the melodic line is needed to lead the people securely into their participation in the song.

Some instruments are not the best to use for clear introductions. For instance, a drum solo or bass guitar lick doesn't provide for a secure entrance to the song. Likewise, merely strumming a series of chord progressions on a rhythm guitar may help the leader, but the people often remain uncertain. It is best if the melody is played on another instrument. Piano/keyboards or

7. Jeffry Rogers, email message to author, March 3, 2014.
8. Ibid.

"C" instruments such as flute, oboe, violin, and others are very well suited to provide melodic introductions and should be used when possible.

Introductions must be rehearsed in advance. Everyone needs to be on the same page to avoid confusion. They need not be long but substantial enough to fulfill their role for the people.

*Tip for creating introductions: Choose a portion of the opening melody of each song as a solid introduction. Make sure it ends on a final **cadence** so that there is a secure landing place before the worshipers are gestured to begin singing. Oftentimes the opening measures of a song combined with its closing measures works well, for they offer a clear statement of the melody and a clear conclusion, which gives the singers confidence for entering.*

Monitoring Volume Levels

The level of sound is another major consideration for effective song leading. Without question, amplification levels have risen over the years. The assumption is that louder is better. Amplification serves two basic purposes: projection of sound and balance of sound. Sound projection is needed when the physical space warrants it—in other words, when the vocal and instrumental forces need help in reaching the entire space. It is not for the purpose of demonstrating power. Amplification of sound is a symbol of power. There is no real reason for amplification to exceed its logical purpose: to help musicians to be heard. Once that is achieved, anything above it could be a power trip. Amplification is also used to mix sounds to bring greater equity among a variety of voices and instruments. This can be a very helpful feature in any size of venue. A good song leader will learn to work with sound technicians to achieve an appropriate mix of sounds. This comes with practice, through trial and error.

One basic principle is absolutely critical to follow: if you can't hear the congregation, you're too loud. The focus of congregational singing must be on the people, not the leaders. Sound is projected so that the congregation can hear the song leader(s) and accompanist(s), then they fill the room with *their* sound. One of the primary reasons for lethargy in congregational singing is that the sound of the music and the leaders' voices covers up the singers' voices. There is really no reason for a community of believers to sing if they cannot be heard. Most of us have had the experience of being in a worship service where we were singing, but the music was so loud that we could not hear our own voices. That is an abuse of power. The same philosophy mentioned above is at play here: just because you *can* doesn't mean you *should*. Another maxim related to sound levels (with biblical overtones) is this: "The congregation must increase and the leaders decrease."[9] One quick way to turn participants into onlookers is to overtake the people's voices with the leaders' own. Song leaders are wise to note:

> Vocal leadership has nothing to do with singing out "over" the congregation or with overpowering them. Vocal leadership should be conceived as coming from within the group. It's like the elementary school teacher who speaks in a whisper in the midst of a noisy classroom so the children have to quiet down in order to listen. It's learning to be community. It involves learning to listen, both on the part of the leader and on the part of those in the congregation.[10]

Tip for monitoring volume levels: During a regular worship service, set the volume levels where you normally would. Let another leader take your place while you become a worshiper who fully engages in the singing. Position yourself in the middle of the worship space. Listen for your voice and those around you. How much of the congregation's voice do you hear by comparison to those of the leaders (vocalists and instrumentalists)? What adjustments would need to be made if you believed that priority should be given to the voices of the people?

Checking Your Attitude

Every leader has an attitude that becomes readily evident to others. Attitude comes across in many different ways: through tone of voice, posture, gestures, type of humor used, even attire. Song leaders should be confident but not arrogant, enthused but not hyper, genuinely humble but not self-deprecating, feel valued but not self-important, one of the crowd but not above the crowd. In the end, attitude is about relationship. Having an authentic relationship with God and others is the best way to shape the song leader's attitude so that his or her servant spirit is evident to all.

Enlivening the Church's Song

Being an effective song leader involves giving direction to singers, but that's not all. It also involves bringing life to the music by capturing the heart of each

9. Harold M. Best, *Unceasing Worship: Biblical Perspectives on Worship and the Arts* (Downers Grove, IL: InterVarsity, 2003), 144.
10. Mark Mummert, Mark Sedio, and Richard R. Webster, "Techniques for Leading," in *Leading the Church's Song*, ed. Robert Buckley Farlee and Eric Vollen (Minneapolis: Augsburg Fortress, 1998), 19.

song. Leaders who apply similar instrumentation, tempo, volume, and so on for every congregational song, regardless of its genre, do a grave disservice to the community. Each song has its own roots, its own way of being related to a historic or stylistic tradition, its own "home." Songs should be set free to exhibit their natural character, or infused with a special setting for helping it to be experienced in a new way. Unfortunately, too often songs, regardless of their heritage, have been flattened out to sound like all other songs in the church by being subjected to the same type of generic accompaniment and leadership. It's as if there is some preconceived, uniform, church-like idea of what sacred music should sound like. This misconception has dulled the perception of music sung in church and drained it of its energy.

There are probably several reasons why leaders have fallen into a predictable pattern for leading songs. Perhaps it is because we all can be lazy at times or lack imagination; more likely we have never been taught how to breathe life into songs. One of today's most well-known song enliveners, Alice Parker, firmly believes that part of our song-leading deficits come from an undue allegiance to the printed score. She writes:

> The page to me is a virtual prison. The music in my head streams in clear profusion, beautifully articulated. But the moment I write it down it is shuttered, corseted into those unwieldy notes, those rigid counts, that visual dullness. Rare is the group that restores it to its free state—and I think this is because we treat the visual page as an end in itself, rather than moving through it to the aural/oral sound.[11]

It's time to enliven congregational singing! Any musical, enthusiastic song leader can learn to enliven songs. Here are a few practical steps to begin.

Step One: Become Acquainted with the Song

Every song has a history; get to know it. Do song **exegesis**; critically examine its text and tune in light of its original context.[12] Like people, a song is always "born out of" and "born into." Songs are *born out of* the songwriter's time in history, their cultural surroundings, their perspective on life, their religious predisposition, and so on. Songs are also typically written with an audience in mind. In that sense they are *born into* a community that will welcome the song and sing it. Here are a few exegetical questions to get started. Of course,

---

11. Alice Parker, "Song Leading," in *Melodious Accord* newsletter, April 2014, 3.
12. Exegesis is most often associated with the process of examination applied to a passage of Scripture. It involves the very methodical system of looking at a passage through the writer's and the original audience's eyes.

complete information will not be available for every song. Nevertheless, do your best to find what you can. Pretend you're a journalist. What information can you discover?

- Who wrote the song?
- When? (What century/decade? What was happening in the world?)
- Where? (Where did/does the author/composer live? What global influences informed his or her thinking? How does this show up in the text or musical style?)
- Why? (What circumstances inspired the song?)
- Audience? (Was it written for a particular group to sing? If so, why?)
- Purpose? (Did the songwriter hope to influence people in a certain way?)

An excellent place to start for exegetical work is to locate a variety of **hymnal companions**. Most major hymnal publishers also publish a companion that provides background information pertaining to the hymns found within it. (Remember, hymnals contain a wide variety of worship songs, not just hymns.) Hymnal companions are often found in libraries of Christian seminaries and universities.

Key question: What background facts inform my leading of this song?

Step Two: Listen Carefully to the Song

Really listen to a song. Imagine yourself hearing it for the first time. Find various recordings (CDs, YouTube, etc.) of it, and try not to make quick assumptions. What is the song really saying? How does the song *sound*? How does it sound differently when different artists perform it? Try to find someone to sing this song for you. (Even if you are a fine singer, it is enlightening to hear someone else's take on it.) Listen carefully as the person sings, and make notes about how you hear the song.

Key question: What sounds inform my leading of this song?

Step Three: Use Your Imagination

Try to imagine how a song would have been sung the very first time. Close your eyes and place yourself in the song's world.

- Pretend you are present the first time this song was sung. Where are you?
- Describe the event.

- Describe the surrounding environment.
- Describe the sound of the group singing the song.
- Describe the music.
- Describe the accompanying instruments (if any).
- Describe the emotion you feel in singing this song.

Key question: What can I imagine that will inform my leading of this song?

Step Four: Experiment

Experiment with various ways of singing a song. Sing it aloud a multitude of different ways. For instance, vary the volume, the tempo, the rhythmic patterns, the harmony, the **voicing**,[13] the musical style, the accompaniment instrumentation, and so forth. Be courageous. The song won't break! Sometimes songs just need to be set free to be what they are trying to be.

Key question: What unique aspect can I bring to the song that will help it be heard in a way that seems natural to it?

Step Five: Communicate Your Vision

Strive to communicate your vision well to others on your team. Work well in advance to ensure that all leaders, vocal and instrumental, are comfortable with how they will lead the congregation. Make sure instrumentalists complement the song rather than overtake it. Build confidence in your song leading team or choir by helping them to internalize the way you will lead the song. Communicate your vision to the congregation as well by sharing brief informational pieces in the church newsletter, the order of service, or on projection screens. Again, little is much. Too much information really isn't necessary and will be ignored. Give people enough to get their bearings and create interest.

Key question: How can I prepare all the leaders involved to give them confidence?

Step Six: Enjoy!

Portray a spirit of delight and enjoyment as you lead. Let the song come from deep within you. Be convincing. This comes from your own preparation. Own the song. Prepare vocally; prepare your gestures for entrances.

13. For instance, could the men instead of the treble voices carry the melody?

Practice how you will introduce the song and lead into and out of it. Then, by all means enjoy what you have prepared. This will go a long way toward the success of your efforts.

Key question: How can I prepare for successfully leading this song?

Additional Practical Considerations

Here are a few other practical considerations for enlivening song.

- Decide where you will stand. There *are* options. Make sure that your decision as to where you stand is fitting to what you are trying to accomplish.
  - in the front, elevated
  - in the front, on the same level as the people
  - from the center of the people
  - from the center of the congregation, with the people turned inward to face one another as in a circle (This is how song leaders historically positioned themselves in Sacred Harp sings, community singing events. The leader stood in the center of "the sacred square" with the four vocal sections facing one another.)
- Decide if instruments are needed. Many songs are overaccompanied. There is something beautiful about unaccompanied singing. Various types of song originated with no accompaniment whatsoever—only the sound of the human voice (the only instrument that God created!). Encourage a cappella singing when the song calls for it.
- Use helpful techniques.
  - *Echo.* A leader sings a line of the song and invites the congregation to echo it as a dialogical approach using statement/answer.
  - *Lining out.* This is a very old practice of the song leader singing an entire phrase, repeated by the congregation. Lining out employs echoing but is done throughout the entire song (every stanza), whereas echoing is a technique that may be used to enhance only part of a song.
  - *Reinforcing the melody.* For new or less familiar songs, consider reinforcing the melody by using octaves in the piano accompaniment or a treble instrument doubling the melody. It gives security to the singers, helping to create a good first-time experience.
  - *Pedal notes.* Invite one subgroup of singers to sustain one note throughout a part (or all) of the song. It resembles an organist holding down one pedal tone throughout a section of a piece, producing a rather

haunting effect. It is very effective, for instance, when done for a chant-like hymn (such as, "Of the Father's Love Begotten").[14]

- *Descants.* A **descant** is an independent vocal line that serves to decorate the melody. It is often done by higher voices on a final stanza. It has the effect of raising the level of exhilaration. Prepare a soloist or select group of singers to adorn the melody for a portion of the song. Often the tenor line of a four-part hymn, sung an octave higher, provides a fine descant. Descant collections are also readily available for purchase.

- *Imitation (round).* This is a great technique to create interest. Many pieces lend themselves to the melody entering at different, predetermined points. Each time the melody is sung in its entirety; it is simply divided among singers who enter at various times. It is also known as singing in a round. The simple song for peace *Dona Nobis Pacem*[15] ("Grant Us Peace") is a lovely example. Even some songs that were not written to function as a round still work well using this technique to create mystical layers of sound.

- *Simple harmonies.* Don't get too involved with harmonies when trying to enliven singing. Keep it simple. One well-placed harmony part in companionship with the melody can be very effective. Four-part singing is a worthy and magnificent achievement these days, but only if the song itself is well suited to it. Classic hymns, metrical psalms, and gospel hymns are usually conducive to four-part singing.

- *Text display.* Whether in a songbook, in a worship folder, or projected, the display of the words makes a big difference in how easily the song is sung. Ask a trained graphics person about font size, font colors, backgrounds, and so forth. Also, pay strict attention to where the lines are divided so that they make sense. Punctuation matters (as seen on a T-shirt: "Let's eat Grandma. Let's eat, Grandma. Punctuation saves lives."). Proper punctuation should be added (even if it is not supplied in the original source), first, for clarity of text and, second, because it is part of being good stewards of every aspect of the art forms we offer to God.

- *Be alert.* Strive to be in the moment. This comes largely through experience. Pay real attention to what is going on around you and respond accordingly. Trust your instincts. Think on the fly. Go with what seems

14. Early fourth-century hymn still in many hymnals. See Aurelius Clemens Prudentius, "Of the Father's Love Begotten," http://www.hymnary.org/text/of_the_fathers_love_begotten.
15. See "Dona Nobis Pacem," http://www.hymnary.org/text/dona_nobis_pacem_canon.

right at the moment. If you have devoted yourself to preparation and
to God, most of the time your inclinations will turn out well.

Worshipers benefit greatly from song leaders who have taken the time to
invest in preparation. If songs are dull, the buck stops with the leaders. Liveliness of singing is a realistic goal for every congregation.

Accompanying the Song: Using Instruments in Worship

Leading congregational songs effectively calls for intentional direction and
creative enlivening, as we have seen. One more important dimension of song
leadership is that of the wise use of instrumentation.

Basic types of musical instruments used in every known culture are referred
to in the Bible, in both Old and New Testaments, including: aerophones
(wind instruments like the trumpet and flute), membranophones (struck
instruments like hand drums[16]), idiophones (shaken instruments like rattles
and timbrels), and chordophones (stringed instruments like the psaltery and
harp). Instruments had many uses in the Bible—warfare, celebrations, cultic
worship, and more. Historically speaking, the use of instruments in Christian
worship has been rather sporadic. There have been periods of time in various
regions where instruments were widely used, while in other places and times,
not at all. Tracing the biblical and historical practices of instruments in worship would be fascinating, but it is not particularly relevant here. Instead, we
will concentrate on how the song leader should incorporate instruments for
the purpose of accompanying congregational song.

Before we do, however, let us affirm that instrumental leadership in worship,
apart from its role in accompaniment, is a vital ministry on its own merits.
Even as the whole creation joins in praise to its Creator, so "wordless instruments reflect the song of creation and are, therefore, called to play their part."[17]
Before discussing their accompaniment role as a primary one, we may note
two examples of beneficial instrumental music: (1) instrumental arrangements
of known worship songs and (2) newly composed pieces for instruments. In
both cases, worshipers benefit from the instruments "speaking" in worship.
They communicate the story of God without words. As N. T. Wright reminds

16. The word *toph* (or *tof*), mentioned frequently in the Bible, is considered to be a drum
constructed by stretching an animal skin over a wooden or metal hoop and played by striking
with the hand. See Mary Hopper, "Music and Musical Instruments," in *Baker Encyclopedia
of the Bible*, ed. Walter A. Elwell (Grand Rapids: Baker, 1988), 3:1511.

17. Paul Westermeyer, *The Heart of the Matter: Church Music as Praise, Prayer, Proclamation,
Story, and Gift* (Chicago: GIA, 2001), 19.

us, lyrics are not the only storytellers in worship; the music (tune) tells a story too.[18] This is a very important reminder. At the same time, art forms that do not use words provide implied story lines at best. Instrumental music written to depict an event or to communicate an idea or emotion provides an impression, not a clearly articulated proposition (program music of the Romantic Period is a good example of this). The same is true for dance, mime, sculpture, charcoal sketches, or any wordless art form. With words the presenter can be very clear about what is being communicated; without words, things are left more open-ended. That is not to elevate one art form above another. It is simply to say that words provide the means to most explicitly communicate ideas, whereas other art forms are more implicit about what is intended. In the case of the instrumental arrangement of a known song, words are drawn on from memory by the listener (who has the benefit of the message running in the background by virtue of his or her recollection). In the case of instrumental music for worship that is newly created and is not depending on any memory of certain lyrics, a general story may be told by the music—even one that is associated with a Bible story—but the listener is left to fill in the gaps. There is a place for instrumental groups to contribute to worship in their own right, and they should not be reduced to producing Muzak or creating a mood; at the same time their limitations must be appreciated.

The primary use of instruments in Christian worship is to assist in telling the story of God. Worshipers sing the story; instrumentalists support and adorn the story. Essentially, instrumental accompaniment functions in two ways. First, it supports the song. Singing a cappella can be a very moving experience, yet the type of singing that takes place in most Christian congregations in the West and many other parts of the world benefits from the support of appropriate instrumentation. Keyboard instruments (organ, piano, synthesizer, etc.) serve very well for several reasons: they provide ample volume; fuller chords can be produced (because ten fingers can be used at once); treble and bass registers can be used together to encourage both male and female singers; the melody can be highlighted clearly while the other notes are still heard; and they are extremely expressive in terms of volume, articulation, and **rubato**. Other instruments also function well in the support role of congregational song. Guitars provide harmonic support through rich chord progressions. They can also provide rhythmic drive through certain types of strumming, as well as a softer, mellow background with picking. Many churches today have the advantage of small ensemble accompaniment (praise bands, brass choirs, woodwinds, strings, handbells) or full orchestral accompaniment.

18. N. T. Wright, "Remembering Not to Forget," *Worship Leader*, May 2012, 21.

In each of these cases, instruments support the singers; they are not intended to overshadow the song. They can provide solid introductions, emphasize the melody, and furnish a foundation so that the singers do not feel timid. But balance is the key. Singers need to be heard above the accompanying instruments. To accompany means, by its very definition, to serve in a support role. To accompany is to escort, to supplement, to partner with. That is the instrumentalists' job in congregational song—to escort the song, to partner with it in giving glory to God.

Appropriate self-restraint is to be encouraged among instrumentalists so as to avoid the approach reported by a student in a reflection paper:

> Our worship pastor told me that he does not care if I play crazy bass lines, or make really cool riffs, but that he just wants me to get up there and worship Jesus while I play. Obviously I was expected to not totally botch the entire thing, but to focus more on playing for God than playing for the people. I really liked this approach as it took a lot of pressure off of us as the band.[19]

It can be tempting for instrumentalists to pursue their own self-expression, but they must be led to think of themselves in the servant role of enhancing congregational song, not overtaking it. Their ministry is valued to the same degree as the singers' ministry, but they are not equal in prominence.

A second significant function for instrumental accompaniment is that of adornment. To adorn is to decorate, to add beauty (through decoration). Most instruments are perfectly suited to provide musical lines that embellish the melody. Together, they offer a very full palette of sounds. The wonder of all of the **timbres**, ranges, and sound qualities of modern instruments today is nothing short of amazing. Use your imagination and a little ingenuity, and you can really expand the color of congregational song.

If you have had limited exposure to working with instrumentalists, don't jump in over your head at first. Start simple. Here are some strategies for taking instrumentation to the next level in your church.

Finding Instrumentalists

Think positively when you are considering instrumentation. There are more people around who play instruments than you may realize.

- Identify instrumentalists in your church. Avoid making all-church announcements for players; it can be very difficult to refuse someone who is

19. Student reflection paper, submitted March 15, 2015.

not ready once you have issued a "come one, come all" invitation. Word of mouth recommendations from other musicians can be a good strategy.

- Ask middle school and high school students to fill out a questionnaire regarding their participation in their local school bands or orchestras. Interview and audition potential candidates.
- Contact directors of community orchestras and bands for a roster of instrumentalists.
- Contact teachers who give private lessons in your area. Ask if any of their students might be ready to play at your church.

Using Instruments for Adornment

Using instruments for adornment in congregational singing is surprisingly easy. Here are a few tips.

- Start with simple descants of a **counter melody** for an existing song in your repertoire. A good place to look for descants is on the website of major church music publishers. Many of them have published collections of descants that match standard hymns and modern songs. (See suggestions at the end of this chapter.)
- As was the case for vocal descants, often the tenor line of a standard hymn that is scored in four-part harmony works very well for an instrumental descant. With a little tweaking you can produce a very effective counter melody from the tenor part. Decide which instrument would match the character of the song. You may need to transpose the descant for the instrument used.
- Compose a descant. You can do it. Just make sure it is interesting and adds to rather than detracts from the melody of the congregational song. Purchase a basic orchestration book that outlines the ranges, clefs, and best ways to feature each orchestral instrument.
- If instrumentalists are absolutely not available, consider using a good synthesizer. Instrumental sound samples have improved vastly over the years and can be strikingly realistic.

Working with People

A basic maxim is "Love people; use instruments" (not the other way around). Show your appreciation for instrumentalists by the way you interact with them.

- Invite them to play for you before you give them a particular piece of music for the service. The first step is to become acquainted with their abilities, style, experience, and so on.

- Find a simple way for instrumentalists to perform at first. It is better to have a successful first run than to overdo it and falter.

- Provide the words to every song an instrumentalist is asked to play, not just the music. Remember that they are interpreting and adorning the text. They must know and internalize the lyrics as the first step to accompanying them.

- Be clear regarding all the details. It's very helpful to put everything in writing, even if it's via text or email. It saves confusion.

- Be clear as to the financial arrangements. If you expect instrumentalists to volunteer their time, say so before you get under way. If you plan to pay an honorarium, let them know in advance how much to expect. It is never a good idea to assume things when it comes to money.

- Be respectful of their time. Whether in a one-on-one rehearsal or a large group rehearsal, you should be prepared and on time. Instrumentalists will greatly appreciate your consideration and feel valued.

- Be able to play or sing each instrumental part in order to help in rehearsal.

- Always thank those who participate in the service. Being thanked is not only basic courtesy but also helps to build lasting relationships.

Song leaders should take full advantage of a wide variety of instruments in worship to accompany and adorn congregational song. Certain worship styles have leaned almost exclusively toward favorite instruments, but there are more ways to mix it up now than ever before. Think outside the box and explore the sound of color all around.

Conclusion

It's true: congregational song *is* the heart of music ministry in worship. Churches must find people they can entrust with this most significant aspect of leadership. Perhaps that's you, the reader. If so, fall in love with congregational singing. Devote your life to helping others sing God's song. I join

Charles Gardner with this exhortation: "Pastoral musicians must learn to love the sound of a singing congregation above any other musical sound."[20] Those you lead will know it when you do.

Key Terms

cadence. The ending (landing place) of major phrases of musical compositions, indicating a musical thought has been completed.

counter melody. An independent musical line written to partner with the melody; it functions like two equal voices forming a melodic duet.

descant. An independent vocal line that serves to decorate the melody; it is commonly performed by higher voices on a final stanza.

directing song. Guiding multiple singers in the corporate act of singing through secure vocal and personal leadership.

exegesis. The critical examination of a written text in light of its original context.

hymnal companions. An encyclopedia of information pertaining to the hymns found in a particular published hymnal.

intonation. The ability to sing or play an instrument with accuracy of musical pitch.

metronome. A device that demonstrates a wide range of tempos according to numeric value.

range. The distance between the lowest and highest notes of any musical piece.

rubato. The freedom to hold the tempo back or move it forward for expressive purposes.

tempo. The speed at which music is sung or played.

timbre. The character of sound that makes an instrument or voice identifiable (e.g., the difference of sound between a clarinet and an oboe).

transpose. To shift the entire musical score to a different musical key (up or down).

voicing. Assigning particular voices (soprano, alto, tenor, bass) to particular parts of the song; the same principle refers to the orchestration of instruments.

20. Charles R. Gardner, "Ten Commandments for Those Who Love the Sound of a Singing Congregation," in *The Singing Assembly*, vol. 6 of *Pastoral Music in Practice*, ed. Virgil C. Funk (Washington, DC: Pastoral Press, 1991), 103.

To Learn More

Books

Barrier, Jim, Julie Hansford, and Mark Johnson, eds. *The Instrumental Resource for Church and School.* Nashville: Church Street, 2002.

Farlee, Robert Buckley, and Eric Vollen, eds. *Leading the Church's Song.* Minneapolis: Augsburg Fortress, 1998.

Flather, Doug, and Tami Flather. *The Praise and Worship Team Instant Tune-Up.* Grand Rapids: Zondervan, 2002.

Music, David W. *Instruments in Church: A Collection of Source Documents.* Lanham, MD: Scarecrow, 1998.

Parker, Alice. *Creative Hymn Singing,* 2nd ed. Chapel Hill, NC: Hinshaw Music, 1976.

Rienstra, Debra, and Ron Rienstra. *Worship Words: Discipling Language for Faithful Ministry.* Grand Rapids: Baker Academic, 2009.

Schultze, Quentin. *High-Tech Worship? Using Presentational Technology Wisely.* Grand Rapids: Baker Books, 2004.

Songbooks

The Descant Hymnal. Durham, NC: Apex Music, 2003.

Hopson, Hal H. *The Creative Use of Descants in Worship.* Carol Stream, IL: Hope, 1999.

Engage

Critique yourself as a leader of song using the following steps. (If you supervise others who do the actual leading, coach them.)

Directing the song:

1. Listen to recordings of your vocal leadership in worship. Invite a trained singer to evaluate your accuracy of pitch.
2. Watch a video recording of you leading singing in worship. Do you portray a hospitable spirit? Do you appear appropriately enthused about the act of corporate singing?
3. Are there any noticeable habits that have crept in that may distract the congregation (unnecessary pacing, closed eyes, "ums" when speaking, etc.)?
4. Is the congregation completely secure in when to begin singing?

Enlivening the song:

1. Explore a new song from a genre not within the congregation's normal experience. Research its background thoroughly; listen to samples of the song; imagine what the original setting might sound like; rehearse your team of musical leaders; lead the congregation in discovering the joy of singing a new song.
2. Create a survey to discover the instrumentalists you have in your church. (Some have been hiding.) Begin to incorporate them according to their level of abilities.

10

Participating in Song as the Body of Christ

Helping Worshipers to Engage through Singing

Explore

Participation in corporate worship is a hot topic. "What can I do to get worshipers engaged?" is one of the most commonly raised questions among leaders today. They share a great concern for the general apathy they perceive in worship, most especially for congregational singing. "I'm pouring my heart out up front, but the congregation doesn't look energized; people are just staring back at me. What can I do?"

Before reading this chapter, reflect on the level of engagement in your church, especially during the time of singing. Find some conversation partners so that your perceptions are as accurate as possible. Invite other staff members or people of various ages from your congregation to have an informal chat over a cup of chai. Really listen to one another, and see what kind of insights come out of that conversation. Try using the small survey below to help get started. Answer each question with a number from 1 to 10.

1 = Strongly disagree, 5 = Neither agree nor disagree, 10 = Strongly agree

1. Worshipers in our church typically seem very enthused while singing.
2. I can hear strong singing coming from the congregation.
3. I can see physical expressions of engagement. (Note what these are.)

4. The singers are louder than the instrumentalists.
5. The amount of engagement seems to have changed over time. (Note when this occurred.)

Now that you have gathered some initial thoughts about the level of engagement for congregational singing in your context, read the rest of this chapter to gain insight into how music architects may disciple worshipers in their vital role of singing.

Expand

The young professor was mystified. The puzzled looks on the faces of his students took him by surprise and left him, well, speechless. He was teaching a graduate-level worship class at a very large Christian university and when he "suggested that Christian worship is about Christ and that our planning of it must consider this fact at every juncture, there were confused glances and an awkward silence. Finally, one of the students asked their burning question: "*If we make worship all about Jesus, how will we keep the people engaged?*"[1] That very question told Brian more about the current situation in worship than he cared to admit was true. He worried about the underlying assumption, so prevalent among young worship leaders today, that it is up to them to produce engagement, that there must be some trick to getting people visibly involved in worship. They had never considered that the real presence of Jesus Christ in worship is the greatest cause for engagement. Instead, they were thinking of human strategies for producing participation. Brian concluded, "I see I have some teaching to do." Knowing Brian, he patiently guided them to better questions about engagement in worship.

Participation. Engagement. Connection. These are buzzwords in worship leader circles, for we long to see genuine and enthusiastic participation—signs that worshipers are engaged in the moment and connected to God. Leaders tend to look especially at the musical portion of worship for outward signs of emotional engagement. If the indicators aren't apparent, they quickly become discouraged. Singing is certainly one place that levels of participation seem to be more readily evident, from the volume of voices to the physical expressions that go with it (clapping, dancing, heads up, hands raised, etc.). Yet these things don't necessarily assure true participation. The place to begin a discussion of congregational engagement is not with the outward signs but with the inward humility of heart needed for devoted followers to fully accept their spiritual role

1. Email message to author, January 19, 2015.

in corporate singing as a vital ministry offered to God and others. Participation has less to do with outward show than with sharing or partnering in an effort. As we have seen, the New Testament Greek word **koinonia**, which is translated as "participation," is also translated as "fellowship" or "partnership." A biblical view of participation in worship primarily has to do with how the members of the Christian fellowship partner with one another to minister to God. Participation is more corporate than private. It is a group investment in the fulfilling of God's expectations for worship. It is about giving rather than receiving.

Singing in worship is a matter of Christian discipleship. It is a means of following Jesus Christ in his devotion to God.[2] The congregation's role in singing is a primary means to partner together in worship, even for those who don't think of themselves as singers per se. If the church is expected to sing, we must devote ourselves to the ministry of singing to help maintain the bonds of Christian fellowship. It is the same for any corporate act of worship—prayer, vows, the presentation of offerings—we learn to enter in as committed participants in whatever aspect of worship is expected. Worship calls for full abandon in our roles as worshipers, one of which is singing, remembering that whatever we do we must do all to the glory of God (1 Cor. 10:31).

With this brief introduction to participation in worship as a backdrop, this chapter sets out to help pastoral musicians equip believers in fulfilling their vital role as singers in corporate worship. Helping worshipers to become full participants in worship should be the primary vocation of worship leaders: "full and active participation by all the people is the aim to be considered before all else . . . and therefore pastors of souls must zealously strive to achieve it, by means of the necessary instruction, in all their pastoral work."[3] In chapter 3 we explored a general theology of the communal nature of song in worship. Here we focus on specifically guiding worshipers into their God-given role in the body of Christ through true participation in song. Understanding five key aspects of participating in corporate song can really make a difference: singing to the Lord, singing in community, singing with the mind, singing with the spirit, and singing a new song.

Singing to the Lord: Participating with the Right Intent

To sing or not to sing—that is the question. Many worshipers find singing in worship to be a thrilling experience. They readily join in under the enthusiastic

2. Jesus sang hymns to God (Matt. 26:30); Jesus sings praise to God in the congregation (Heb. 2:11b–12).
3. Second Vatican Council, "The Constitution on the Sacred Liturgy," *Sacrosanctum Concilium*, December 4, 1963, chap. 1, sec. 2, no. 14, http://www.vatican.va/archive/hist_councils /ii_vatican_council/documents/vat-ii_const_19631204_sacrosanctum-concilium_en.html.

leadership of the instrumentalists and vocal leaders. When the people around them are giving their all in song, it's easy to join with the crowd and be "lost in wonder, love, and praise."[4] But other worshipers don't participate through singing. They may be uninterested or perhaps they feel inadequate. Some people don't sing because they just enjoy listening to good musicians, others because they feel self-conscious. There are a variety of reasons why some folks don't participate in singing songs in worship.

While there may be a legitimate reason why a particular person refrains from singing, too often leaders accept or even encourage nonparticipation in song as a means of extending personal preference to worshipers. Whether worshipers are enthusiastic participants or not, we can't deny that to sing in worship is an urgent expectation for God's people throughout the Old and New Testaments. "Sing" occurs in more than one hundred verses of Scripture.[5] The word is used both descriptively ("I will sing of your steadfast love, O LORD, forever; with my mouth I will proclaim your faithfulness to all generations" [Ps. 89:1]) and proscriptively ("Sing to the LORD, bless his name; tell of his salvation from day to day" [Ps. 96:2]). In other words, to sing in worship is both the normative practice that is assumed through common experience and also a command to heed. It turns out that we really *must* sing, for it is a means of being faithful to the primary recipient of the song.

In worship, we sing to the Lord.[6] The Lord, the triune God, is the primary recipient of our song.[7] The starting place for congregational engagement in song is to recognize that singing is a ministry we collectively perform *to the Lord*. There is someone listening to our community's song, someone receiving the song, someone delighting in it, someone longing for each voice to join the chorus of song—and that someone is God. The imperative admonition to "sing to the Lord" is found often in Scripture, frequently in command form.[8] If Scripture urges us—even directs us—to sing to the Lord, this must become our heartfelt intention. We participate not because of the quality of our voice or our level of interest in the music. No, we participate because

4. This phrase is taken from the last phrase of Charles Wesley's hymn, "Love Divine, All Loves Excelling."

5. The results of a search on Accordance Bible Software.

6. Elsewhere in the book I have highlighted the appropriateness of addressing worship songs to the community, a matter also addressed later in this chapter.

7. When the phrase "sing to the LORD" appears in the Hebrew Scriptures, "LORD" is YHWH (Yahweh, reverently pronounced "Adonai"). However, in light of New Testament teaching, it is appropriate for Father, Son, and Holy Spirit (Three in One) to be the recipient(s) of the congregation's song.

8. The results of a search on Accordance Bible Software indicate the imperative of "to sing" occurs in the Hebrew fifteen times.

it is unto the Lord. The divine recipient is reason enough to give our all to singing in corporate worship.

To sing to the Lord is a matter of proper intention. Intention has to do with purpose. To intend to do something is to purpose to do it. Singing becomes a matter of the will. William Temple, ninety-eighth Archbishop of Canterbury, understood the connection between singing and the intention of the will:

> In 1931, at the end of the Oxford Mission (what is known in many Protestant circles as a Revival Meeting), he led a congregation in the University Church, St. Mary the Virgin, in the singing of the hymn, "When I Survey the Wondrous Cross." Just before the last stanza, he stopped them and asked them to read the words to themselves. "Now," he said, "if you mean them with all your heart, sing them as loud as you can. If you don't mean them at all, keep silent. If you mean them even a little and want to mean them more, sing them very softly." The organ played, and two thousand voices whispered:
>
> > Were the whole realm of nature mine,
> > That were an offering far too small;
> > Love so amazing, so divine,
> > Demands my soul, my life, my all.[9]

We must bring our intentions into submission so that we will be willing to sing the songs of Zion in order to participate as one voice among many as citizens of the earthly kingdom. The aim of singing is to please God, not to please ourselves. There are people who refuse to sing songs in a musical style that they don't appreciate. They simply keep their mouths closed because they don't prefer or resonate with the style. They withhold their participation. We may need divine assistance to help with our intention to sing with enthusiasm. Some hymns actually call on God for spiritual help to sing with proper intention:

> Come, thou Fount of every blessing, tune my heart to sing thy grace;
> streams of mercy, never ceasing, call for songs of loudest praise.
> Teach me some melodious sonnet, sung by flaming tongues above.
> Praise the mount I'm fixed upon it, mount of God's redeeming love.[10]

Occasionally our heart must be tuned to sing God's praise for it may not always come naturally. But sing we must, for God's unceasing mercies call

9. James E. Kiefer, "William Temple, Theologian, Archbishop of Canterbury, 27 October 1944." http://justus.anglican.org/resources/bio/61.html.

10. Robert Robinson, "Come, Thou Fount of Every Blessing," 1758, public domain, http://www.hymnary.org/text/come_thou_fount_of_every_blessing.

for songs of loudest praise. Even David, who had proper intentions ("My heart is steadfast, O God, my heart is steadfast; I will sing and make melody" [Ps. 108:1a]) also engaged in some self-talk for inspiration: "Awake, my soul! Awake, O harp and lyre! I will awake the dawn. I will give thanks to you, O LORD, among the peoples, and I will sing praises to you among the nations" (Ps. 108:1b–3). If worshipers lack zeal in singing, they should pray that a song is awakened within them—a song to the Lord.

Singing in Community: Participating for the Sake of Others

When worship leaders perceive that the engagement of the people is low, they are tempted to initiate various strategies to correct the situation. Unfortunately, sometimes they launch a plan based on assumptions and not on interviewing worshipers as to why they seem unengaged.

One of my students, Jarod, asked to speak with me one day after class. He was discouraged. He told me that he led popular worship songs at the Wednesday night youth meetings at his church but that the kids made no effort to participate. They looked bored. He asked what he could do to create interest in the music.

"Tell me about your kids," I said.

He shared that the youth were not from the church; they were from the rough neighborhood nearby, the result of a recent outreach program. None of them were Christians; they'd never been in church before.

I suggested to Jarod that he was asking the wrong question. Perhaps he should not ask how he could get them interested in the music, but how he could get them interested in relationships with loving Christians and ultimately with God. It might even involve not singing at all for the time being.

Jarod had a problem with engagement, which he tried to address through programming a particular type of popular music, hoping for good results.

"It's pretty hard to be enthused about singing love songs to Jesus," I said, "when you don't yet know Jesus." This led to a great discussion about worship leaders' expectations in general when it comes to the level of participation as the people sing.

It's not uncommon to address lethargic singing through external means such as increasing the volume of the instruments, choosing more upbeat songs, changing the musical style altogether, or admonishing the congregation with comments like, "Sing as if you really mean it." Ordinarily, browbeating isn't effective. Instead, one of the wisest approaches toward increased engagement is for leaders to disciple worshipers in their role as singers in community.

The starting place is to teach worshipers that, at its core, congregational song is a group activity, a corporate event that depends on their commitment to it. The gathering of God's people for worship, sometimes referred to as "the assembly," is the most fundamental symbol of worship. Whether two or three—or many thousands—gather in Christ's name, it is the physical assembly of worshipers that symbolizes the reality of the existence of the church of Jesus Christ. It is not *only* a symbol, of course; the assembly is also a *reality* of earthly citizens of the kingdom of God found in the presence of their risen Lord in a unique way by virtue of the very act of gathering. This is why our understanding of the role of individual worshipers is so crucial. Those "who take the trouble to be seen and heard, and to be touched, render a holy service because by their very presence and action they constitute the symbol that is the *church assembled*."[11] When each worshiper is a coparticipant in the song, we render a service to one another through our participation. Randall Bradley states, "There is no community without participation. To stand on the sidelines is to give up our place within the local worshiping community. . . . Community, worship, and singing are all built around participation, and each symbolizes God's participation in our lives and our offering gratitude back to God through hearty involvement."[12]

There is no community without participation. Full participation is necessary in order for independent individuals, who join in when and as they wish, to move toward singing for the sake of the body of Christ. True worship calls us to selfless singing. We surrender our inclination to call the shots according to our desires—to alternate between passivity and participation in order to satisfy our own needs at the moment. Instead, we offer control to the Holy Spirit who strengthens us to sing for the sake of others, to contribute to the authenticity of the community's worship voice.

Even as the gathered assembly was a *visible symbol of unity*, the sound of singing is an *audible symbol of unity*. To the earliest believers, singing with "one voice" became an expression of the spiritual harmony within the community. While writing to the church in Rome, Paul connects their ability to live in harmony with one another to glorifying God with one voice (Rom. 15:5–6). Singing with one voice was a prominent theme among the early church fathers who also made the connection between the unity of

11. Lawrence Madden, "The Congregation's Active Participation Is Performance," in *The Singing Assembly*, vol. 6 of *Pastoral Music in Practice*, ed. Virgil C. Funk (Washington, DC: Pastoral Press, 1991), 52 (emphasis in original).

12. C. Randall Bradley, *From Memory to Imagination: Reforming the Church's Music* (Grand Rapids: Eerdmans, 2012), 124.

faith and the unity of song.[13] Early on, unison singing was considered to be the purest form of unity of spirit; "'with one voice' became an ideal for Christian song, an ideal that found its natural expression in unison, communal singing."[14] There is no doubt that singing together as the body of Christ in worship both contributes to and expresses a kindred spirit among believers. Perhaps the popular proverb, "The family that prays together stays together," can be reworded to suggest, "The family of God that sings together clings together."

While our priority in this chapter is that of singing as the body of Christ in local church Lord's Day worship, any time Christians gather for worship and/or fellowship is a wonderful time to sing. The body has multiple dimensions. Corporate singing in small groups is a great way to experience Christian community. Encouraging corporate song in small groups could pay big dividends in renewed singing in church. Likewise, singing together as families in individual households should be reclaimed. Whether during family devotions or riding in the car or singing around the house, I encourage pastoral musicians to provide resources for helping family groups to sing as another dimension of the body of Christ. It doesn't require trained musicians to make a joyful noise unto the Lord. Perhaps most of all, we must remember that the body of Christ consists of the saints of God past, present, and future who are performing their glorious duty of worship through endless song. When we participate enthusiastically in Lord's Day worship, our song mystically merges with that of the great cloud of witnesses having gone before us who now, with the heavenly beings, day and night worship without ceasing (Rev. 4:8b). Corporate singing is an eternal, cosmic activity.

Given the significant ministry of congregational song that is expected of the body of Christ, certain practical guidelines are helpful so that individual members can know how to take up their role with discipline and grace. Various religious leaders in their respective eras have provided the church with specific guidance for corporate singing in worship. Surprisingly, it seems they faced some of the same concerns that we do today. Two prominent figures from vastly different periods and locations share amazing similarities in their advice to worshipers. A bishop in the early church, Niceta of Remesiana, admonished the faithful in detail concerning the discipline of corporate song. Fourteen centuries later, an Anglican priest, John Wesley, attempted the same thing. Their advice is still relevant to worshipers today.

13. Calvin R. Stapert, *A New Song for an Old World: Musical Thought in the Early Church* (Grand Rapids: Eerdmans, 2007), 25.
14. Ibid., 27.

Niceta (4th–5th centuries) was bishop of Remesiana, a region in modern Serbia that was politically aligned to the church in the East but also held ecclesiastical associations with the bishop of Rome.[15] Niceta is best known for six books of pastoral guidance for catechumens (persons undergoing extensive educational and spiritual preparation for Christian baptism).[16] One of his sermons, *De utilitate hymnorum*, "is one of the central patristic documents on ecclesiastical music."[17] It provides fascinating insights into the significance of corporate song in worship. A portion of his sermon is quoted here at length (words in parentheses are from Niceta's original Latin):

> Thus, beloved, let us sing with alert senses and a wakeful mind, as the psalmist (*hymnidicus*) exhorts: "Because God is king of all the earth," he says, "sing ye wisely" (Ps. 46.8), so that a psalm is sung not only with the spirit, that is, the sound of the voice, but with the mind also (1 Cor. 14.15), and so that we think of what we sing rather than allow our mind, seized by extraneous thoughts as is often the case, to lose the fruit of our labor. One must sing with a manner (*sonus*) and melody befitting holy religion; it must not proclaim theatrical distress but rather exhibit Christian simplicity in its very musical movement (*ipsa modulatione*); it must not remind one of anything theatrical, but rather create compunction in the listeners.
>
> Further, our voice ought not to be dissonant (*dissona*) but consonant (*consona*). One ought not to drag out the singing (*protrahat*) while another cuts it short (*contrahat*), and one ought not to sing too low (*humiliet*) while another raises his voice (*extollat*). Rather each should strive to integrate his voice within the sound of the harmonious (*concinentis*) chorus and not project it outwardly in the manner of a cithara as if to make an immodest display. . . . And for him who is not able to blend (*aequare*) and fit himself in with the others, it is better to sing in a subdued (*lenta*) voice than to make a great noise, for thus he performs both his liturgical function and avoids disturbing the singing brotherhood.[18]

Niceta's concerns may be summarized as an admonition to worshipers to sing with a keen and focused mind to avoid distraction, to demonstrate appropriate restraint so as not to draw attention to themselves (avoid theatrics), to sing in tune, to sing in time, to sing so as not to be louder or softer than others, and to contribute to the liturgy rather than to detract from it. The emphasis is clearly on offering songs as with one voice, a familiar theme for

---

15. Maria Grazia Mara, "Niceta of Remesiana," in *Encyclopedia of Ancient Christianity*, ed. Angelo Di Berardino (Downers Grove, IL: InterVarsity, 2014), 910.

16. Ibid.

17. James McKinnon, *Music in Early Christian Literature* (Cambridge: Cambridge University Press, 1987), 134.

18. Ibid., 138.

the author who is credited with first penning the phrase "the communion of saints"[19] in the West. The phrase eventually made its way into the Apostles' Creed.

Like Niceta, Wesley emphasized the unity of sound and purpose among worshipers. John Wesley, eighteenth-century Anglican priest, along with his brother Charles and other key leaders, led a movement in England focused on the renewal of the Anglican Church. In time this effort became known as the Methodist movement. The Methodists often gathered in the open, in preaching houses, and in various venues for their meetings—all of which included singing. Wesley, who was well known for his methodical approach to the spiritual life, became concerned with the rather undisciplined, individualistic nature of corporate singing and so established procedures for singing. His famous "Directions for Singing" first appeared in *Select Hymns with Tunes Annext* (1761). Wesley's purpose was clear: "That this Part of Divine worship may be the more acceptable to God, as well as the more profitable to yourself and others, be careful to observe the following Directions."[20]

I. Learn these tunes before you learn any others; afterwards learn as many as you please.

II. Sing them exactly as they are printed here, without altering or mending them at all; and if you have learned to sing them otherwise, unlearn it as soon as you can.

III. Sing all. See that you join with the congregation as frequently as you can. Let not a slight degree of weakness or weariness hinder you. If it is a cross to you, take it up, and you will find it a blessing.

IV. Sing lustily and with a good courage. Beware of singing as if you were half dead, or half asleep; but lift up your voice with strength. Be no more afraid of your voice now, nor more ashamed of its being heard, than when you sung the songs of Satan.

V. Sing modestly. Do not bawl, so as to be heard above or distinct from the rest of the congregation, that you may not destroy the harmony; but strive to unite your voices together, so as to make one clear melodious sound.

VI. Sing in time. Whatever time is sung be sure to keep with it. Do not run before nor stay behind it; but attend close to the leading voices, and move therewith as exactly as you can; and take care not to sing too slow. This drawling way naturally steals on all who are lazy; and it is high time to drive it out from us, and sing all our tunes just as quick as we did at first.

19. Mara, "Niceta of Remesiana," 911.
20. John Wesley quoted in Carlton R. Young, *Companion to the United Methodist Hymnal* (Nashville: Abingdon, 1993), 320.

VII. Above all sing spiritually. Have an eye to God in every word you sing. Aim at pleasing him more than yourself, or any other creature. In order to do this attend strictly to the sense of what you sing, and see that your heart is not carried away with the sound, but offered to God continually; so shall your singing be such as the Lord will approve here, and reward you when he cometh in the clouds of heaven.[21]

Summarizing Wesley's concerns, Wesley emphasized that worshipers should perform each song with respect for both the composer's and the author's exact intent, join in as often as possible, view corporate song as a spiritual discipline, sing with enthusiasm, sing so as not to draw attention to oneself, maintain the tempo, and sing with great devotion to God. Like Niceta, Wesley emphasized the unity of sound and purpose among worshipers.

It is amazing to note the substantial overlap in the issues addressed by the two leaders. The points of mutual concern they share offer the modern worshiper much wisdom for today. Both leaders begin with advice stated positively while not shying away from rather abrupt "don'ts." I will follow this approach in my summary paraphrases here.

- Strive for simple, clear, unified singing that is fitting for a service of worship. Let all voices blend together as a sign of harmony. Don't try to be heard above others; avoid musical theatrics.

- Sing in the tempo set by the leader(s). Don't drag behind; it's a form of laziness.

- Sing in order to please God; offer each song to God continually. Don't get distracted with wandering thoughts or absorbed in the beauty of the sound.

It's interesting that both leaders urge worshipers to attend to singing as a *spiritual vocation*; in fact, it is their primary concern. Niceta begins with this thought, and Wesley ends with it. The vitality of song within a congregation is a sort of spiritual barometer. Distinguished hymnologist Hugh T. McElrath claimed that "the depth and breadth of participation in congregational song is a good indicator of the depth and breadth of a congregation's spiritual life."[22]

Also, both leaders share a concern for the technical skills of making music together. Learning to sing by listening to one another and attempting to

---

21. John Wesley quoted in *The United Methodist Hymnal* (Nashville: United Methodist Publishing House, 1989), vii.

22. Hugh T. McElrath, "Hymnology," lecture at Southern Baptist Theological Seminary, Louisville, KY, fall 1980.

contribute to the overall beauty of shared song takes congregational song to another level. Instead of providing singers extreme options—either opt out entirely or sing your lungs out regardless of what anyone else is doing—congregational singing is best rendered in loving self-deference. In honor, preferring one another, worshipers should offer courteous regard, respect, and compliance with another's wishes, as together we seek to offer selfless song with one voice unto the Lord. Part of the pastoral musician's duties is to instruct worshipers in both the spiritual disposition and the artful skill needed to "make song" together as the body of Christ.

Singing with the Mind: Participating with the Intellect

In his first letter to the church at Corinth, the apostle Paul spends a good deal of time guiding the church in matters related to public worship (especially 1 Cor. 11–14). When addressing the use of spiritual gifts in worship, Paul concludes: "What should I do then? I will pray with the spirit, but I will pray with the mind also; I will sing praise with the spirit, but I will sing praise with the mind also" (1 Cor. 14:15). Singing with the spirit and singing with the mind were not two separate entities for Paul. Rather, they were two sides of the same coin. "He represents an integration, a wholeness in his life and in his expression of his faith. . . . Paul does not compartmentalize the life of faith into some segment of the person; instead, the whole person, mind and spirit and heart, is renewed and is placed in service of God, its Creator and redeemer."[23] Paul consistently aspires for the whole person to participate in worship: bodies presented as a living sacrifice (Rom. 12:1), minds renewed (Rom. 12:2), and praying with the spirit and mind (1 Cor. 14:15).

Still, for all of Paul's interest in the integrated person as a full participant in worship, he personally favors the value of praying and singing with the *mind* in public worship. Why? For one primary reason: edification. Paul indicates that when he speaks in tongues (prays in the spirit), the outsiders gain no benefit (1 Cor. 14:16) and others are not built up (v. 17).[24] Paul argues, "For if I pray in a tongue, my spirit prays but my mind is unproductive" (v. 14). Paul is emphatic: "In church I would rather speak five words

23. J. Paul Sampley, "The First Letter to the Corinthians: Introduction, Commentary, and Reflections," in *Acts; Introduction to Epistolary Literature; Romans; 1 Corinthians*, vol. 10 of *The New Interpreter's Bible: A Commentary in Twelve Volumes* (Nashville: Abingdon, 2002), 963.

24. The need for interpretation is stressed precisely for the purpose of knowing what is said/prayed in the spirit (1 Cor. 14:5).

with my mind, in order to instruct others also, than ten thousand words in a tongue" (v. 19). The operative phrase is "instruct others." The use of the mind is not just a matter of worshipers employing their cognitive powers; it is using our minds to contribute to the building up of the body of Christ. This is exactly what Paul is referring to in his letter to the Colossians when he says that the songs we sing in worship must employ the mind as we (1) let the word of Christ dwell in the community richly; (2) teach and admonish one another in all wisdom; and (3) and instruct one another through the singing of psalms, hymns, and spiritual songs (Col. 3:16). Unproductive minds in worship are problematic. Paul longs for all believers to experience the renewal of their minds so that they can discern God's good, acceptable, and perfect will (Rom. 12:2).

Paul's clear instruction to sing with the mind suggests the importance of participating intellectually as the body of Christ. First, we must sing the truth (the whole truth and nothing but the truth) so that Christians *know* the truth. Worship songs must be clear, be faithful to Christian beliefs, and state truths that invite wonder at the mysteries of God. They must be understandable while at the same time call us forward into deeper apprehension of the truth. When we sing the truth about God and Christian faith, we participate in proclamation and witness.

Second, singing with the mind helps us to participate in accountability. Songs serve as vehicles for admonishing ourselves and other believers—for advising one another in matters of Christian faith and for warning us of the consequences of disobedience. They help us to sing of our intentions to love the Lord our God with all our heart, soul, mind, and strength and to love others as ourselves (Mark 12:30–31). In short, when we sing we testify to one another of our successes and failures as we participate in helping the members of the community to remain honest and faithful.

Third, singing with the mind helps us to participate in the edification of believers. We are called to build one another up in the faith. Paul champions edification consistently in his letters. It is a hallmark of New Testament worship.[25] To edify is to help someone improve in knowledge and character. Singing songs of encouragement is a primary means for edification. Singing with the mind enables the community to grow in grace and to become more deeply aligned with Jesus Christ in his death and resurrection (Phil. 3:10).

Let us sing with our minds, for we desire the renewing of our thoughts and imaginations for the glory of God and the encouragement of the church.

---

25. Ralph P. Martin, *Worship in the Early Church* (Grand Rapids: Eerdmans, 1971), 132–33.

Singing with the Spirit: Participating with a Heart of Love

In worship, the community is expected to sing praise with the mind *and* with the spirit. At this point, having examined one half of the equation, the reader may expect that I will return to the same verse as a basis for discussing the other half—what it means to sing with the spirit. Instead, I go to the very heart of Paul's discussion of spiritual gifts in worship: the profound apostolic instruction of 1 Corinthians 13. Here, indeed, is a summarization of what it means to sing in the spirit; it is to love the community in which one sings. Participation in song must be done in the spirit of love for one another.

To sing with the spirit is impossible without love. When Paul mentions "sing with the spirit" in 1 Corinthians 14:15, he is addressing only one of the spiritual gifts at that point—speaking in tongues. But when leading into his discussion of love in chapter 13, Paul offers a list of many spiritual gifts at the end of chapter 12 (speaking in tongues is one among several). Paul's main point of this section of the letter is that all the gifts are meaningless without love. Regardless of the gift endowed, it does not exceed the more excellent way: the way of love.

While the apostle is not speaking explicitly of congregational song in chapter 13, I do not think it is taking too much license to apply chapter 13 to singing in community. After all, Paul connects love and corporate song in Colossians: "*Above all, clothe yourselves with love*, which binds everything together in perfect harmony" (3:14, emphasis added), and "sing psalms, hymns, and spiritual songs" (v. 16). All the songs we sing in community are meaningless without love. Singing beautiful songs written in the tongues of mortals and angels is only noise without love. All the knowledge conveyed in songs is nothing without love. Having the greatest faith when one sings is nothing without love. Generosity and self-surrender gain us nothing without love. Participating in song with hearts full of genuine love will yield some remarkable results. If we have love, our services of congregational song will be places where we exhibit patience and kindness to one another. We will not find ourselves envious, boastful, arrogant, or rude. We will not insist on our own way, or be irritable or resentful. We will not rejoice when others stumble but celebrate the truth. When we sing with Christian love, we will bear all things, believe all things, hope all things, endure all things.

If Paul were to learn of the widespread lack of engagement in worship today, I feel confident that he would say the same thing to us with which he concluded this portion of his letter to the Corinthians: "Pursue love" (1 Cor. 14:1a). Love will revitalize the energy in the room during worship far beyond what any hit song or impressive instrumentation will do. Love will warm hearts. Love will deepen community. Love will summon one and all to enter into singing with zeal because it is for God and others.

Pursue love. But how is this done? Love is both a gift from God and something to be developed. Pray for Christian love. If it is honestly desired and intentionally sought, God will not refuse the gift of love to the human heart. Also, cultivate love. Practice it. Don't depend on affectionate feelings to come first. Rather, perform loving acts before you even feel the love you hope for. Offer gestures of love to others in the community; feelings will follow. Paul uses the Greek word *agapē* in chapter 13. While there are several words used in the New Testament to indicate different types of love, *agapē* in this context speaks of love not driven by feelings or natural inclinations but love that seeks the welfare of all.[26] Action may need to precede affection. It does not mean you are artificial if your intent is truly to pursue love; it means that you are on a sincere journey that will result in the real thing.

There are practical steps we can take to cultivate love while singing. First, open your eyes when you sing. Corporate song isn't about private moments with God. Actually look at those around you. Visualize the community singing its praise to God. Celebrate their presence in song. Second, pray for others as they sing, that they will have strength to offer their song to God and be touched by the Spirit. Pray for the worship leaders as they lead. Third, take up the song on behalf of others. Sing songs of faith when others can't do so. Sing the song for the one who lacks faith or will or energy. Step in and present *their* song to the triune God on their behalf.

Sing with the spirit—the spirit of love—and you will find that participation increases greatly in the congregation.

Singing a New Song: Participating in the Song of Jesus

One final means of participation in congregational song is to sing a new song. The phrase "new song" occurs nine times in Scripture, five of which appear as an invitation for the worshiper(s). Examples include the following:

- "O sing to the LORD a new song; sing to the LORD, all the earth" (Ps. 96:1).
- "Praise the LORD! Sing to the LORD a new song, his praise in the assembly of the faithful" (Ps. 149:1).

26. W. E. Vine, Merrill F. Unger, and William White Jr., eds., *Vine's Complete Expository Dictionary of Old and New Testament Words* (Nashville: Thomas Nelson, 1985), s.v. "*agapē*."

- "Sing to the LORD a new song, his praise from the end of the earth!" (Isa. 42:10).

It is very common to interpret "new song" to mean the composing of original music to be sung in worship, which is one realistic interpretation. The writing of new material is an ongoing need of the church. One way to increase participation is through encouraging new songs to be sung. But with this comes a great challenge. Too many churches are incessantly intrigued with singing exclusively what is new. We have an infatuation with the new and easily dismiss the old, even if "old" is only last week. Worship songs have become as disposable as yesterday's newspaper. Fortunately, some worship leaders are beginning to seriously question the spiritual wisdom of allowing Western culture's preoccupation with whatever is new to define what is valued. The importance of establishing a canon of song (see chap. 5) is to *expand* your worship music repertoire, not to *replace* it week by week. The constantly revolving door of new songs in worship must be reevaluated.

One reasonable interpretation of singing a new song to the Lord no doubt includes creating fresh expressions of song for worship. But is it all? There just might be additional meanings that can shed light on our call to participation in worship. Another possibility is that to sing a new song has much to do with singing songs "newly"—singing existing songs in a way that breathes new life into them. In making this claim, no one is suggesting that new songs not be written. Instead, rather than discarding long-standing worship songs, we are called on to sing them with the full energy of the present. Bible teacher and worship leader Mark Roberts makes this very point:

> Biblical scholars see two possible meanings of the phrase New Song (*shir chadash* in Hebrew). Some emphasize the literal newness of the lyrics. Others explain that a new song needn't be recently written. The psalmist can use this language to refer to a familiar song sung with new meaning and passion. Both literal and figurative meanings of New Song may well be present in the Psalms.[27]

Meaning and passion come from our experience of God, not from new music. If we depend on a constant influx of new songs in order to engage, we have misplaced our source of engagement. The Holy Spirit, not a new song, is our source for empowered singing. That's why congregational singing is one type of spiritual barometer; the deeper the corporate faith of the church, the more vibrant the corporate song.

27. Mark D. Roberts, "The True Source of a New Song," in *Worship Leader*, January/ February 2010, 14.

Harold Best also shares the view that one meaning of new song is to "sing to the Lord a song *newly*."[28] He proposes that "biblical newness is first of all a newness that arises out of a life of faith. . . . [W]hether the song is borrowed, repeated or upsettingly different, faith alone makes it new."[29] After all, a song is truly new only once.[30] Therefore, any repetition of its use requires us to sing it as if it were for the first time, or we could be guilty of the vain repetition about which Jesus warned his disciples (Matt. 6:7).[31] To sing a song newly is not a matter of drumming up energy on the spot. Both Best and Roberts emphasize that what is required for participants to sing a song newly is devoted and sustained attention to our spiritual lives so that any passion in our song is the result of our ever-deepening walk with God. This actually requires more effort than finding new songs. For instance, it requires more work to search the Scriptures for truth to form us than to search the internet for songs to excite us. It resembles the frustration that some leaders face when they discover that their people would rather read books about the Bible than read the Bible. Whatever the cost, when the Scriptures call the church to "sing to the LORD a new song, his praise in the assembly of the faithful" (Ps. 149:1), we must intend to sing our songs newly, reflective of the renewing life of the Spirit that dwells within us.

A third meaning of singing a new song refers to Jesus Christ *as* the **New Song**. In early Christianity the term "New Song" emerged in the writings of the church fathers as a metaphor with very special meaning; it referred specifically to Jesus Christ. As one example, Clement of Alexandria (c. 150–215) identified the New Song as Christ the Logos[32] (the Word). Christ the Word, co-creator with God (John 1:1–3), sang the world into being, so to speak. In doing so, the New Song presided over the music of the cosmos, bringing harmony to its sound.[33] In his writings and also as a teacher at the Catechetical School of Alexandria, Clement contested the predominant cultural view of music that was tied to mythological figures of ancient Greece who, "under cover of music . . . were the first to lead men by the hand to idolatry."[34] His fellow

28. Harold M. Best, *Unceasing Worship: Biblical Perspectives on Worship and the Arts* (Downers Grove, IL: InterVarsity, 2003), 145.

29. Ibid.

30. Ibid.

31. Ibid., 146.

32. McKinnon, *Music in Early Christian Literature*, 29.

33. Ibid., 30.

34. Oliver Strunk, "Clement of Alexandria—From the Exhortation to the Greeks," in *Source Readings in Music History: From Classical Antiquity through the Romantic Era* (New York: Norton, 1950), 61.

Greeks explained the Harmony of the Spheres[35] in terms of mythological stories and musical theories related to the emotional and behavioral powers of certain tonal systems. Clement called it all discord and maintained that the New Song, as Lord of the music of the cosmos, was responsible for the harmonious arrangement of the universe in its entirety.[36] Clement says that the Lord (Christ) made humans to be "beautiful, breathing instrument[s], after His own image; and assuredly He Himself is an all-harmonious instrument of God, melodious and holy, the wisdom that is above this world, the heavenly Word . . . worthy of power, the Christ—I have called Him a New Song."[37]

Jesus Christ *is* the New Song! To fully participate in the songs of worship is to realize that Jesus is not only the leader of the song but also the song itself. Singing becomes much more than an activity in which we participate; it serves as a means of grace—an avenue through which God, in Christ, can change us through the power of the Holy Spirit.[38] We sing with Christ as he sings his song to the Father. Christ is both subject and verb of the church's song. He *is* the New Song. "New" is what Jesus does. The final establishment of a new heaven and a new earth rests on Christ's promise: "See, I am making all things new" (Rev. 21:5). To participate in worship is ultimately to sing to the One who makes all things new, the one who is both the singer and the song.

True participation is forever connected with singing to the New Song. As Robert Lechner summarizes:

> It is not chance that the over-all, the all-embracing word that we use to speak of the act that is proper to the assembly is not love, not knowing, not sensing, but *participation*. An assembly only exists when a group within the Church is actually sharing. And the goal of this participation is the realization of *a presence*. We might say that the grace proper to the assembly is the heightened presence of Christ in the midst of God's people. And the more deep the presence of Christ, the more the assembly is the place where salvation is going on and glory is given to the Father.[39]

35. Also referred to as the Music of the Spheres, this ancient philosophical view (accredited to Pythagoras) proposed that movements of celestial bodies were arranged by mathematical ratios corresponding to musical intervals.

36. Ibid., 62.

37. Ibid., 63.

38. I wish to emphasize that music is not a sacrament. It in no way is promised as a means of God's divine action on behalf of his people. However, there are various means of grace which God providentially uses in order to shape us into the image of his Son. Several elements of worship are often used in this way (prayer, exhortation, music, anointing with oil, etc.).

39. Robert F. Lechner, "The People of God in Assembly," *Worship* 39, no. 5 (1965): 259–64.

Conclusion

We have come full circle. If worship is all about Jesus, how will we keep the people engaged? Let's restate the question: If worship isn't all about Jesus, with what are we engaging? Technologies? Staging? Lighting? Song sets? Instrumentation? Clever videos? Movie clips? Presentational software? The music we adore? Overpowering sound systems? Ultimately (and worst of all), are these things assisting us in engaging with ourselves? Any or all the above can be useful mediums in worship. But the question remains: What produces true participation? If none of these was available to us, would authentic participation exist? *Could* it exist? If it could, what would we depend on to become fully engaged participants? What or who would be the source for our engagement? We must distinguish between the power of the "what" (examples listed above) and the power of the "Who" (Jesus, the New Song).

Being disciples in worship is one of the most urgent needs in the church today. Instructing believers to become informed and dedicated worship participants has been significantly slighted in past decades. For some reason leaders have assumed that worship just happens—that folks will automatically discover what is needed for them to become worshipers. Unfortunately this hasn't worked too well; those who attend church often have no clue what worship is all about. In the end, we can prioritize our efforts in searching the cultural landscape for external means to attract the attention of worshipers, hoping to preoccupy them at least, or entertain them at best. Or instead, we can reprioritize; we can assume our rightful and urgent duty as leaders and choose to disciple all worshipers to sing to the Lord, sing in community, sing with the mind, sing with the spirit, and sing a new song. Participation will rise from within the community rather than from without. The difference will be remarkable.

Key Terms

agapē. A Greek word translated as "love"—a type of love not based on feelings but on intentions to seek the welfare of all.

koinonia. A Greek word translated as "participation," "fellowship," or "partnership"; used often in reference to the unique relationship among believers.

New Song. A metaphor for Jesus Christ in early Christian writings.

To Learn More

Bonhoeffer, Dietrich. *Life Together*. New York: Harper & Row, 1954.

Funk, Virgil C., ed. *The Singing Assembly*. Vol. 6 of *Pastoral Music in Practice*. Washington, DC: Pastoral Press, 1991.

Engage

To improve participatory singing in your church, try these practical steps:

1. Pretend you are the leader of a movement to renew passion for singing in worship. What "Directions for Singing" would you create? Imitating the list composed by John Wesley found in this chapter, write your own seven directions for singing (keep your current context in mind).
2. List three ways you can encourage singing beyond your primary worship service(s). For instance, how could singing be introduced or strengthened in Sunday school, small groups, family units, or church business meetings?
3. Assemble a small group of church leaders (pastoral staff, music staff, accountability partners, etc.). Try paraphrasing 1 Corinthians 13 by substituting "sing" and "songs" for some of the action verbs ("speak," "have prophetic powers," "have all faith," etc.). Discuss what this means for participatory singing in your church.

11

Forming Disciples
through Song

Worship as Spiritual Formation

Explore

Has there been a time recently when a song from your past that you hadn't thought about in a long, long time suddenly popped into your head? Maybe it was a popular song on the radio twenty years ago, or a Sunday school chorus from your childhood, or a song from summer camp. Did it seem to come out of the blue? It may have even taken you a while to recall exactly what song it was. Little by little the soundtrack in your mind got stronger; soon you started to hum the melody aloud. Before long you recognized it, and the words came rushing back. So did the memories. You were able to recall an occasion or a place where that song meant something special to you. It had been playing inaudibly all along, but something unexpectedly turned up the volume, and the song made its way from its quiet resting place into your consciousness once again. It felt like an old friend. Before reading this chapter, think about the staying power of songs. To help, here are a few questions you can toss around on Facebook or text with some friends:

1. Name a favorite pop song from your high school era.
2. Describe an occasion where you recall it was playing.
3. Using only one word, what emotion comes to mind?
4. What Christian song do you most associate with your conversion? Why?

5. What song, of any type, would you say tells the story of your life?
6. How does it tell your story?

Songs are related to the stories of our lives. Now that you have begun to think about the power of song, read the rest of this chapter to discover just how powerful songs can be in one's spiritual formation.

Expand

Songs tell the stories of our lives. One doesn't have to be a singer to appreciate the power of song. Many people identify with the story lines of blues, country, or gospel songs. Songs describe realities that we have experienced at some point in time, and we find our own place in the singer's story as the words unfold. Songs influence us. They both express who we are and call us to who we can become. The opening measures of a national anthem stir within a nation's citizens a deep emotional fervor, not only for what it has meant in the past but also for what it will mean in the future. It both expresses pride in the nation's history and calls people forward to future duty. The songs of a culture deeply impact the character of the persons who live in that culture. Plato had it right: "Let me write the songs of a nation and I care not who writes its laws." The songs of our lives shape our lives.

Likewise, the songs of worship naturally play a powerful part in the formational process at work in corporate worship. Many elements of worship are vital, but songs of Christian faith are especially well suited as vehicles for spiritual formation simply because music reaches into the depths of our being so readily, so deeply, joining text and tune for incredible impact. Disciples of Jesus Christ are formed in worship, and songs play a key role in the process.

In this chapter we will first take time to explore how corporate worship is transformational in character. Music architects must understand the formative nature of worship. After examining the big picture, we will look at congregational singing in particular to see how music plays a very significant role in enabling spiritual formation within the context of worship. We will look at music as a means of grace to facilitate formation. Ultimately, our purpose is to see how disciples are formed in worship in general and through song in particular. If we can see how profoundly effective songs are in shaping our spiritual journeys, we will lead with great care and intentionality, realizing that, to a large degree, we disciple worshipers through song.

Worship as Spiritual Formation

Corporate worship changes us. That's quite a claim. Is it true? We spend a lot of time discussing and planning how *we change worship*, but have we thought much about how *worship changes us*? Many leaders have never been challenged with such a provocative thought—provocative *and exciting*! And yet the corporate worship event is transformational at its very core. When a particular Christian community devotes itself to intentional, regular, biblical, corporate worship over time, participants will begin to be internally shaped by that experience and will live out their faith externally by that experience. That is because when we worship, whether we realize it or not, we are placing ourselves under the influence of the liturgy. (Reminder: every church has its liturgy—the collection of actions, words, gestures, and symbols that facilitates worship in one's context.)

The phrase "under the influence" is used in various contexts. Parents warn their children not to hang out with friends who could lead them in the wrong direction. The law enforcement community uses it to refer to driving while intoxicated by either drugs or alcohol. When someone drives while under the influence, they have chosen to surrender themselves to conditions that hold the possibility of real danger to themselves and others.

When we choose to worship God in community, we are choosing to place ourselves under the influence of the liturgy of that community—of surrendering to conditions that hold the possibility for life-changing results. (I am not speaking of random times of worship in various settings here and there; I am speaking of the primary, ongoing worship in a local church.) Both the *content* and the *manner* of that liturgy affect worshipers. If this is true, *what* liturgy we place ourselves under really matters. When we choose a worship tradition, we are, in fact, choosing a trajectory for our spiritual lives. This may not be the only spiritual influence on the life of a worshiper, but it is a primary one. So consider these key questions: When worshipers place themselves under the influence of your services week after week in good faith, over time, what type of transformation is likely? What transformation would you have a right to expect?

To be clear, I am not speaking about the *style* of worship, though it too can play an influential role (style is not neutral). I am primarily speaking of the content of worship and the manner of worship. By *content* I mean the actual dialogue that is communicated in the conversation with God—the substance of the prayers, the songs, the sermons, and so on. Most of the content transpires through the use of words but not all. Some of the content comes in the form of symbol, gesture, fine art forms, expressive art forms, and so forth. Nevertheless, the text of our conversation shapes us. We are transformed by what we sing, pray, hear, and do over time. By the *manner* of worship I referr to the attitudinal approach leaders take when they lead the content of worship—the sense of humility (or not), reverence (or not), and so on—the virtues that they bring to the worshiping experience. For instance, does our worship ethos seem to expect that worshipers will come prepared to give or to receive? To participate or to be passive? To be consumers or to be producers? The joy, sincerity, hospitality, even competence with which we lead all shape our understanding of God and faith. The very outlook of a Christian community worshiping God in Christ through the Spirit can be transformational.

An ancient formula, dating back to the fifth century, is the Latin phrase *lex orandi, lex credendi*, translated, "The rule of praying is the rule of belief."[1] Essentially, the proposition is this: what we pray becomes what we believe (in the context of worship). The idea is that all corporate worship is prayer and that the words that we use to pray ultimately shape what we believe. The songs we are given to sing shape what we believe. The creeds, the passages of Scripture that the community hears, the baptismal and Communion liturgies—all of it forms us. In short, the doctrine of the church comes under the influence of worship. What I suggest is that the majority of belief comes through what worshipers say and do in worship rather than what they hear from systematic theologians or learned preachers. We can argue whether this *should* be the case, but reality remains: the doxological act of worship deeply shapes us.

Now, *lex orandi, lex credendi* can go both ways—and does. Certainly there are times when what a faith community comes to believe reforms the liturgy. The liturgical changes made as a result of the Protestant Reformation come to mind. It happens any time a leader makes intentional adjustments to what is said and done in worship as a direct result of new understanding and commitment. Really, a dynamic partnership best describes the rule of praying and the rule of belief. Yet while one influences the other, it's not equal influence. It is likely that worship shapes belief to a greater degree than belief shapes worship.[2] Regardless, the point is this: we must never underestimate the power of any worship's content and manner in shaping the spiritual lives of its participants.

Like a biological family, we take on values, beliefs, language, priorities, and so forth, simply by participating in the events of the family. Some of

1. Attributed to Prosper of Aquitaine. See Simon Chan, *Liturgical Theology: The Church as Worshiping Community* (Downers Grove, IL: InterVarsity, 2006), 48.

2. Ibid., 48–49. Chan notes that both Alexander Schmemann and Aidan Kavanagh hold this position.

this we learn through words that the family speaks and repeats as members share life together; some we learn merely through observation of the family's actions. Some of it is positively forming (e.g., when families serve the poor as an act of mercy); some of it is de-forming (e.g., when parents teach little ones to hate persons of another race). Much of who we are by nature is caught rather than taught.

It is the same with worship. When we place ourselves under the influence of the liturgy of our church, we find ourselves becoming transformed by that which we hear, speak, think, taste, feel, and imagine. We pray (*lex orandi*) only to find that we come to believe (*lex credendi*) what we are saying and doing through worship. A Christian worldview is partially caught from the liturgy.[3] We worship in faith and then find ourselves shaped by that to which we have surrendered ourselves. This is one reason why intergenerational worship is so urgent. It is very important to have young children and youth together with all ages of adults in worship in the local church, for we are discipling young believers in the faith, forming their Christian understanding as together we sing the songs and pray the prayers through which we all are simultaneously formed.

Lex orandi, lex credendi happens both informally and formally. Informally, the transformational aspect of the liturgy just happens over time as a result of sincere worshipers participating fully in communal worship. We take on the outright beliefs and commitments so evident in corporate worship, then we slowly discover that we are *becoming* the liturgy. It is argued that we know we are becoming true worshipers when it is no longer necessary to follow the rules for worship; the form has become native to us, and we aren't just *doing* the liturgy anymore—we are *living* the liturgy. At the same time, wise and godly leaders see that formation happens formally as well. They intentionally shape the worship event through the use of appropriate and rich content, and they foster admirable Christian virtues that encourage worshipers to approach worship with proper attitudes as they engage in proper worship acts.

Whether through formal or informal means, transformation leads to a new way of living. A third (and vital) term is sometimes included in the phrase: *lex vivendi*, meaning "so we come to live."[4] The late Robert Webber, founder of the Institute for Worship Studies, routinely visited each of the classes when in

3. I do not mean to suggest that all Christians hold identical worldviews or that there is only one way to see the world as a Christian. Here I am referring to the larger, universal, orthodox views central to Christian faith (the centrality of Christ, the kingdom of God, etc.).

4. Keith Fournier, "Lex Orandi, Lex Credendi, Lex Vivendi: As We Worship, So We Believe, So We Live," *Catholic Online*, November 8, 2010, http://www.catholic.org/news/hf/faith/story.php?id=39029.

session. He so enjoyed face-to-face time with the students. He would share a few salient thoughts and then open up the discussion for some general questions and answers. I vividly remember one session in which a doctoral student asked Webber, "How do you know if you have truly worshiped?" Without hesitation Webber replied, "You have truly worshiped when you find that you are ever increasing in your day-to-day obedience to God." He went on to suggest that worship is questionable if one finds that he or she is not growing in obedience. Obedience is evidence of the way that worship has shaped us. *Lex orandi, lex credendi, lex vivendi*: "How we worship reflects what we believe and determines how we will live."[5]

When worship influences us to this degree—when lives are transformed from disobedience to obedience as a result of sincerely being in God's presence as full participants in the community's worship—we are engaged in *primary theology*. We *do* theology first. Doing worship, investing in the costly enterprise of fulfilling God's expectations for worship as found in Scripture is our highest calling. It is primary theology (1) because it is first in importance and (2) because it amounts to an experience *with* God rather than discussion *about* God; God is encountered firsthand. *Secondary theology* is the organized reflection on primary theology. It consists of doctrinal conclusions that are a means for explaining the reality of primary liturgical theology. It is worship seeking understanding. "Secondary liturgical theology seeks to explain as fully as possible this primary experience of the church in its encounter with God which is expressed in its public act of worship. Its goal is . . . to make explicit what worshipers know mostly in an implicit or tacit way."[6] Yet secondary liturgical theology isn't just for cognitive understanding; its most important function is that of "intending to enable a more profound participation in [worship] by the members of the assembly."[7] We seek to understand not to *know* more but to *be* more fully devoted worshipers of the triune God. A third type of theology, after primary and secondary theology, is called *pastoral liturgical theology* and is described by theologian Gordon Lathrop as the "critical, reforming edge"[8] of bringing about "urgently needed renewal of the form [of worship] under way in our time."[9] Worship is always in need of reforming (*Ecclesia semper reformanda est*).[10] To become the worshiping church envisioned by

5. Ibid.
6. Chan, *Liturgical Theology*, 51.
7. Gordon W. Lathrop, *Holy Things: A Liturgical Theology* (Minneapolis: Fortress, 1993), 6.
8. Ibid., 7.
9. Ibid., 7–8.
10. *Ecclesia semper reformanda est* is translated, "The church is always to be reformed." The term, first used by Karl Barth, has become a rallying cry in some circles to pursue continuous reexamination of the church's orthodoxy for the sake of orthopraxy.

God is an ongoing process. Therefore, all worship leaders must constantly critique worship in light of biblical, theological, historical, missiological, and pastoral considerations for faithfulness in our time. Worship's reexamination is always in order. Lathrop neatly summarizes matters this way:

> Primary liturgical theology: participating in the pattern.
> Secondary liturgical theology: discerning the pattern.
> Pastoral liturgical theology: renewing the pattern.[11]

A profound postresurrection story from the Gospel of Luke (24:13–35) is a perfect example of primary, secondary, and pastoral liturgical theology in interdependent relationship. On the day of Jesus's resurrection, two of his disciples were traveling from Jerusalem to the village of Emmaus, presumably returning home after witnessing the crucifixion of Jesus. They were distraught and confused, for the Rabbi they had followed had been left for dead. Even though the women disciples had reported Jesus to be alive, the two followers had their serious doubts. While in discussion between themselves, Jesus mysteriously appeared and joined them as they walked, but they did not recognize him. As the journey progressed, Jesus "interpreted to them the things about himself in all the scriptures" (v. 27). And yet their confusion remained.

Later at a meal in their home when they engaged in worship, they recognized Jesus. Jesus, the guest, had become the Host. He "took bread, blessed and broke it, and gave it to them" (v. 30). These two had likely seen or heard about Jesus performing this same fourfold action on other occasions at other meals: the feeding of the five thousand (Luke 9:16) and the Passover meal the night before his death (Luke 22:19). But here, on *this* occasion, their eyes were opened, and they recognized Jesus. They experienced the risen Lord first, and they found themselves *participating in the pattern* (primary theology). Next, they reflected on what had happened in worship: "Were not our hearts burning within us while he was talking to us on the road, while he was opening the scriptures to us?" (v. 32). They thought about what had occurred in worship and were able to make sense of it; they sought understanding, and their faith was rewarded. They were *discerning the pattern* (secondary theology). Last, the disciples immediately left to head back to Jerusalem, where they found other disciples dazed in wonderment at what they were hearing. In turn, these two shared what had happened to them. They told how Jesus was made known to them in the breaking of the bread

11. Lathrop, *Holy Things*, 8.

(v. 35). The experience of the presence of Christ at the Table of the Lord changed everything. They had experienced an urgently needed renewal of worship that was under way in their time. They found themselves *renewing the pattern* (pastoral theology).

Primary, secondary, and pastoral theologies are ways of apprehending *lex orandi, lex credendi, lex vivendi*. We worship, we reflect on our worship, and we live in ways that embody the renewal of worship in our time. In the end, as we worship, so we believe, and so we will live.[12]

What I am proposing is that the ongoing corporate worship of a community offers us an opportunity for intentional spiritual formation. Richard J. Foster considers worship to be a corporate spiritual discipline "because it is an ordered way of acting and living that sets us before God so he can transform us."[13] As we meet to offer worship to God regularly, sincerely, and intentionally, we create an opportunity for God to meet us and change us for his glory. Often the changes that take place in us as a result of true worship are unexpected, perhaps even unseen at first, but they are happening nevertheless. The fruit of the spiritual disciplines is most often slow-growing, rarely noticeable immediately. We must be patient as we look for ways in which God transforms us through corporate worship. When we view worship as a spiritual discipline that we undertake to honor God, when we commit ourselves to the work of worship, when we intentionally participate personally, and when we contribute to the worship experience of others, we are engaging in formal (intentional) formation.

Like any spiritual discipline, there are certain practices that typically enable the fruitfulness of the discipline. In the case of worship, these practices include corporate prayer, *lectio divina*,[14] the giving of offerings, singing, exhortation, and, of course, the sacraments/ordinances. Others could be named, but these are some of the practices that we take up when we enter into the spiritual discipline of worship for the purpose of letting God change us; they provide us a means of engagement with the discipline. If you think I have suggested that we use some spiritual disciplines to facilitate other disciplines, you are right. Let me explain.

The particular discipline to which we are called at a given moment by God is a *primary discipline* (for this point in time). When God summons

12. Ibid.
13. Richard J. Foster, *Celebration of Discipline: The Path to Spiritual Growth*, rev. ed. (San Francisco: Harper & Row, 1988), 166.
14. *Lectio divina* ("divine reading") is an ancient approach to the devotional reading of Scripture that includes silence, meditation, and contemplation for the purpose of hearing God speak and ultimately for the transformation of daily living.

the community to worship, we engage in a primary discipline (primary for the moment) as we place ourselves *as a community* on a "path of disciplined grace."[15] But in order to answer God's invitation to transformation through worship, we offer other practices to give us the means of engagement in the undertaking of our primary discipline. For now, these are functioning as *support* disciplines because they are disciplines placed in service to the primary spiritual discipline at hand (corporate worship), though they are not the primary focus. Each of the support disciplines is, of course, a primary discipline in its own right and may be used as such when God invites us to do so at other times.

To take full advantage of the potential transformation inherent in Christian worship, we may employ various spiritual disciplines such as:

- offering *corporate prayer* by voicing praise, confession, petition, listening prayer, intercessions, and so on
- engaging in *lectio divina* as we contemplate the Holy Scriptures
- bringing, presenting, and dedicating our *offerings* in obedience to God
- *singing* with one voice—energetically and devotedly
- *exhorting* one another publicly to encourage and to hold one another accountable
- feasting at the *Table* and remembering our *baptism*

These (and other) spiritual practices enable the discipline of corporate worship. As we engage in them, we present ourselves to God, trusting that he will use these as transformational moments. Intentional participation in these practices is an important means for individuals and communities to be transformed through worship for God's glory and for the sake of others.

Thus far I have been speaking of the transformative nature of Christian worship in a positive manner. But remember that any discipline holds the potential to be de-forming as well. When disciplines are undertaken for the wrong reason or for selfish motives, when disciplines are carelessly or half-heartedly exercised, the result may not be neutral in effect. It may corrupt. This poses a very great challenge to leaders; our humanly derived religious programs that we call worship may de-form us as opposed to reform us. Anthropomorphic worship comes to mind here (see chap. 1). When worship is undertaken for selfish or ulterior motives, or when we carelessly plan and lead it, we risk de-forming participants. If we're not careful, our worship can

15. Foster, *Celebration of Discipline*, 7.

represent our attempt to change God, rather than allowing God to change us. We do this when we alter God's vision for worship. We do this when we begin with ourselves. We decide *if* we will worship, *when* we will worship, *how* we will worship, *where* we will worship, with *whom* we will worship, *what* we will do in our worship, and even *why* we will worship in the first place. Robert Webber spoke of this dilemma as "self-situated spirituality."[16] In many circles, worship has become highly narcissistic.

Participating in corporate worship will change us over time. The only question is, what way will it change us? "Have it your way" worship—worship that is centered primarily on us, our needs, our desires, and our wills—shapes us in a self-centered way. We will quickly learn that the worshiper is to be gratified. *Christ-centered worship forms us in a different direction.* God's vision of worship becomes our vision of worship, and we lay aside our rights for immediate satisfaction by pursuing the gratification of God and by seeking to serve other worshipers in their pursuit of the same.

Let's return to Luke 24. The Emmaus disciples found their encounter with Christ to be transformational. The context didn't initially start out as a worship service, but it ended up that way. The story has so many of the central features of worship:

- Jesus approached the disciples and initiated the encounter.
- Jesus accepted them where they were but moved them forward into deeper relationship with him.
- Jesus explained the Scriptures to them.
- There was deepening affection between Jesus and his followers.
- They experienced a holy meal.
- They recognized him in the action at the Table.
- They eagerly ran to the others to testify that Jesus was alive.

Notice the transformation that took place throughout this event. The story began with the disciples being grief-stricken and confused; the story ends with them ecstatic and convinced.

This remarkable transformation happened both informally and formally. Much of the time they did not know transformation was happening; some of the time they became aware of the transformation under way. Informally, as the two followers went step-by-step toward Emmaus, they were also being

16. Robert E. Webber, *The Divine Embrace: Recovering the Passionate Spiritual Life* (Baker Books, 2006), 95.

drawn step-by-step into the Risen Lord. They were unknowingly getting closer to the truth. They were beginning to feel something—at least they were intrigued, for they compelled him to stay with them. Their transformation began simply by being in the presence of their Master, even though they did not yet recognize him. They were experiencing the transformation even before they knew they were. At the same time, their transformation happened formally. Jesus instructed them systematically, as he began with Moses and then went through the prophets. He taught them; he reasoned with them; he admonished them. The disciples experienced careful instruction from the Rabbi. *All of this* that was transformational—spontaneous and systematic, relational and propositional—all of it contributed to their formation.

Notice also the various support disciplines found in this marvelous story: holy conversation, inquiry, theological reflection, admonition, accountability, contemplation of Scripture, prayer, the breaking of bread, illumination, and witness. All of these became avenues that culminated in profound spiritual worship!

Corporate worship shapes us in ways we are unaware of. Often we are clueless to this wondrous work. We, like the disciples, might recognize it only when we look backward. Their transformation went unnoticed at first. It was only after the fact that the disciples exclaimed, "Wait! We see it now! Our hearts were burning all the while we were journeying with Jesus!" Once the disciples suddenly saw things differently, they knew they were different people. This propelled them forward into the next action—the action of telling their colleagues that Jesus was, in fact, raised from the dead! They were living the experience of worship. This was transformation realized for the sake of others.

We too will likely need to look backward from a different vantage point in order to view the unseen, unnoticed work of formational worship. It has been going on; we are just not always able to see it at the time. We should not be surprised. Jesus taught that "unless a grain of wheat falls into the earth and dies, it remains just a single grain; but if it dies, it bears much fruit" (John 12:24). Germination takes a while for the unseen to be seen. Perhaps, like the disciples, we have been kept from recognizing it, or maybe it is just that subtle or that slow. Rest assured, the transformational work of worship *has* been going on all the while. At other times God is gracious to reveal how worship truly has formed us. We look forward, eager to bear the fruit of the transformation in our lives that has been revealed. This revelation comes in God's way, at God's time. Worship "shapes us backward," and "worship shapes us forward." Either way, it's all good.

Music as a Means of Grace: Informal Spiritual Formation

The music of worship serves as an active participant in the transformational process that takes place in worship. It functions as a means of grace from the generous heart of God to his people. "**Means of grace**" refers to God-appointed channels through which God chooses to meet us and change us for his glory.[17] The phrase is used widely in many denominations and not at all in others, although virtually all Christians would acknowledge its reality even if they do not use the terms. While "means of grace" has a range of meanings across traditions, essentially it is the acknowledgment that God has various ways and means to communicate his grace. Many of us grew up with a one-dimensional view of grace—saving grace. But God's grace consists of so much more! God is faithful to offer continuing grace and strengthening grace too.[18] Grace consists of all of God's actions on our behalf that work for our benefit—things that we cannot do for ourselves that God provides out of his abundant love for his creation. Whenever God graciously speaks to us and works in us to conform us to the image of his Son, grace happens. Grace is not only a noun (we not only receive grace); grace is also a verb (we also experience it and are graced). Grace is what God is doing from creation to re-creation. It consists of all the initiatives that God takes for our good, noticed or unnoticed.

Think of means of grace in terms of media. "Media" refers to avenues of delivery: for information, art, advertising, and so on. Today, given the ever-increasing media possibilities for transmission of ideas, it is common to hear folks clarify the primary medium for their work or interest, such as, "I have a career in online journalism" or "I paint exclusively in watercolors." Means of grace function like various media—they are avenues for God to "deliver" transformation (in partnership with us). Like the journalists or artists invested in their mediums, Christian believers are invested in various means of grace—God-ordained medium for shaping us in Christlikeness. While the worship service itself is a means of grace in that worshipers become more and more like the One they adore (this principle is true for idol worship as well), within the service are multiple media, each a means of grace, that are available to serve God's purposes for our transformation. These include such primary things as the reading and hearing of Holy Scripture, preaching, the sacraments, and prayer.

17. Constance M. Cherry, *The Special Service Worship Architect: Blueprints for Weddings, Funerals, Baptisms, Holy Communion, and Other Occasions* (Grand Rapids: Baker Academic, 2013), 22.
18. Philip E. Hughes, "Means of Grace," in *Evangelical Dictionary of Theology*, ed. Walter A. Elwell (Grand Rapids: Baker, 1984), 482. Some traditions refer to God's action of imparting continuing and strengthening grace as "sanctification."

In the context of Christian worship, music also serves as a means of grace.[19] It is a channel through which God speaks to us and works in us for our good. It provides an avenue for God to continue the ongoing process toward Christlikeness in his children. Music itself doesn't change us, of course, but God often uses music to work in us on our journey of transformation. It is a way through which we are continued and strengthened in faith. While the action is all God's, we have an important role to play. First, we open ourselves to God's gracious initiatives. We make ourselves vulnerable to God and one another in surrendering control to God when we sing. (This is all the more reason to be cautious about which songs qualify as beneficial in worship.) Second, we watch to see what God is doing. We await God's action with expectancy and great anticipation. Our spirit reflects that of the prophet Habakkuk: "I will stand at my watchpost, and station myself on the rampart; I will keep watch to see what he will say to me" (Hab. 2:1). Third, we intend to invest in the process by giving ourselves to the song. We will sing with devotional abandon as a means of doing our part, for "Great is the LORD, and greatly to be praised" (Ps. 145:3a). When we open ourselves, keep watch, and invest in the process of congregational song, we become coparticipants with God in our spiritual formation.

In the action of singing, intent and disposition matter (as is true of all means of grace). God's actions in and through us as we sing must be rightly received. This involves our singing in faith and with gratitude.[20] Simply being in the room while music is occurring with no awareness of one's role in song or intention to invest in it does not avail oneself of the marvelous transformative work that God hopes to do. Means of grace are not automatically bestowed. Foster makes this clear in describing the spiritual disciplines as means of grace:

> [They] are God's way of getting us into the ground; they put us where he can work within us and transform us. By themselves the Spiritual Disciplines can do nothing; they can only get us to the place where something can be done. They are God's means of grace. The inner righteousness we seek is not something that is poured on our heads. God has ordained the Disciplines of the spiritual life as the means by which we place ourselves where he can bless us.[21]

---

19. John Wesley differentiated between "instituted" means of grace (means that Christ instructed believers to do, such as the Lord's Supper, fasting, prayer, searching the Scriptures, and Christian fellowship) and "prudential" means of grace (other means that are beneficial for advancing spiritual growth). I am proposing that music in worship is considered to be a prudential means of grace. I am indebted to and recommend the work of Rob L. Staples, *Outward Sign and Inward Grace: The Place of Sacraments in Wesleyan Spirituality* (Kansas City, MO: Beacon Hill, 1991), 97–102.

20. Ibid.

21. Foster, *Celebration of Discipline*, 7.

When we engage in congregational song as a means of grace, we "place our-selves before God so that he can transform us."[22] Foster continues, "It is 'grace' because it is free; it is 'disciplined' because there is something for us to do."[23]

To summarize thus far, the music of worship serves as a channel through which God changes worshipers. As such, it is a means of grace that functions more or less informally. Our part is to position ourselves before God through participation in each song, anticipating that God will use the songs of the church as means for speaking to and shaping us. Our participation consists of opening ourselves, watching, and investing in the song as an act of trust and surrender. God is faithful to work in and through this means of grace, along with others, to form us according to his plan, not ours. It is informal because there is little that we can actively do to influence the particular results. By faith we receive the benefits God has in mind for us for the sake of his glory and kingdom.

Music as Catechesis: Formal Spiritual Formation

Another word that teases out the formational nature of worship music fur-ther is **catechesis**, a Greek word meaning "to resound" (*katēchéō*) and refers to teaching the elements of religion by word of mouth.[24] Many Protestants (Presbyterian, Reformed, Lutheran, etc.) have a long history of the use of catechisms. Catechisms simply take the teachings of the church and place them into a question-and-answer format to disciple believers in the faith (by word of mouth). Apostolic leaders in the earliest centuries of Christianity instituted a very rigorous catechetical process that took years for seekers to become Christians who were well formed in faith. Catechisms have a long and distinguished history in the church. As the definition suggests, catechisms depend largely on oral transmission of doctrine. Central beliefs are posed in the form of questions to which young disciples respond with memorized answers, all for the purpose of being formed in the Christian faith.

Worship music is the new catechesis. Traditional means of formal Christian education have languished in many places today. While there are exceptions, generally Sunday schools have diminished in attendance and influence. Confir-mation classes have shrunk in length. Vacation Bible schools have gone from two weeks to two days. Bible reading and instruction in families is extremely low.[25] Is it possible that as standard means for Christian education have declined, the

22. Ibid.
23. Ibid., 7–8.
24. *A Lexicon Abridged from Liddell and Scott's Greek-English Lexicon* (Oxford: Oxford University Press, 1935), s.v. "*katēchéō*."
25. Forty-six percent of Americans are non-Bible readers (i.e., they read the Bible one or two times per year or less). *The State of the Bible Report 2014*, Barna Group, Ventura, CA,

teaching ministry of worship has increased? Is that why sermons have moved from preaching to teaching in many churches? At this point, worship is the one and only avenue of church involvement for many people, and that not always weekly. Therefore, songs and sermons are the primary or only means for instruction in the faith today in too many places. By default, worship music has become the new catechesis—a means for the oral transmission of the faith. Doctrine is recited through song. Albert van den Heuvel prophetically spoke of this current situation many decades ago when he wrote, "[Hymns] are probably, in our age, the only confessional documents which we learn by heart. As such, they have taken the place of our catechisms."[26] If this is true, a lot of responsibility is placed on songwriters and music architects. The doctrine of the church is presently at the mercy of what is sung in worship. If so, we have some work to do to answer the call.

Occasionally leaders object to singing songs that feel theologically challenging. But there is a difference between songs that are doctrinally dense and doctrinally rich. There is no need for highly complex language and difficult words. True, many aspects of our faith are difficult to comprehend. Much of what we believe we will never fully grasp. Nevertheless, we persist in singing and studying the truth, trusting those from whom we have learned it (2 Tim. 3:14). Understanding comes as the light of dawn—increasing incrementally until its brightness sheds enough light for us to see more clearly. The sunrise takes time; sometimes it's a slow dawn. We must therefore persist in singing some songs that are beyond us in depth. There is real benefit in singing that which we cannot fully grasp at first pass, songs that we must grow into. As we sing such songs, our prayer should be that of the father who brought his son to Jesus for healing: "I believe; help my unbelief!" (Mark 9:24). There's real wisdom in paying attention to our song texts in light of their catechetical strengths. "In this way we feed our people, nourish them, as pastoral musicians should, and give them something not just to sing about *then*, but something to sing about in the whole of life."[27]

Conclusion

I have claimed that worship songs are spiritually forming—both informally (as a means of grace) and formally (as a type of catechesis in faith formation).

2014, http://www.americanbible.org/uploads/content/state-of-the-bible-data-analysis-american -bible-society-2014.pdf.

26. Albert van den Heuvel, *New Hymns for a New Day* (Geneva: World Council of Churches, 1966), preface, 6.

27. Rembert Weakland, "Claim Your Art," in *The Singing Assembly*, vol. 6 of *Pastoral Music in Practice*, ed. Virgil C. Funk (Washington, DC: Pastoral Press, 1991), 112.

One final consideration draws our attention as we conclude this chapter: *What* is formed in us?

Barry D. Jones offers four suggestions: "Worship redefines our identity, worship reorders our affections, worship repatterns our imagination, and worship reorients our life in the world."[28] All these formational benefits are worthy results of spiritually transforming worship. As helpful as these are, there is yet a better question to ask: *Who* is formed in us? The ultimate goal of transformative worship is Christlikeness. Pastoral musicians identify with the apostle Paul, who compared the spiritual formation of those under his care to the pains of childbirth until Christ is formed in them (Gal. 4:19). Worship is the delivery room. "Through engagement with the body of Christ, bathed with God's Word, nourished by the sacraments, people of faith become more like the One in whose image we are made. We become better at imitating God . . . [a]nd we become more like the person we worship: Jesus."[29]

Key Terms

catechesis. To teach by word of mouth; from the Greek word *katēchéō*, meaning "to resound."

means of grace. A God-appointed channel through which God chooses to meet us and changes us for God's glory.

To Learn More

Abernethy, Alexis D., ed. *Worship That Changes Lives: Multidisciplinary and Congregational Perspectives on Spiritual Transformation*. Grand Rapids: Baker Academic, 2008.

Foster, Richard. *Celebration of Discipline: The Path to Spiritual Growth*, rev. ed. San Francisco: Harper & Row, 1988.

28. Barry D. Jones, *Dwell: Life with God for the World* (Downers Grove, IL: InterVarsity, 2014), 142.

29. Clayton J. Schmit, "Worship as a Locus for Transformation," in *Worship That Changes Lives: Multidisciplinary and Congregational Perspectives on Spiritual Transformation*, ed. Alexis D. Abernethy (Grand Rapids: Baker Academic, 2008), 26.

Engage

Here are a few practical ways to engage with the content of this chapter.

1. Review your church's vision statement for worship. (If you don't have one, write one!) Does it refer to the formational nature of Christian worship? Write one simple statement that affirms worship as formational that you would insert in your present or future vision statement if you had the opportunity to do so.

2. Listed below are a few samples of questions found in most any standard Protestant catechism.[30] If your church has its own catechism, start there. Look through your church's canon of song (the list of songs your church draws on for worship). Find all songs that explicitly provide an answer to each of the questions. (Don't force the issue with vague possibilities. List only songs that clearly address each question.) The purpose of this practical application is to determine where any gaps may exist theologically if your church were to depend on worship songs as the primary means for Christian education.

   a. Who is Jesus Christ?
   b. What is meant by the incarnate life of Jesus Christ?
   c. What is the kingdom of God?
   d. What is the nature of God's love?

30. *The Standard Catechism* (Nashville: Abingdon, 1929), 2–3, 7.

12

Pursuing Spiritual Leadership through Excellence

Explore

What does the word "excellent" mean to you? This word is used often in many different ways: to describe a carpet sample or the price of a vacation package; to compare coffee blends or receive a word of commendation from your guitar instructor; to assess the quality of water drawn from a well or refer to the weather for planting spring crops. Prior to reading this chapter, try this little exercise to begin thinking about what is meant by the word "excellent":

1. When I hear the word "excellent," I think of _____.
2. Excellent worship music is _____.
3. I would describe an excellent worship music architect as someone who _____.

Keep your ideas in mind as you read this chapter. At the end, compare your answers to these questions with your answers at the end of the chapter. How has your view changed by the end of the chapter? Why?

Expand

We have arrived at the final stage of our journey—at least for now—of discovering what it means to be a music architect in today's church. We've covered a lot of territory, but let's examine briefly how this book begins and ends. In chapter 1, the focus was on *becoming*—becoming a pastoral musician, not a musician who just happens to work in a church but a person called to serve the church who happens to be a musician. It is my prayer that the first chapter opened a big, new window through which music architects can see their profound significance in the world of worship. This closing chapter is about *pursuing*—pursuing excellence as a music architect. "Becoming" *launched* us on the journey; "pursuing" will *keep* us on the journey. Our ministries are a work in progress until our services are no longer needed in the eternal kingdom when all God's people will sing heaven's worship songs together perfectly. Until then, we are called to pursue excellence. Together chapters 1 and 12 form bookends that speak mostly of who we will be in light of what we do. We have come full circle.

To that end, excellence will not be portrayed as some arbitrary standard of achievement. Rather, it will be explained much more broadly, as an ideal that comes into clearer focus as we mature and are able to discern between realistic versus unrealistic expectations of ourselves and others. The title of this chapter uses the word "pursuing" with that in mind. To pursue is to follow after something or someone with the intent to capture. Those who pursue an education in cancer research will follow after the curriculum path set before them in order to capture a degree that will qualify them to fulfill their aspirations. The apostle Paul wrote of pursuit and capture to the Corinthians. His words are direct: "Run [pursue] in such a way that you may win [capture] it" (1 Cor. 9:24b). The "it" Paul refers to is the prize, the imperishable wreath received in the future based on our quality of pursuit now. Paul emphasizes the persistence of the runner; the goal is important, but it is not really the focus of the passage. What we have now is the race. Our pursuit of excellence is a course we run over time. The prize will come later.

This chapter approaches the idea of excellence by mirroring the same three categories found in chapter 1: person, vision, and role. Excellence is pursued in several arenas at once. We will look at the person of excellence, the vision of musical excellence, and the role of excellence. In the end, music architects understand that they are giving themselves to a lifelong pursuit of pleasing God both in who they are becoming and in how they undertake their ministry.

The Person of Excellence

In the previous chapter, we discovered that the worship service itself is formational. What we experience in worship changes us over time, and music has its role to play in the formational process. If this is true, music architects are spiritual guides. We accompany God-worshipers in their journey of transformation each week when the assembly is gathered. To play that role properly we must take seriously our own matter of **spiritual formation**. We must pursue excellence in Christlikeness personally as a way to set the example and guide others along the way.

The term "spiritual formation" is used in different ways today.[1] I am using the term in the classic sense to refer to our growth in Christlikeness, that comes when we intentionally cooperate with God for our transformation, especially through the ongoing use of the spiritual disciplines. M. Robert Mulholland Jr. offers a helpful definition: "Spiritual formation is a process of being conformed to the image of Christ for the sake of others."[2] The key words and phrases of this definition provide much insight. First, spiritual formation is always a *process*. It is not instantaneous.[3] It happens over a long period of time—a lifetime, in fact. Unfortunately, spiritual formation is often talked about as if it were an object by the use of such phrases as "my spiritual life." In doing so, we suggest that it is an entity in itself—a tangible reality, much like when we use the terms "my physical condition," "my emotional wellness quotient," and so on. Instead, our spiritual development is a journey we are on with God in control. As such, it is a dynamic course, a forward motion in which we are invited to participate as partners with God by virtue of God's gracious initiatives taken to produce necessary change within us. This takes time. There are no shortcuts. The first step to pursuing excellence through spiritual formation is to see it as a process rather than as a goal.

Second, spiritual formation is a process of *being conformed*. This suggests that surrender is involved. While our contemporary culture shouts, "Be yourself," God's Spirit is calling, "Surrender yourself." The point of spiritual formation is to become what God has in mind and to resist what we first have in mind. We must comply with the initiatives God is taking to shape us. We must learn to sing a different song—not, "I Did It My Way," but, "I Surrender All." Mulholland writes, "Spiritual formation is the great reversal: from acting to bring about the desired results in our lives to being acted upon by God and responding in ways that allow God to bring about God's purposes."[4]

1. For instance, some people use it to refer to Christian education programming.
2. M. Robert Mulholland Jr., *Invitation to a Journey: A Road Map for Spiritual Formation* (Downers Grove, IL: InterVarsity, 1993), 12.
3. This "longer way" of sanctification does not discount the "shorter way" of sanctification. God's prerogative to achieve sanctification in the believer is simply that—*God's* prerogative.
4. Mulholland, *Invitation to a Journey*, 30–31.

Third, spiritual formation has only one goal: growth in Christlikeness. Spiritual formation is not about *knowing* more or *doing* more; it is about *being* more—more like Jesus. Information and formation are not mutually exclusive, of course, but gaining knowledge does not necessarily result in transformation. There is a big difference between acquiring knowledge that informs your actions and knowing the One who transforms your attractions. The difference is between controlling your behavior with your best guess at what Jesus would do (i.e., WWJD) and being conformed by God so that Christ in you causes you to do the right things naturally as your first impulse.

The final part of the definition is incredibly significant: our pursuit of Christlikeness is *for the sake of others*. We often have the mistaken idea that we are to become like Jesus so that we can be more "spiritual." Not really. Any progress in Christlikeness has a more important goal, that of benefitting others in their perception and experience of the triune God. "For the sake of others" refers to all others. Christlike service is offered wherever and to whomever God wills, believers and nonbelievers alike. It comes in many manifestations, including caring for the poor and reversing patterns of injustice. The more we are like Christ, the greater the chances that others will apprehend who God is and experience aspects of God's love.

Still, the question remains, how does spiritual formation happen? One of the primary ways through which we are formed, as we have seen, is the time-honored practice of spiritual disciplines. **Spiritual disciplines** are those means that believers employ to place themselves before God in order for God to change them according to his will. Richard J. Foster refers to engaging the disciplines as placing ourselves on "paths of disciplined grace."[5] They are things we intentionally do (disciplines of engagement) or intentionally cease to do (disciplines of abstinence)[6] in order to open ourselves to God for intervention—for allowing God's Spirit to transform our ungodly nature into God's holy nature. Spiritual disciplines are useful avenues that help to facilitate the sanctification of the believer. It is in and through the disciplines that we cooperate with God in our transformation. We have a part (offering ourselves to God by engaging with the disciplines), and God has a part (transforming us in the process). Simon Chan states it very well:

> We do the work, and yet it is ultimately the work of grace, something freely given to us, something that we could only receive as a gift. . . . We cannot

5. Richard J. Foster, *Celebration of Discipline: The Path to Spiritual Growth*, rev. ed. (San Francisco: Harper & Row, 1988), 7.
6. Dallas Willard, *The Spirit of the Disciplines: Understanding How God Changes Lives* (New York: HarperCollins, 1988), 158.

predetermine the outcome of our practices no matter how correctly they are carried out. For ultimately it is grace that forms us and not practices per se, and yet it forms us not apart from practice.[7]

Paul understood this dialectic of coparticipation in transformation. He wrote to the Philippians: "Therefore, my beloved . . . *work out your own salvation* with fear and trembling; for it is *God who is at work in you*, enabling you both to will and to work for his good pleasure" (Phil. 2:12–13, emphasis added).

Excellence does not begin with identifying a performance standard for music or worship. It doesn't even begin with a performance standard for the leader, at least in terms of personal achievement. It begins with becoming the person God has in mind for each of us to be. Pastoral musician Cynthia Serjak affirms the urgency of such a pursuit: "It is more than time for musicians, even pastoral musicians, to be comfortable with the call to be excellent. Excellence is less a state of being than a *way* of being."[8]

Pursue personal excellence by becoming intentional about your own spiritual formation. It will not only strengthen your life in Christ, but it will also equip you to serve as a spiritual guide in worship services that are, in themselves, formational opportunities for believers.

The Vision of Excellence

A second arena in which music architects must pursue excellence is in their vision of what excellence is all about when it comes to making music in worship. At the risk of oversimplification, I have noticed two predominant but somewhat opposing perspectives as to what is meant by excellence in music in the church. One view, which I will call the "performance view," emphasizes the quality of performance based on standard musical criteria. Excellence is depicted as achieving an agreed-upon level of musical accomplishment (this will naturally vary according to cultural norms and standards). Excellence is also yoked with aesthetics—one's understanding of beauty. What is excellent is beautiful and vice versa. One highly regarded church musician of the twentieth century describes excellence this way: "Excellence in the aesthetics of musical worship to the glory of God is achieved through a skilled performance of theologically true and poetically sound words set to well-crafted

7. Simon Chan, *Liturgical Theology: The Church as Worshiping Community* (Downers Grove, IL: InterVarsity, 2006), 94.

8. Cynthia Serjak, "The Musician: Transformed through Excellence," in *The Pastoral Musician*, vol. 5 of *Pastoral Music in Practice*, ed. Virgil C. Funk (Washington, DC: Pastoral Press, 1990), 49.

music that is meaningfully placed in the liturgy."[9] Notice the performance-driven words and phrases that are used. This definition emphasizes skill in the midst of the liturgy.

An equally highly regarded church musician offers an alternative view: "*Excellence is the process*—note that word *process*—*of becoming better than I once was.*"[10] Notice how different this view appears to be from the first. I call this view of excellence "the dynamic view." It portrays excellence as something that is always developing. It isn't static; there is no magical place of perfection, where we plant the flag of success and declare ourselves having arrived at the destination. Instead, we move forward to simply improve on our level of giftedness at which we find ourselves today.

I refer to the performance view and the dynamic view as somewhat opposing because the center of each definition emphasizes quite different things. One emphasizes the *arrival at* a destination; the other emphasizes the *journey as* the destination. In the end, the dynamic view describes excellence essentially as *who one is* in music ministry more than *what one does* in ministry. (Sound familiar?) Harold Best elaborates:

> In the face of all this glut of power, size, and glory, what is excellence anyway? The answer is brief. Excellence is authenticity. Excellence is temperance in all things. It is servanthood. It is loving-kindness. It is sojourn. It is esteeming another better than oneself. It is meekness, brokenness, personal holiness, greatness of soul. It is peaceableness, gentleness, perseverance, hunger and thirst. . . . It is a process, not an event. And, in the final analysis, there are no earthly measurements for it. The pursuit of it is entirely personal and the final judge as to its validity will be a God whose wise creatorhood, sustenance, and expectations are worth far more than blue ribbons, accolades, recording contracts, or Grammys.[11]

The pastoral musician will not dismiss the performance view of excellence out of hand. Indeed, we must pledge ourselves to the necessary, ongoing pursuit of developing musical expertise, both for those we lead and ourselves. We do want to become better musicians; we surely seek to play skillfully (Ps. 33:3). However, we will lean into the dynamic view with all our hearts, for in the end excellence will always be deeply connected to the quality of person we are becoming and calling others to become as well. After all, this is how God

9. Donald P. Hustad, *True Worship: Reclaiming the Wonder and Majesty* (Carol Stream, IL: Hope, 1998), 200.

10. Harold M. Best, *Music through the Eyes of Faith* (New York: HarperSanFrancisco, 1993), 108 (emphasis in original).

11. Ibid., 113–14.

and others will ultimately measure our lifetime of ministry. Serjak agrees: "When one aspires to be excellent, one never totally 'arrives,' or at least one does not arrive finally, but rather reaches moments of excellence, clarity, and integrity. . . . And the rest of the time we work at sharpening our skills, looking for better ways to sing what has been sung thousands of times already."[12]

Authenticity is an equally significant aspect when pursuing a vision of excellence. Best describes inauthenticity as "pseudoexcellence," which he defines as "the substitution of production for content."[13] Modern worship leaders sometimes depend on technological enhancements to suggest that their musical performance is better than they are capable of. Best posits an interesting point to consider:

> Perhaps we have it all backwards or upside down. Instead of little people trying to become someone they are not—trying to overpower with technique—God might just be wanting all the little people, *created that way in the first place*, to stay their own size so that divine power can come down on them and break down strongholds the divine way, with the straightforward foolishness of the gospel.[14]

One's vision of excellence must include the value that is placed on the power of God to work in and through the musician in his or her best prepared yet unenhanced performances. Artificial techniques are not wrong to apply, but if our musicianship depends on them for effectiveness, it is likely that our musicianship needs more development in the first place.

The Role of Excellence

A third arena to consider is one's approach to leadership. Music architects have a role to play in the pursuit of excellence among their people. While they are caring for their own spiritual formation and developing a healthy vision of the meaning of musical excellence, they must also learn to lead others in an excellent manner. That is the role of the **servant leader**.

Leadership styles for church leaders have been a very big topic in the past fifty years. A large number of books, conferences, seminary courses, and webinars have appeared on the landscape that promise answers to underequipped or frustrated leaders. Many of these resources have supplied very helpful information and played a part in equipping the saints. Yet even

---

12. Serjak, "Musician," 49.
13. Best, *Music through the Eyes of Faith*, 113.
14. Ibid. (emphasis in original).

with the wide variety of perspectives from which leaders can select to apply to their own situations, none can surpass the servant leadership model. This is not to say that all the approaches promoted are incompatible with servant leadership (although some are); in the end, however, servant leadership ultimately transcends all models, even though bits and pieces of others may be valuable to enhance servant leadership. It can be argued that servant leadership isn't really a leadership style at all; it is not in the lineup among other styles from which to choose. Instead, it is a way of life. While servant leadership may not be entirely one or the other, we will lean toward servant leadership as a way of life as we explore what is expected in leading God's people as music architects.

Servant leadership is rooted in Jesus's words in the Gospels.[15] In response to a dispute among his disciples as to who was the greatest of them, Jesus took the opportune moment to instruct them in the way of life to which he was calling them:

> You know that the rulers of the Gentiles lord it over them, and their great ones are tyrants over them. It will not be so among you; but whoever wishes to be great among you must be your servant, and whoever wishes to be first among you must be your slave; just as the Son of Man came not to be served but to serve, and to give his life a ransom for many. (Matt. 20:25–28)

Jesus stands against the predominant view of leadership well known in his culture and sets forth a new way: not leading from the top down but from the bottom up, not from the outside in but the inside out. This plan is as threatening and misunderstood today as it would have been in Jesus's context. No leader worth his or her salt would refuse the opportunity to call the shots and take charge by making demands of others—except for Jesus. The approach is threatening because it is downright bizarre. It is misunderstood because meekness is assumed to be weakness.

To help flesh this out, I turn to the remarkable work of J. Robert Clinton.[16] Clinton describes the servant leader as someone who "uses leadership to serve followers."[17] Note the definition's consistency with Jesus's teaching. Followers are served and leadership is the means. If we were to transpose the words in the definition, we would have a secular model of leadership: "A leader uses followers to serve the leader." Jesus's view is one of using leadership to serve people,

---

15. See these accounts in the Synoptic Gospels: Matt. 20:20–28; Luke 17:7–10; 22:24–27.

16. I commend J. Robert Clinton's website: http://bobbyclinton.com/.

17. J. Robert Clinton, *A Personal Ministry Philosophy: One Key to Effective Leadership* (Pasadena, CA: Barnabas, 1992), 13.

whereas the common view is to use people to serve leaders. Let's address some key features of servant leadership and try to dispel any confusion as we do so.

First, servant leadership is more about attitude and values than it is a job description or leadership style. The servant leader is spiritually formed to naturally assume this role over time. If leaders pursue excellence in spiritual formation as described above, they will find themselves gravitating to the servant leader mind-set. Once we offer control of our formation to the Holy Spirit, we will discover that we are becoming more and more comfortable as servant leaders. No one becomes a servant leader just by wishing or praying. It comes through the school of hard knocks, through trial and error, through experiencing mountains and valleys. The main thing to realize is that servant leadership is crafted in us by God's Spirit to the degree that it becomes unlikely that we could lead in such a way that would *not* be servant in nature.

Second, servant leadership is about meekness, not weakness. Some leaders resist the idea of servant leadership because it appears that the leader is weak, and weakness is not an ideal attribute to possess by anyone's standards. Weakness is an impoverished internal state wherein an individual does not have the fortitude to take logical and needed steps toward success (however that is defined). This is true in both our personal and professional lives. For whatever reason, weak leaders do not have or are not able to demonstrate courage to move toward healthy and good choices for their own welfare or the welfare of those around them. Servant leaders, however, do have an adequate supply of internal strength and character formation so as to act positively on behalf of others. They strategically pour themselves into the lives of others around them to empower their colaborers with strategies and skills to do effective ministry in their context. This is meekness. It is a matter of self-control. The leader confronts his or her own desire and/or need to be at the head and assumes, rather, a subservient role of promoting others forward into their appropriate places. In the Scriptures, meekness is portrayed as a virtue (see Zeph. 2:3; 2 Cor. 10:1; Gal. 5:23; Col. 3:12; etc., KJV).

Servant leadership can be confused with being a doormat. Whether someone is a doormat has largely to do with his or her self-control and intention. If persons are weak, allowing others to walk all over them because they cannot prevent it, they run the risk of becoming doormats. If, however, persons are servant leaders, they are intentionally choosing to surrender the prominent role that is theirs by right in order to help others become who God has called them to be. This is exactly what brings God honor, as seen in Jesus's self-surrender and what we are urged to emulate as his followers:

> Let the same mind be in you that was in Christ Jesus, who, though he was in the
> form of God, did not regard equality with God as something to be exploited,

but emptied himself, taking the form of a slave, being born in human likeness. And being found in human form, he humbled himself and became obedient to the point of death—even death on a cross. (Phil. 2:5–8)

It is this very attitude of self-submission that God honors and that brings him glory (vv. 9–11).

Third, servant leadership is not just a matter of working hard in the church. It is possible to work many long, hard hours and not be a servant leader. Some leaders have the mistaken idea that servant leadership is about spending an excessive amount of time in service to the church, even at the expense of their own or their family's well-being. The number of hours one invests does not define servant leadership. The real difference between working hard in one's ministry and servant leadership has to do, again, with attitude and values. A servant leader is invested in leading others through intentional downward mobility. Ministry will always make many demands on our time. It is how we spend our time that counts, rather than impressing our constituents through logging excessive hours. To be honest, some leaders like the credit that a lot of hard work earns them. But if we are finding our identity in the number of hours we are reporting versus the number of persons transformed through servant leadership, we should check our motives promptly.

Last, servant leadership is not a free pass from leading. We have emphasized the servant nature of leadership, but we must not understate the leadership component. Unfortunately, leaders can fall into the trap of thinking that servant leadership is a matter of passing leadership responsibilities along to the laity. They erroneously conclude that their job is to simply set others free to be leaders, without equipping them for the task by investing in their success. This is the lazy leader's approach and is the cause for many a leader's demise. There is no integrity in passing off responsibility without contributing to others' effectiveness through sharing with them your own gifts and experience. Servant leadership *is* leadership, after all.

Servant leadership is especially fitting for music architects who pursue excellence of leadership. Premiere pastoral musician Joseph Gelineau sees the role of the leader as essentially that of service—one that serves others, serves the rites, and serves music.[18] Of particular note in our discussion of servant leadership are Gelineau's words regarding the service of others:

> We have to serve humanity for the service of God. I do not celebrate liturgy to make music that pleases *me*. I must search unceasingly for music that will help

18. Joseph Gelineau, "The Importance of Prayer for the Musician," in *The Pastoral Musician*, vol. 5 of *Pastoral Music in Practice*, ed. Virgil C. Funk (Washington, DC: Pastoral Press, 1990), 72.

my fellow believers, gathered here together, to pray better. I must keep each and every one in mind, the young as well as the elderly; the cultivated as well as the more simple folk; those who are waiting to be helped by lots of joyous and expressive songs; but also those who will pray more profoundly, with less exuberant songs, and lots of silence. I may not impose my tastes on anyone, but I must find for myself some taste in all I set about to do, in order to do it well.[19]

Conclusion

Music architects, as leaders in the church, are called to pursue lives of excellence: in their personal spiritual formation, in their vision of musical excellence, and as servant leaders among fellow worshipers. This kind of leadership is vital to successful music ministry. It is challenging, but it is also invigorating. Our communities await the breath of fresh air that such a pursuit of excellence will bring. Good enough has been good enough for too long. Holy shoddy is still shoddy. Like Paul, because we desire the eternal prize, we do not want to run aimlessly or box as though beating the air; we bring our lives and our ministries under subjection to the lordship of Jesus Christ so that after proclaiming to others the excellence that is possible, we do not find ourselves disqualified (see 1 Cor. 9:24–27).

Key Terms

servant leader. Someone who uses leadership to serve followers.[20]

spiritual disciplines. Formative practices we intentionally engage in as acts of devotion in order to offer God an opportunity to do a work of inner transformation in us leading toward the holy life.

spiritual formation. "A process of being conformed to the image of Christ for the sake of others."[21]

To Learn More

Clinton, J. Robert. *The Making of a Leader: Recognizing the Lessons and Stages of Leadership Development*. Rev. ed. Carol Stream, IL: NavPress, 2012.

19. Ibid.
20. Clinton, *Personal Ministry Philosophy*, 13.
21. Mulholland, *Invitation to a Journey*, 12.

Covey, Stephen R. *The 7 Habits of Highly Effective People: Powerful Lessons in Personal Change.* New York: Simon & Schuster, 2004.

Engage

How have any of your views about excellence changed since reading this chapter? Before reviewing the responses you gave at the beginning of the chapter, how would you answer these questions now?

1. Excellent worship music is _____.
2. I would describe an excellent worship music architect as someone who

_____.

Now review your initial responses to these questions. How do they compare?

Next, ask several persons in your music ministry program to define excellence with one word. Collect the words. Meet informally at someone's home and have a discussion about the meaning of excellence in your context. Try to write a definition of excellence for your music ministry context.

Postlude

The sound of singing saints is the most beautiful sound this side of heaven. It is a foretaste of the glorious things to come. But for now we must use our imaginations as we anticipate the music of the new kingdom. The book of Revelation gives us only hints. The choirs? They will be on a much grander scale—millions of voices, both human and angelic, comprising the mighty chorus (Rev. 5:11; 7:9). The theme? "Worthy is the Lamb!" (Rev. 5:12). The instruments? We will hear harps and trumpets and whatever else God places in the hands of worshipers to add to the splendor of heaven's praise (see Rev. 5:8; 8:6). We can only imagine the sound of eternity's song to be as attractive to the ear as the bejeweled streets are to the eye. But whatever its magnificence will be like in praise of the triune God, the music of eternity will far exceed what we experience now.

That's okay. Until then, we will make music for our Lord to hear among the sisters and brothers whom God has given us in community. For now our primary occasions for offering sung worship are on the Lord's Day in a local church, whether that is a thatched shelter, a warehouse-turned-church, a cave, or a grand cathedral. Our weekly rhythm of coming to worship as the assembly in which the risen Lord is present becomes the duly constituted event whereby God's people gather to continue the song in finite space and time in preparation for when we are ultimately gathered in infinite space, and time is no more. What is now our avocation will become our vocation. To paraphrase the apostle Paul: For now we sing through a glass, darkly; but then we shall sing face-to-face (see 1 Cor. 13:12 KJV).

Come, Lord Jesus!

Appendix A

Assessing Your Canon of Song

Song Title	Revelation	Response	Vertical	Horizontal	Praise	Lament	Declarative	Expressive	Corporate	Personal	God's Story	Our Story	Shorter Songs	Longer Songs	Names for God	Titles for God	Universal Tradition	Particular Tradition	Older	Newer	Eternal	Temporal	Comforting	Disturbing	Personal Holiness	Social Holiness	Lord's Day	24/7	Adults	Youth

Appendix B

Antiphon for Congregational Use

Psalm 130:1–8
Congregation

I cry to You; I wait for You, O Lord, my God! Hear me in love, and for - give.

Leader: Out of the depths I cry to you, O Lord.

Lord, hear my voice!

Let your ears be attentive to the voice of my supplications!

Response

Silence

Leader: If you, O Lord, should mark iniquities, Lord, who could stand?

But there is forgiveness with you, so that you may be revered.

Response

Silence

Leader: I wait for the Lord, my soul waits, and in his word I hope;

        my soul waits for the Lord more than those who watch for the morning,

        more than those who watch for the morning.

Response

   Silence

Leader: O Israel, hope in the Lord! For with the Lord there is stadfast love,

        and with him is great power to redeem.

        It is he who will redeem Israel from all its iniquities.

Response

Psalm 130:1–8
Accompaniment

Psalm 130: C Instrument Descant

Prayerfully

Index